THE EFFECTIVE TEACHING OF RELIGIOUS EDUCATION

second edition

Brenda Watson and Penny Thompson

Routledge
Taylor & Francis Group

LONDON AND NEW YORK

First published 1994 by Pearson Education Limited
Second edition published in Great Britain 2007

Published 2013 by Routledge
2 Park Square, Milton Park, Abingdon, Oxon OX14 4RN
711 Third Avenue, New York, NY 10017, USA

Routledge is an imprint of the Taylor & Francis Group, an informa business

ISBN 13: 978-1-4058-2410-1 (pbk)

British Library Cataloguing-in-Publication Data
A catalogue record for this book is available from the British Library

Library of Congress Cataloging-in-Publication Data
Watson, Brenda, 1935–
      The effective teaching of religious education / Brenda Watson and
   Penny Thompson. — 2nd ed.
         p. cm.
   Includes bibliographical references and index.
   ISBN-13: 978-1-4058-2410-1 (pbk.)
   ISBN-10: 1-4058-2410-7 (pbk.)
   1. Religious education.   I. Thompson, Penny.   II. Title.
   BL42.W37 2006
   207′.5—dc22
                                                2006047526
Typeset in 11.25/13pt Stone Print by 35

CONTENTS

LIST OF FIGURES AND TABLES

FIGURES

TABLES

PREFACE

This is a revised edition of the Longman book published in 1994 under the same title. In setting about the task of revision, Brenda Watson was most grateful to have the collaboration of Penny Thompson. This has proved to be a fruitful and interesting experience. We don't agree about everything but have gone through a process of 'give and take', not dissimilar from the process an agreed syllabus conference goes through when reviewing the RE syllabus. The result, we hope, is the stronger for realistically facing difficulties. We hope that readers may find stimulus in what we have written to continue what must always be an on-going debate.

Much has changed in the fifteen years since the first edition. Globalization has continued apace, and ever-developing technology has brought opportunities for fresh approaches in education. Intellectually there has been a phenomenal extension of a post-modernist mind-set which has impacted on educational policy for schools making much more pronounced tendencies operating since at least the 1970s. The values of breadth, non-judgementalism, celebration of diversity of forms of expression, and providing a curriculum in which all can excel now seem by many to be taken for granted.

The latter we may approve, but when it is allied to a commitment to a presumed value-free society, it can result in serious dumbing-down. An example is the anxiety over the future of physics because so few schools outside the independent sector are producing students capable of doing physics.

We argue in this book therefore for an RE which is both accessible and intellectually rigorous. The importance of this has been underlined by the events of 9/11 and 7/7 which have alerted the West to the continuing power of religion and the need to learn greater discrimination concerning it.

Certain chapters have warranted considerable rewriting, notably Chapters 4 and 10 on, respectively, the purpose of religious education and its relationship to other subjects. There is also a new chapter on the place of Christianity in RE, and an Appendix on tackling assessment and syllabus requirements.

A new feature is the website which will give practical examples and back-up material, and promote the role of ICT.

We have found that much of the book is still pertinent and necessary. This is because the 1994 publication deals with fundamental underlying issues, approaches and truth-questions, and not primarily with practicalities or flavour-of-the-month suggestions. The book assumes that teachers are responsible people who want to approach work in the classroom in their own way, responsive to the particular needs and interests of those whom they are teaching.

We hope therefore that this second edition will afford encouragement and support to teachers wrestling with a demanding but exhilarating and important subject. Misunderstandings concerned with religion are so rife today that the safety of the world may be at stake unless real insight becomes possible for both religious people and the many in the West who are not.

The book is written with the needs of specialist and non-specialist teachers in mind, in both primary and secondary schools. The intention is to integrate theory and practice so that the discussion of ideas is closely related to what is feasible in the classroom. We therefore hope that the book will prove an encouragement and stimulus to all who care about Religious Education and want to teach it as well as possible.

ACKNOWLEDGEMENTS

We gratefully acknowledge the help of many people in preparing the material for this book. The thinking expressed in its pages is the result of innumerable conversations with colleagues and pupils over the years, and we especially mention Professor Edward Hulmes, Professor Basil Mitchell and Dr Elizabeth Ashton.

We acknowledge valuable help given us regarding particular chapters: by Farid Panjwani of the Aga Khan University-Institute for the study of Muslim Civilizations, Rabbi Dr David Goldberg of the Liberal Jewish Synagogue London, and Rt Rev. Dr David Jenkins for Chapter 6; by the late Dr Terry McLaughlin of the Institute of Education London, and Dora Ainsworth for Chapter 7; by Dr Mark Pike for Chapter 10; by Dr Penny Jennings for Chapter 12; and by Mark Chater for helping to clarify our thinking about the website which accompanies the book. The website accompanying this book was developed with the help of Paul Hopkins. Paul Hopkins is a freelance consultant working with educational technology. He works nationally and internationally advising on religious education. He has published widely in books, journals and electronic media.

We are especially grateful to Dr Marius Felderhof, Professor Roger Trigg and Dr Andrew Wright for their endorsement of the book.

We acknowledge kind permission to reproduce the following copyright material: Dr Adrian Thatcher for the quotation in Chapter 5; Julie A. Gage for the poem 'Lavender Lily' in Chapter 7. Excerpt from 'Creed or Chaos' reprinted by permission of Dorothy Sayers and the Watkins/Loomis Agency.

PART I

ROLE OF RE IN SOCIETY TODAY

CHAPTER I

THE EFFECTIVE TEACHER OF RE

'Education is not about skills and jobs; it is part of a quest for truth . . . It seems glaringly evident that what competes with the open search for knowledge is not the perspective of committed belief, but the closed mind of boredom.' (Elaine Storkey)[1]

What makes a good teacher of RE? We explore the question of commitment and openness, and suggest a six-fold approach to valuing as the essential basis for effective education. This can help teachers marry professionalism with values with which they engage personally and publicly. We then relate these values to the teaching of RE.

The most fundamental factor in effective RE, as in the effective teaching of any other subject, is the teacher. Guidelines, syllabuses, books, aids of various kinds, all depend upon the teacher who actually applies them within the classroom situation. The same topic, with the same age and ability range of pupils, and the same general style and method of teaching, can yield entirely different results, depending upon the teacher. One lesson can really take off, and another be dead. For a good teacher is able to establish rapport with pupils and infectiously share enthusiasm for the subject.

IS RELIGIOUS FAITH A HINDRANCE OR AN ASSET FOR RE?

The question of a teacher's commitment is a crucial one. It used often to be assumed that a religious person would teach RE better than someone who is an atheist or agnostic. But that depends on the nature and content of the commitment. A religious person who is extremist or narrow-minded, uninterested in views different from his/her own, may do much damage and close off pupils' incipient interest in religion and capacity to think intelligently and sensitively about it.

A case is sometimes made for a position of agnosticism as being one which is most congenial to teaching with openness. We know some excellent teachers of RE who would see themselves as agnostic. But a dogmatic kind of agnosticism is also possible: agnosticism just as much as religious faith rests on its own assumptions which can betray key-hole vision. Furthermore, a strong case can be made for arguing that religious commitment is the only way to understand the depths of religion which from the outside may remain sheer enigma. As in the teaching of science or music, for example, the scientist or the musician has normally far more to offer than the non-scientist or the non-musician.

Experience and knowledge of the subject obviously yield dividends in the classroom. Especially in secondary schools, considerable sophistication is called for in order to sustain the interest of older and often religiously alienated pupils. In both primary and secondary schools there is a need for as highly qualified teachers as possible to act as coordinators, helping and encouraging those whose main expertise lies elsewhere. The website accompanying this book will have material to help specialist teachers of various kinds. RE does, however, have to call on the services of many non-specialist teachers, that is, some teachers in secondary schools, and most teachers in primary schools.

We would like therefore to reassure them, as well as those specializing in the subject, that most teachers who are willing to try to teach RE well *can* do so. For if education includes enabling pupils to take responsibility for their own ongoing self-education through life, the more limited experience that the teacher may have can nevertheless be deployed in a professionally helpful way. This can happen if the teacher has a willingness to engage at some depth with the concepts, ideas and questions evoked by the material, together with a desire to give space to pupils to think for themselves rather than presuming their agreement with everything that is taught. Above all, a teacher needs to model the kind of reflectiveness and weighing of issues which is expected of pupils.

BASIC ATTITUDES ESSENTIAL FOR BOTH SPECIALIST AND NON-SPECIALIST RE TEACHERS

This kind of character and professional behaviour results from holding certain fundamental values. It is important to discuss what these are. A major weakness of what is usually dubbed 'the Western liberal tradition' is a certain incoherence about fundamental values. It tends to see values such as tolerance, freedom for self-expression, and equality as fundamental, and yet they are not. For their desirability rests on their conforming to something more deep-seated. Thus tolerance of intolerance is a dangerous contradiction enabling the intolerant to use the tolerance of others as a stepping-stone to power. Similarly, much self-expression is at the expense of the self-expression of others, thereby rendering some people more equal than others, as George Orwell famously put it in *Animal Farm*.[2]

In the last two decades there has been more concern to find a common basis for our pluralist society by identifying shared values. Thus the 1999 *National Curriculum*

Handbooks for Primary and Secondary Teachers lists these as The Self, Relationships, Society, and The Environment.[3] The non-statutory national framework for RE sees these basic values as 'truth, justice, respect for all and care of the environment'.[4]

Values may be expressed in many different ways, and we respond in the following way to the excellent work which has so far been done (see Figure 1.1). Three from the *Handbooks'* list appear to be the same, although the gloss on them is different in some respects. But we miss out *Society* and put *Truth* as a separate value, for to subsume the latter under *Society* makes a mockery of what we mean by *Truth*: truth relates to reality as it is, not just to how any particular group of people think it is. Truth is especially important for understanding religion which sees a supreme place in the scheme of things for God or the Transcendent. Religious people claim that God does exist and is not just a figment of their imagination.

Truth is present in the framework list, as is *respect for all* which is understood to include oneself. We feel, however, that there is a need specifically to distinguish the self from others. We consider that *justice* is an inherent part of respect in that to be unjust towards others is to fail to show them respect. We also widen the valuing of the environment to include human traditions and cultures.

To both lists we add *beauty*, because valuing the aesthetic dimension to life contributes so much to civilized life and well-being. Similarly, *beauty* relates to that sense of awe

Figure 1.1 *A six-fold approach to valuing*

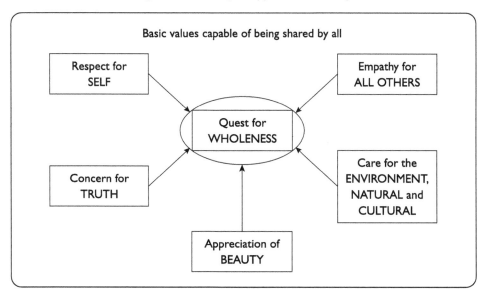

and wonder which is so often lacking when people talk about God as though God is just a human concept.

A list by itself is inadequate to convey the real import of each value. We therefore give more detail on how we understand the six-fold approach to valuing.

1   Self-respect – a basic self-affirmation and awareness, concern for integrity and openness to guard against prejudice and delusion. A certain self-respect is crucial, for without respecting the one person one is with all the time and can know from the inside, what possibility is there of respecting anyone else? But this self-respect must be more than simple self-esteem or a 'feel-good' factor. Respect for oneself acknowledges also limitations, difficulties and failures and the need for criticism. We need to affirm ourselves, but critically. (See discussion of this on pp. 8, 63–5 and 133–5.)

2   Respect for all other people – a basic attitude of empathy towards others and generousmindedness towards what is especially meaningful to them. It is very important to understand that there must be respect for *all* others, not just for those whom we happen to like or whose opinions agree with ours, nor just for those who wield power or are gifted with charisma. In meetings of all kinds, for example, this translates into respect not just for the dominant member of the group, nor just for people immediately present, but also for the people who will be affected by any decision made or not made.

3   Respect for the environment natural and cultural – a basic care for the natural world and interest in diverse human traditions with concern to play fair with them. This valuing involves acknowledging that people are part of these worlds, each with their own autonomy yet powerfully influencing one another. It helps to guard against two dangerous misunderstandings: regarding nature as just to be used by humans, and being dismissive towards human traditions which may seem strange or uncongenial.

4   Respect for beauty – a basic sense of wonder and awareness that there is more to life than the mundane, pragmatic and purely factual. The word *beauty* suggests a heightened awareness and delight in qualities such as shape, proportion and colour which the environment, either natural or manufactured, can display. Quite apart from the vexed question as to whether beauty is in the eye of the beholder or whether it has objective reality, the appreciation of beauty has been one of the hallmarks of every civilization.

5   Respect for truth – a basic search for truth, that is, for what actually is the case, seeking to avoid ignorance, misunderstanding and falsehood. Truth is fundamental for without it there can be no respect for the self that one really is, for other people as they are, or for the world which happens to be in existence. Even awareness of beauty is, for most writers, artists and musicians, in a deep sense linked to awareness of how things actually are. Chesterton once spoke of it like this: 'The startling wetness of water excites and intoxicates me; the fieriness of fire, the steeliness of steel, the unutterable muddiness of mud.'[5] The pursuit of knowledge understood as the opposite of ignorance, blindness and delusion is central to education and to being a person.

6   *Respect for wholeness – a basic concern for seeing the inter-connectedness of everything and a desire to sort out contradictions, not resting satisfied with fragmented and perhaps schizophrenic understanding.* It is important to appreciate that the other five basic values are not in watertight compartments but constantly interact. The search for wholeness reinforces each one without marginalizing any; it asks what makes most sense of the totality of experience without, so far as possible, ignoring any aspect of life.

Openness and commitment

In some ways the word *openness* can pinpoint this six-fold approach to valuing, but only provided that openness is not misunderstood. It can very easily be taken as meaning sitting on the fence about anything controversial, or as refusing to hold any strong convictions. But of course belief in the importance of openness is itself a conviction, and one normally held very strongly today! Furthermore, life does not permit us the luxury of constant academic neutrality in an ivory tower. Decisions have to be made on one basis or another. Not to choose is in fact to choose in a weak and unintended form, just as failing to answer a letter is itself answering it. True openness is paradoxically only possible on the basis of firm convictions. The opposite of firm commitment is not no commitment but a confusion of weakly held or conditioned commitments, mostly unarticulated and imprecise.

Education cannot avoid advocacy as well as elucidation, but if the values it encourages are educationally valid, as we believe those we are advocating are, there need be no fear of inappropriate influencing by the teacher. As far back as 1955 M.V.C. Jeffreys summed up what was needed: 'The guarantee of freedom is not the teacher's neutrality, but his or her respect for the integrity of the pupil's personality.'[6]

What therefore will save teachers from unacceptable dogmatism, whether of a religious or non-religious nature, is not the absence of commitment even were this possible, but the integrity with which the teacher pursues and models such openness. Teachers are then able, as Edward Hulmes has argued, to use their own commitment regarding religion as a valuable resource.[7] (See Figure 3.3 and further discussion on pp. 46–8.)

WHAT RE CAN DO TO IMPLEMENT THESE VALUES

Whether formally qualified in RE or not, the effective teacher in the classroom will seek to exemplify such values in relation to RE. We discuss these in some detail below.

The list may appear daunting and unattainable, especially in view of the enormous pressures placed on teachers in today's schools. Research undertaken by Mark Chater into teachers' vocations and values 1997–2004[8] suggests how risky and fragile an enterprise it is to sustain personal commitment of this nature in the over-bureaucratic, efficiency-dominated atmosphere which tends to pervade the education system in the UK. We hold, however, that if teachers really understand what the basic values of sound education are, this will enable them not to be seriously deflected from pursuing them. Furthermore, only such teachers will be able responsibly to challenge the system for its own good when other values inimical to education threaten it.

Good RE can express and develop the six-fold approach to valuing set out above. We invite readers to respond to such questions as these relating to the list we give below:
- Can you prioritize these values?
- Could any be said to depend on the others?
- Would you drop any?
- Would you add any?
- What answer would you give to a pupil who asked you why he should respect other people, the environment etc.?
- Would it be appropriate to ask pupils these questions?

1   *Respect for self – acceptance of oneself together with the capacity also to be self-critical and flexible enough to change if needed, able*:
(a) to appreciate the necessary limitations of one's knowledge and experience, because without this there can be no glimpsing of what religious people mean by God or the Transcendent;
(b) to trust the insights which one's experience of life accumulates as a basis for going out into the unknown, accepting that we all need constantly to add the insights of others to our own, and see life as a pilgrimage towards ever greater understanding;
(c) consequent on this, to develop willingness also to be critical of one's own beliefs about religion and be prepared to modify, enlarge, or revise, what has so far been thought and felt.

2   *Empathy for all other people – a willingness to look for and acknowledge what is helpful and insightful in other people's views, able*:

(a) to learn how to affirm others, both as people and regarding what is meaningful and important to them. It is especially important to do this in relation to those people whose views on religion are very different from one's own;

(b) to appreciate the power and attractiveness of religion, whether one is religious or not, and to be able to get on the wavelength both of religious people and of those who have non-religious commitments;

(c) to be aware in a meaningful way of the kind of experiences and arguments upon which religious people base their convictions.

3 Care for the environment, natural and cultural – a welcoming curiosity towards diverse traditions and prepared to engage in questions of how they relate to each other, able:

(a) to care about the natural world and that it is not selfishly exploited;

(b) to appreciate the fact of religious diversity and be able to give respect to others as persons without marginalizing their religious commitment – to be able therefore to contribute towards a tolerant harmonious society;

(c) to perceive the crucial area of common-ground between almost all major religious traditions, and that differences and disagreements are only meaningful against that background of what is held in common;

(d) to learn how to disagree courteously and get beyond just tolerance in a pluralist society. This is only possible if we first give other people respect without rubbishing their outlook.

4 Appreciation of beauty – perceiving the aesthetic dimension of life and its links with religion, able:

(a) to foster one's capacity for imagination which is essential for realizing that reality can be greater and other than it often seems. People can easily be imprisoned within a flat two-dimensional approach to life which is not the only option available;

(b) to understand that religious faith expresses itself in a variety of forms, many of which are close to the arts, and to realize also that religious language is often used in symbolic or metaphorical ways;

(c) to appreciate the emotional power of religious commitment and how this can be beneficial or harmful depending upon its focus and how or whether people live up to their convictions.

5 Concern for truth – reflecting on the nature and purpose of life and the importance of finding meaning which rings true to how reality is, able:

(a) to challenge secularist assumptions and to appreciate that religious truth-claims cannot be easily dismissed;

(b) to understand what is distinctive about religion, that is, what it essentially concerns, and be able to distinguish between that and features of it which can vary and perhaps be dispensed with altogether;

(c) to realize, in particular, in how many different ways religion can masquerade as something else, and fail to be what it claims to be;

(d) to appreciate the highly controversial nature of religion and of almost everything that is said about it by anyone, whether religious or not;

(e) to have a firm grasp of criteria by which to evaluate precise examples and manifestations of religion in practice;

(f) to appreciate the ways in which world-views, both religious and secular, need to be questioned for their failures, negative attitudes, and hypocrisy.

6   *Quest for wholeness – joined-up thinking which sees how all these values are linked, and especially how they find expression in God or the Transcendent, able:*

(a) to reflect as deeply as possible about the totality of life's experience and the views one comes across;

(b) to appreciate the interlinking of everything and the force of cumulative evidence, and that what is done and learnt in school cannot be divorced from what happens outside;

(c) to appreciate that religion challenges head-on any view that regards knowledge as something arrived at only by reasoning and scientific experimentation. Religion does not preclude reasoning and experimentation but is not limited to these ways of knowing;

(d) to develop conviction concerning religion, but to be open to evidence and to experience – not to have the answers all neatly sewn up, but to see life as a journey of exploration with exciting prospects. A sense of fulfilment can be found in moving forward and, if necessary, changing in order to accommodate fresh insight.

THE CONTENT OF RE

Nothing has been said so far about precise content, for example, which world religions should be included, or whether the focus should be mainly on Christianity, how far non-religious stances such as Humanism should feature in RE, or what to do about the occult, and so forth. Nor has anything been said about precise method. This is deliberate because:

1 The most impeccable and well-prepared content, and the most exciting and suitable method, will fail as RE unless plugged in to what is its central purpose. Furthermore, if this is really understood, this purpose can be achieved through a great variety of approaches with regard both to content and method. The teacher can adapt almost any and every available item. Even something from the day's newspaper can be all that is needed as an effective starting-point, just as the latest or the most interesting work done in other subject areas of the curriculum may be used. Materials that happen to be available in the school, including even seriously inadequate ones, can be brought into play and yield educationally valuable material if approached from a point of view of real understanding on the teacher's part.

2 What is essential or helpful or inspiring for any one pupil, group of pupils, or class will vary enormously, and therefore effective RE is inescapably dependent on the teacher's skills and perceptiveness within a particular situation. There are no blueprints which can be given. It is the role of the Agreed Syllabus to specify precise content, and the purpose of this book is to help teachers so to understand the nature and purpose of RE that they can relate such content appropriately to the particular pupils or actual classes being taught.

3 There has to be a freshness about teaching – it cannot be pre-arranged and pre-packaged, for that almost always loses the attention of pupils, even if not also of the teacher. Teaching must be alive and it can only be alive in the present moment; it is time-consuming to try to make stale bread palatable, and why bother when fresh bread is available? Fresh bread is the interests, concerns, questions and problems of the moment which pupils bring and which the teacher as a person brings.

4 The teacher always has to operate within a number of constraints such as agreed syllabuses, governors' wishes, heads of department, parental pressures, and so on, which mean that he or she is the only person who is competent to decide on content and method. Other people, such as the authors of a book, do not have the right to do more than offer suggestions which are a few among the thousands possible.

5 The possible content of RE is so enormous, and the possible interpretation so varied, that we have to be careful about assuming that there is one standard core of content which can be target-set as it were in tablets of stone. There are three particular points to notice here:

(a) RE must find space for current needs and interests and therefore have a degree of flexibility built in. If teachers feel that following the syllabus is more important than making the subject live for the pupils in front of them, then the syllabus is getting in the way of effective teaching, instead of enabling it. It is a matter of balance.

(b) Whilst clearly teachers must conform to the target-setting required of them by governing bodies in education, they must be aware of the inadequacy of all such formulations. See the discussion on page 85 on pupils 'knowing' that Christians believe that Jesus is the Son of God and yet perhaps seriously misunderstanding and misapplying that 'knowledge'. Again, the heart of RE is not being able to recite the 'Five Pillars of Islam' but actually to catch a glimpse of what it means really to believe in Allah and seek to worship Him.

(c) Teachers need also to bear in mind that many targettable generalizations can be simplistic and carry dogmatic messages which are in fact controversial and so masquerading as being objective. Selection itself – the choice of this material rather than that – can be a hidden form of indoctrination, and the more so if it comes in the garb of so-called publicly agreed authority.

THE NEED TO LOOK AT THEORY

Because teaching RE effectively depends upon understanding the nature of RE and developing those skills and attitudes essential to it, there is a certain amount of theory to be mastered. This can sometimes be rather hastily dismissed as irrelevant to the classroom. But time spent with a map at the beginning of a difficult and complicated journey is time well-spent – failure to do so can be disastrous, causing much frustration and waste of time and the real possibility of never reaching the destination at all.

Impatience is justified if theory moves off into the stratosphere, so to speak. Provided however that it is properly grounded, failure to engage with it may be termed irresponsible. This is because the effectiveness of RE depends first and foremost on the teacher perceiving the underlying challenge it presents, and why, so that what is negative can be countered.

There is another important reason for attending to theory: it needs to be shared with pupils. Edward Hulmes has many times noted that RE is for teachers as much as for pupils. We would want to add that the theory of RE is for pupils as well as for teachers. This is the only way in which indoctrination can be avoided and any real understanding of religion conveyed. We cannot expect pupils to learn the sophistication necessary for handling difficult concepts if we constantly draw a veil over them and shut pupils off from the real debate.

The next two chapters introduce basic issues with which any teacher of RE needs to engage. Pupils as well as teachers should be aware of secularist tendencies in what is taken for granted in our society and in the educational world, and they should realize that these are not beyond being questioned. Again, they need to appreciate the problems posed by the fact that there are so many different religions, and be alert to possible responses. It is also most important that the abuse of religion with its destructive consequences is faced, and that pupils are helped towards levels of discernment. A consideration of these basic issues is the theme of Chapters 2 and 3.

TO THINK ABOUT

Mark Twain is said to have complained, 'My education was interrupted by my schooling'.

1 What do you think this means?
2 Would you say that it is true in your own case, or in the case of any people you know?
3 How can RE be taught in such a way as to be really creative as education?

NOTES

1 Storkey, E. (2005), from her article in *The Independent*, 22 January.
2 Orwell, G. (1984), p. 97.
3 This statement of common values was first drawn up by Talbot, M. and Tate, N. (1997) in 'Shared Values in a Pluralist Society' (pp. 10–14) in Smith, R. and Standish, P. (1997) (eds), pp. 1–14.
4 The non-statutory national framework (QCA2004).
5 Chesterton, G.K. We are indebted to Charles Barnham for this quotation.
6 Jeffreys, M.V.C. (1955), p. 9f.
7 Hulmes, E. (1979).
8 Chater, M. (2005), pp. 249–59.

CHAPTER 2

RE – ERRATIC BOULDER?

When Terence Copley questioned the supermarket manager about selling hot cross buns on Chrismas Eve, he received the horrified reply 'What! are they past their sell-by date?'[1]

Here we examine the status of religion in society in the West today. Noting the shock caused by the perceived violence of religious extremism and the apparent failure of education to counteract this, we enumerate twelve factors which have tended to be inimical to religion. We then argue that secularization, especially in schools – through the explicit, implicit and null curricula – must be taken seriously and challenged.

Geographers speak of a rock deposited by the Ice Age perhaps hundreds of miles from its place of origin as an erratic boulder, and it often seems to us that that is how RE appears in the landscape of today's schools. What is it doing there – strange, alien, even threatening? Of fascination to some, many would prefer to have it taken away or at least effectively cordoned off so that its presence could largely be ignored.

Sixty years ago most people would not have thought of RE in such terms. They would have preferred the analogy of the soil which supports vegetation and the wherewithal to live. Very few seriously asked how education could flourish without the sustenance provided by religion. This was why religion was the one subject required by British law to be taught in schools. Even in the 1988 legislation, RE has been referred to as 'basic', although in most people's minds any substance to that interpretation has long since evaporated.

We want however to argue that RE remains one of the most important subjects on the curriculum. The secularized Western system of education finds it hard to acknowledge this. The end of religion has long been predicted by those who do not believe in God. As the events of 9/11 and 7/7 have shown the West, religion remains stubbornly powerful in the modern world. Indeed, this has caused some change in many people's reaction to RE. They can see today that children need information about religion even if only to be inoculated against it! But this is a far cry from the earlier emphasis on RE because religious belief was considered important *per se* as fundamental for the good of society.

IMPACT OF EVENTS SUCH AS 9/11 AND 7/7

From one point of view, indeed, these events serve to reinforce the secularist view of religion as dangerous and needing to be superseded. But such a view has immediately to confront the fact that the vast majority of religious people abhor the violence and extremism as much as any atheist. As Rowan Williams put it in his paper on RE: 'The question is not so much why some Muslims are suicide bombers as why most aren't and couldn't conceive of being.'[2]

This suggests that one of the lessons the West needs to learn from these events is that religion is not a monolithic entity but exceedingly varied and ranging from some of the finest aspirations and achievements of human beings to some of the most ferocious and evil. Blanket dismissal of religion is inept and does not begin to address this issue, and does much harm because based on untruth and ignorance.

This is why RE in school is crucial. The case for understanding religion could not be more powerful, for the very survival of civilization may depend on it. It is easy, for example, to misunderstand the motives of those responsible for bombing innocent people and call them suicide bombers and murderers. This makes such acts understandable and provides a frame of reference that allows us in some way to deal with them (murderers can be imprisoned and suicides buried and forgotten). Yet they regard themselves as *martyrs* not as *suicidal*, for the Qur'ān does not permit suicide (see comment by N. Hassan[3]). Nor do they think of themselves as murderers but as soldiers fighting a holy war on behalf of justice which they see as doing the Will of Allah. Their goal is what they call 'sacred explosions' not acts of terrorism.

This is in line with one of the most disconcerting facts to emerge from recent studies of those responsible for the violence: that they are not usually penniless victims of social deprivation, nor people of a criminal tendency, but educated, well-heeled and often courteous, and seemingly responsible citizens. Their motivation may indeed have all kinds of psychological explanations – for example, the way in which immature young people who feel alienated or isolated are worked on by cult extremists who start by giving them the attention for which they crave. But by itself that is an insufficient explanation, for the real trigger for what the West calls suicide bombing is faith in Allah understood in a particular way.

Before dismissing all this as warped thinking, it is essential that we do our best to understand properly what they think that they are doing. Criticism without empathy of this kind is itself a blight because largely failing to connect with what is being criticized. The real issue is the interpretation of religion, in this case of Islam and of the Qur'ān. If they are misinterpreting the Qur'ān – as all moderate Muslims insist they are – then the criteria for correct interpretation of religion and scriptures needs to be taught. Of course this is a responsibility for religious communities themselves, but the task ought to be helped by the kind of sensitive and intelligent work they do in school RE.

IMPACT OF SCHOOLING

So we can ask: what help did those who attended British schools receive in helping young Muslims to think clearly and to judge wisely regarding how their religion should be understood? For so long ostracized from serious study, discussion or casual conversation, religion has been isolated as just a private preserve which our society allows people to pursue much on the level of a hobby. Most higher education routinely starts from the assumption that God does not exist. George Marsden notes that 'our dominant academic culture trains scholars to keep quiet about their faith as the price for full acceptance in that community.'[4] Later he puts it like this: 'So far as the academic dimensions of a university are concerned, religion is expected to have no more importance than would membership in a bridge club. Bridge players are not discriminated against; it's just that their pastime is irrelevant to academic life.'[5] John Webster in his inaugural lecture at Oxford University in 1997 spoke of that 'benign indifference' which is meted out to theology in modern western universities.[6] Terence Copley in his powerful book *Indoctrination, Education and God: The Struggle for the Mind* considers that 'What is happening at present in education and in wider British society is tending to eliminate or deny the possibility of God.'[7]

By contrast an aggressive secularism is not far from the surface. It manifests itself in different ways. The idea that religion is something vitally important or has something significant to offer society is rarely expressed. Religion is more often than not presented in terms of what some people believe. The idea that the millennium had anything to do with Christian faith came as a surprise to many. The population today has little sense of its Christian legacy. (See Chapter 5 for further discussion of attitudes to Christianity.)

Where religion is concerned, the question of truth and how to come to an understanding of truth has on the whole been removed. Secularists assume religion is not true and leave it at that. So it has been left to religious organizations and communities to nurture their young more or less as ghettos in Britain, as elsewhere in the West. They have been cut off from that proper spirit of criticism and openness to the insights of others which is the most positive heritage from the Enlightenment. There has been little two-way traffic.

The educational system has not helped to redress this social trend. It has largely assumed a secularist view of religion in attitudes to learning and curriculum. RE has had to conform to what is acceptable to such a view in bracketing out questions of truth in its approach and content in favour of facts about religion as a social/psychological phenomenon and a vague personal 'learning from'. In the interests of teaching tolerance, truth-claims tend either to be glossed over or simply described in apparently neutral academic fashion, leaving their truth or otherwise undebated. It is not that RE theory precludes debate on truth-claims, but that it usually has little to offer teachers by way of examples of how to do it. RE can often therefore be superficial, asking children to make judgements without being given sufficient help on how to set about doing so. So it becomes a matter of subjective opinion in which the pupil may think that no opinion is any better than any other.

RE experts are not unaware of this problem. Robert Jackson, for example, raises this issue in an important book.[8] He acknowledges the place of the discussion of truth-claims in RE, but sensitivities to the religious communities with whom he was producing classroom texts meant that he felt unable to include controversial issues which existed within these communities. He gives helpful suggestions as to how this might be done, but his own textbooks are silent on the matter. Sue Hookway's recent book[9] is an attempt to put critical thinking centre stage. Despite much that is excellent in this book (not least that it makes truth centre stage) we wonder if it gives sufficient direction to pupils. They are given the right questions to ask but the necessary skills and knowledge are sometimes lacking. To take just one example, more needs to be done to help pupils understand the milieu in which Muhammad was living, the ways in which Islamic views of Jesus resonate with views expressed within Christian thinking at the time, and the matter of evidence for Islamic claims about Jesus. We offer our own attempt to do this in a later chapter.

Fear of addressing truth-claims is indeed part of the wider general trend of avoiding judgementalism.[10] (See further discussion of this in Chapter 4 about the Agendas governing education.) This so-called value-free approach to RE is of little help to those who are deeply committed to the truth of their religion. It simply fails to connect.

THE NEED TO MOVE BEYOND JUST TOLERANCE

RE should look further than promoting tolerance to actually encouraging positive and affirming relationship between people of different cultures and religions, so that what may be false thinking can have some chance of being exposed. For there is a strong case sometimes for intolerance as discussed in Chapter 1 (p. 4). Intolerance is not always wrong; should we not indeed be intolerant of evil, including that within ourselves?

Talk of tolerance, furthermore, is often preaching to the converted whilst the hard-liners who are regarded as intolerant are not addressed, and little help is given to moderates to counter infiltration by extremist or fundamentalist groups which are intolerant. In a perceptive article, Juliet Ipgrave, drawing on classroom experience of teaching RE to Muslim pupils, notes that the dialogue must be 'much more than Westernised liberals talking to one another'.[11]

This really is a crucial issue. It is more than teaching the young that violence is wrong – it is supporting them in their commitments to help them make sure that those commitments are as sound and as true as possible. For if it is the case that Allah does not teach hatred and violence, then those who believe He does are seriously misguided. The young can easily fall prey to manipulation if they have not been helped to understand this for themselves.

The urgent need therefore is for far more subtlety and a more nuanced approach to both religion and secularism – which is why RE is so important. Instead of running away from the issues, and especially from the question of truth, RE must embrace controversy and seek to help all pupils, whatever their religious or secularist beliefs, backgrounds and affiliations, to think about the beliefs and values which are essential for civilized life.

FEATURES OF WESTERN SOCIETY TODAY

In order to do this it is important for the teacher of RE to understand the nature of those facets of life in the twenty-first century which should be RE-friendly but which, if religion is misunderstood, may not be. Figure 2.1 notes some of these. The reader will probably want to add many more. These are all, from one point of view, immensely positive and exciting achievements, and they could all help to reinvigorate interest in religion and sensitivity in pursuing it. Yet all these facets also carry negative implications with regard to religion which have had the effect generally of marginalizing religion.

1   *The success of science in extending the frontiers of knowledge has led to scepticism about religion.* The achievements of science have encouraged the view that scientific method provides the *only* route to genuine knowledge. As religious beliefs cannot be proved scientifically they are to be doubted, for it is assumed that religion is just a matter of subjective opinion. Positivism, more popularly known as scientism, is so pervasive and damaging that it will be examined in detail in Chapter 3. RE must be able to discuss the degree to which its basis is faulty.

2   *The achievements of technology have promoted the distractions of a utilitarian approach to life.* The spectacular achievements of technology have dazzled people into

Figure 2.1 *Features of Western society today*

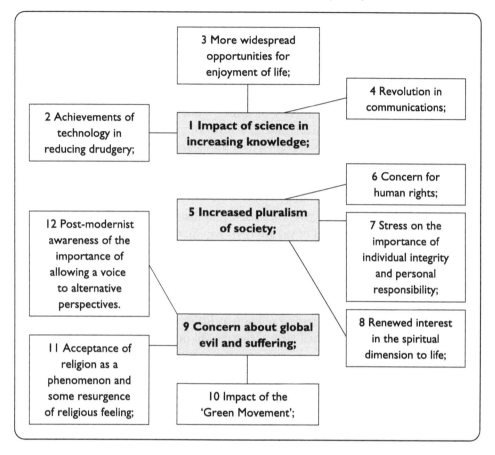

awe at the marvels of human inventiveness and mastery over the natural world, as well as promoting an unprecedented emphasis on mechanical and organizational efficiency. This has greatly encouraged a utilitarian attitude to life, and inflated the notion that human beings are the measure of all things. Both of these developments have tended to have the effect of dulling sensitivity to religion.

3   The attractiveness of a materialist way of life in encouraging consumerism, individualism or the pursuit of pleasure. A materialist way of life is enjoying a heyday. This shows itself in a variety of ways: in the all-consuming craving for more money and possessions, more power and social status, and more pleasure and entertainment. In such an environment it is hard to take religion seriously which requires that all these things – good as they may be – must take second place to the cultivation of spiritual values and the worship of God, not gods. It is not that these things are in themselves opposed to religion, but the possessiveness and distractedness which they tend to promote are.

4   *The restlessness of constant change and novelty, promoting activism*. Technology has brought speed of travel, and the almost instantaneous dissemination of information from one part of the world to another, such as has been unheard of in the history of the world. It has created a world of mobility: of rapid and constant change, with attention focused mainly on novelty or utility – a world eager to break free from tradition which has become irrelevant to a restless, fast-moving age. Although this can help religions come together, their traditions are under threat. It also affects religions in another way: religious sensitivity needs stillness in order to develop – a stillness almost impossible for most people in today's noisy world.

5   *Pluralism leading to relativism*. Increased pluralism has brought different problems for religion, notably that of yet another -ism, namely, relativism. Out of bewilderment at such diversity of views and the need to promote some level of harmony between them, the view has become quite widespread that differences are *entirely* due to cultural context and are not therefore contradictions to be resolved. This on the surface may not seem to be hostile to religion, but it causes severe re-interpretation encouraging many people to regard religion as little more than a culturally derived dressing-up game. How justified such a view is will be looked at in Chapter 3.

6   *A pragmatic basis for the human rights movement*. The emphasis in the human rights movement supported by this relativism is more and more in the direction of a hidden pragmatism. There is a marked reluctance to arguing why people should be accorded such rights – 'It just is so and things work better if you accept it – racism, for example, causes instability and prejudice and violence, so it must go'. Religious support is normally little called upon – indeed the record of most religions with regard to these issues is not regarded as good, and so it is not surprising that many see religion as the suppressor of human rights rather than as its advocate.

7   *Personal responsibility seen as the pursuit of autonomy*. Religion is often castigated for encouraging an attitude of dependence upon authority or tradition, which is at loggerheads with the attitude of taking responsibility for oneself. Religion has been accused indeed of keeping people docile and naïve. Assertiveness training has rarely featured much in religious traditions. They have often not promoted the idea that human nature is basically sound if encouraged, but rather emphasized the need for a concept of divine grace. This does not seem to fit in at all with the demand for autonomy.

8   *The spiritual dimension seen as separate from religion*. It may seem that the renewed interest in spirituality would be wholly to the benefit of religion, yet it is

not necessarily so. The word *spiritual* has become for many fundamentally dissociated from religion and so serves to encourage an alternative, one that is more attractive because lacking both definition and the incubus associated with religion. The search for spirituality can become diverted also into extremist cults or fascination with the occult, and if it avoids these dangers it can become simply another form of aesthetic experience and move away from the major religious traditions. Many people, for example, see the arts as a kind of substitute for religion.

9   The problem of global evil and suffering can be seen as an indictment of religion. Awareness of the enormity of global evil and suffering, aggravated by the potential powers now within human grasp, has been augmented by the speed and change of life and the challenges and displacements this brings. All this, often broadcast by the media too, has had a detrimental effect on religion causing the age-old cry of the heart, 'If there is a God why all this suffering?' to be raised with ever-greater seriousness and urgency. The dilemma is worse still in that religion often appears to be inextricably and centrally involved in the perpetration of crime. The anti-semitism associated with Christianity is such an example.[12] These questions will be discussed in some depth in Chapters 3 and 5.

10   The 'Green Movement' is often critical of religion. The 'Green Movement' is not necessarily the friend of religion – it can displace it as understood within the great religious traditions, giving rise to a neo-paganism which challenges them. It is deeply critical in particular of the exploitation of the earth which it often considers the three Semitic religions of Judaism, Christianity and Islam are guilty of pursuing. Christianity especially has come in for great criticism as being the major religion in the history of Western civilization, and therefore the one which must take most blame.

11   Acceptance of religion as a phenomenon has not weakened critique of religious institutions. The shortcomings of organized religions, especially in having within their ranks and amongst their leadership large numbers who do not live up to their beliefs, have had a serious effect on attitudes towards religion. A huge battery of criticism is levelled against religion, including charges of hypocrisy, smugness, dogmatism, narrow-mindedness, imperialism, naïvety and prejudice. Criticism of religious institutions, leadership and policies is rife, and religious people have on the whole been tardy in responding creatively to justified charges and pointing out the inappropriateness of false charges; an approach of burying one's head in the sand has been a characteristic of many religious people. Hatred of religious bigotry, and of the violence and injustice it can produce, is a major reason for people turning their backs on religion (see discussion in Chapter 3, pp. 43–7).

12   Post-modernism serves often to undermine religion in three respects. Whilst the celebration of diversity which reflects a major post-modernist mood gives encouragement for the expression of a variety of religious beliefs, it also poses a severe challenge in taking any of them seriously. As a newer phenomenon we discuss this in more detail.

Comment on post-modernism

Post-modernism impacts negatively on understanding of religion in at least three ways. First, post-modernism has indeed effectively challenged the all-pervasiveness of positivism which sees scientific method as leading to absolutely reliable knowledge; it interprets this -ism as one vulnerable *meta-narrative* amongst others. Theoretically this should have helped to raise the status of religion by counteracting scepticism of religion based on scientific considerations. However, because it discounts all meta-narratives, it discounts the meta-narratives behind all the major religions too. Thus attempts to incorporate post-modernist insight by religious people have tended to privatize religion still further, emphasizing its purely subjective and personal nature as this person's or that person's *micro-narratives*. By denying the possibility of any objective truth post-modernism puts a question mark beside all forms of traditional religious belief. All the religions offer meta-narratives which it discredits on grounds of their being purely local. It thus powerfully reinforces a relativist assessment of all religious truth-claims.

Second, the extreme emphasis on the power motif behind all agendas reinforces the general suspicion of society as a whole to authority of any kind. Because post-modernism does not take the notion of truth seriously it tends to reinterpret people's claims to truth as disguised claims to power. We are all hopelessly entangled with individual desire for power which affects our judgement. This makes ancient religious traditions appear to be even more outmoded than before as being also despotic. Its emphasis on power seeking and power keeping agendas serves to reinforce the suspicion of all hierarchical authority structures. It makes it appear childish and damaging to accept any religious authority whatsoever.

Third, post-modernism effectively marginalizes the historical dimension thus treating deference to tradition of any kind as a kind of hangover from the past. It insists on meaning being what we as individuals find now, and focuses so strongly on the present and perhaps the future that it breaks links with the past. A sense of history and a knowledge of history are not highly regarded in our society today. It often appears contemptuous of what previous generations have discovered and lived by, and arrogant in its belief in the creative possibilities of the present day, especially in the light of continuing technological advancement. Thus if we today do not see any need to talk about God, the fact that other people at other times have done so does not matter. Those who still do – and particularly attention is drawn to ethnic minorities in the West who continue to be interested in religion – can be treated with tolerance but their truth-claims can be ignored and not considered at all.

THE RADICAL SECULARISM OF SOCIETY

All these factors fan a bias against religion which produces a fundamental obstacle for RE. Some argue that the secularization thesis is in trouble and that it is really just a turning away from institutional religion. For they consider that the religious impulse is very much alive still, as the rise of New Age religion and other forms of 'spirituality' testify.

On the other hand, the assumption that religion does not matter because it is not true – that it is an illusion – is prevalent among the leadership of society in the West, especially in the professions, in politics, in the business world and in the media. The notion that there is no God tends to be routine, together with seeing the spiritual dimension to life as being simply an aspect of human personality which human beings create for themselves.

In such a society it is not 'done' to admit to taking religion seriously. David Hay, who was director of the Religious Experience in Education Project at Nottingham University, draws attention to the taboo about religion in British society. Research conducted at the Alister Hardy Research Centre suggests religion is widely regarded as 'a culturally mediated prejudice'.[13]

A question of vocabulary: secularist *and* secular
It is important to note at this point two very different ways in which the word *secular* can be used. One meaning relates to this-worldly matters – how things get done, efficiency, practical points, anything to do with what we see, hear, touch, feel and taste, how we find out about these things, and so on. But the word can also be used to denote the idea that religion does not matter because it is not true.[14] The distinction is a very significant one, because all the great religions of the world have emphasized how important it is that religion and life are bound up together, that religion does not hive off into some remote corner unrelated to the real world; all religions do bother about the *secular* in the first sense of the word; about how life is actually lived and what people are and do, and not just about what they say and believe. But if *secular* is used in the second sense, as meaning the abandonment of religion, it is obviously the enemy of religion. Its presence will indicate indifference, if not hostility, towards religion and make it very difficult for people to take religion seriously.

Some Christian theologians such as John Macquarrie[15] have tried to indicate the difference between these two uses of *secular* by coining specific terms: *secularity* and *secular* as referring to the straight-forward neutral sense, and *secularism* and *secularist* to the anti-religious stance. Although this distinction is not widely known, we think it a helpful one because when words mean radically different things it is useful to have some way of explicitly distinguishing them.

The legacy of religion

The widespread presence of secularism does not mean that the legacy of religion does not live on. (See Chapter 5 for further discussion on the extent to which Britain should be described as a post-Christian society.) Michael Polanyi drew attention to the way in which people can unconsciously share certain basic assumptions or beliefs even if, at a conscious level, they express something else. He suggested a reason for this – the power of habit: 'People can carry on a great tradition while proposing a philosophy which denies its premises. For the adherents of a great tradition are largely unaware of their own premises, which lie deeply embedded in the unconscious foundations of practice.'[16] Its roots are tenacious and most people still wish to acknowledge the ideal of Christian values. Religion is far from being totally eclipsed or reduced to the status of a literally insignificant minority interest.

Nevertheless Polanyi considered that our society is a secularist one, not in its values but in its rejection of the beliefs supporting those values. Values enshrined within Christianity may still be widely held, but this does not mean that Christianity is believable for the vast majority. The vehicle may still be moving forward under the impact of the initial push but, if the source of the pushing is removed, how long will it continue in motion? Are there other pushing agencies available, and if so will they push in the same direction?

This poses the interesting question which only the future can resolve: how long can values survive without the beliefs which sustain them? Peter Fuller, the atheist art critic who died in 1990, pursued the question rigorously as to how art can flourish in a secular society. He saw the discontinuity with religion as the dilemma of modern art and asked, 'Can work be reinvested with its spiritual-aesthetic dimension when tradition has in fact gone, and we have lost the illusions of faith?'[17] It is significant however that he referred to religious faith as *illusions*. This is a key indicator of the presence of secularism.

IMPACT OF SECULARISM ON SCHOOLS

It would be surprising if education escaped being profoundly influenced by secularism. Indeed education has played a huge part in encouraging secularization for, despite the radical thrust at work in much educational policy, many of the characteristics of a society have been internalized too deeply.

In schools the assumptions of society show themselves in three ways: through what has been called the explicit, the implicit and the null curricula. These three curricula

Figure 2.2 *The received curriculum*

Seven factors influence what is either learnt or indoctrinated

2 METHOD
how it is taught

3 AUTHORITY
with what status it
is taught

EXPLICIT CURRICULUM

IMPLICIT CURRICULUM

I CONTENT
what is taught

4 RECURRENCE
how often it is
taught

UNIQUE FACTORS

NULL CURICULUM

7 PERSONAL
how attentive a
pupil is

5 DEFAULT
what is not taught

**6 OUT-OF-SCHOOL
CONTEXT**
what is or is not encouraged

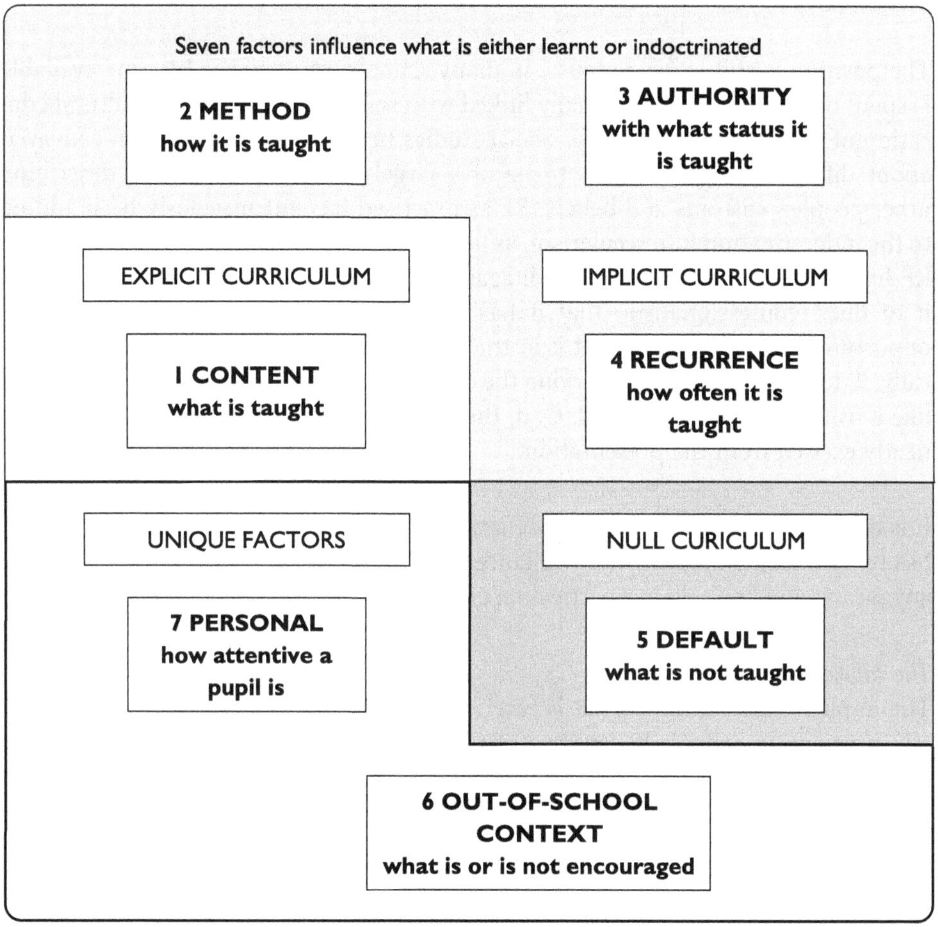

play their part in what is *the received curriculum* for any one particular pupil (see Figure 2.2).

The explicit curriculum
The explicit curriculum refers to what is openly expressed as the intention of the school, and to what is actually taught – the content *per se* which is put across. In the majority of schools this is mostly devoid of any reference to religion; thus the teaching of science, maths, history, geography, PE, art etc. normally have little specifically religious content. The subject area RE continues to have low profile. Despite the best efforts of organizations like the REC[18] and initiatives at QCA, in the schools

themselves RE is often struggling to achieve recognition and status. This is hardly surprising given the widespread view that it is all illusion.

The position is still worse because, in many schools, most of the RE time available is spent on content only marginally linked with religion: on moral and cultural education of one kind or another, or social studies in which the information conveyed about different religions tends to be of a largely sociological nature, describing other people's customs and beliefs. RE as practised has unconsciously been adding to the indoctrination into secularism, as has already been hinted at on page 24 above. RE has had to defend itself so much against the secularist objection raised against it of illicit confessionalism, that it has often effectively removed from teaching opportunities to reflect on what is at the heart of religion. As Copley notes graphically, 'Education is visibly preserving the discourse of religion, but sometimes rather like a fish that has been filleted. God, the backbone of religion, has too often been neatly excised from the presentation.'[19]

It is difficult to avoid the conclusion that, with regard to the explicit curriculum, RE has to fight for its life; constant vigilance is the necessary price it pays for retaining any meaningful foothold in a curriculum groaning under the weight of other priorities.

The implicit curriculum

The implicit curriculum is what is received through the total impact of what actually happens in school. It covers attitudes, relationships, behaviour, selection of content, manner of teaching, way of speaking to pupils, and many other factors. The implicit curriculum includes the messages conveyed by the ethos of the school and the total approach to pupils, as well as to how the explicit curriculum is delivered.

One powerful message put across by the curriculum in most schools is that knowledge can be divided into compartments. This has the effect of divorcing religion – like other subjects – from the rest of the curriculum. If practical considerations make it desirable to put RE with another subject, then the one chosen is usually humanities or social studies, it being taken for granted that religion is an aspect of what people believe. It is assumed to have nothing to do with, for example, science.

We need to remember that the implicit curriculum works especially through style of teaching. Pupils can pick up many notions from the very methods we use. Thus discussion lessons can often give the impression that everything is just a matter of opinion – there need be no rigour, for 'it's all subjective anyway'.[20] Talk of problem-solving becomes translated into a message to pupils that all matters of controversy can and should be resolved; the idea that not everything is a problem to be solved is barely entertained. The use of role-play can similarly often give the impression that façades are more important than being oneself, acting a part more significant than reflective evaluation.

Thus the implicit curriculum rests on beliefs and values also – not necessarily the same as those behind the explicit curriculum, for there is often considerable double-talk and hypocrisy, mostly unintentional but sometimes not. The existence of a powerful taboo against religion in society as a whole, together with the lack of opportunity given by the explicit curriculum for questioning the taboo, ensures that most of this implicit curriculum operates against religion – against its being taken seriously.

The null curriculum
The null curriculum exists by reason of the fact that it does not exist – it is what is conveyed by omission, avoidance, bypassing, as well as by ridiculing, criticizing, and putting-down. Its allies are boredom, distraction, prejudice and narrowness of out-look. It refers to excluded knowledge, failure to give pupils opportunities to appre-ciate, areas left out of consideration, ideas not addressed, concepts not offered or discussed. Pupils cannot think about or develop sensitivity and discernment concerning what they are in deepest ignorance about, even as not to appreciate that there is anything of which they are ignorant is an even greater indication of the degree of deprivation. It also relates to the way in which subjects are not presented – to pro-cesses and procedures and methods which are rarely or never employed. This is not neutral – it indoctrinates more successfully than anything else. As Maria Harris has noted:

> The point of including the null curriculum is, of course, that ignorance – not knowing something – is never neutral. If we do not know about something or do not realise what is addressed can be understood in another manner or seen through another lens, it skews our viewpoint; it limits our options; it clouds our perspective.[21]

Religion is most notable by its absence, and, where it appears, by the omission of any serious discussion of its truth-claims. A good example of this is the way in which sex education is approached. It is remarkable how little generally any religious perspective on this is ever mentioned. Issues such as abortion which are widely acknowledged as controversial in society do find a place in PSHE (personal, social and health education) or RE lessons, but the crucial de-coupling of sexual activity from any intention of long-term loving relationship is barely questioned. It tends to be simply assumed that everyone has the right to sexual pleasure if they wish, provided the partner gives consent and precautions are taken to prevent unwanted pregnancy or the spread of Aids.[22] This is an approach which no major religion countenances. Nor do any of them see sex education as just a matter for lessons in biology, health education, social studies or PSHE.

It is true that official publications, such as the DfES booklet *Sex and Relationship Education Guidance* (2000), include reference to teaching about relationships, love and care, and the responsibilities of parenthood. As Halstead and Reiss say in their book, *Values in Sex Education* (2003): 'most serious books on sex education nowadays acknowledge the importance of value'. But they immediately add that 'many give the topic comparatively brief attention before moving on to what they present as more pressing matters.'[23] The impression can easily be given, especially in a culture in which propaganda for sex is put across forcefully in so many ways, that the problem of unprotected sex is a mechanistic problem, and therefore that mechanistic solutions are all that are needed. Marvellous opportunities for discussing depth in personal relationships and the development of an attitude of genuine love are routinely missed. Indeed, as recent surveys reported on by Mark Pike[24] show, many teachers fear even to discuss questions of family life or promote family values, in case they offend someone or appear moralistic.

Whilst many today are beginning to see that a hedonist philosophy of life is seriously inadequate, in an area where some revision is so clearly relevant the matter is rarely raised in schools, never-alone taken seriously and discussed.

The scales are not neatly balanced as between secularism and religion in our society. In most societies the world has known, the balance has been in favour of religion; in ours it is the other way round. This is the background against which RE has to happen.

REACTION AGAINST THE PRIVILEGED STATUS OF RELIGION

It is interesting to note that there appears to be great resistance to acknowledging the full impact of secularism on schools. The real situation RE has to contend with is now very different from how many, perhaps most, people have generally thought it to be. Historically, the Christian churches had exceptionally close links with education: indeed in the early nineteenth century almost all the impetus for setting up schools and teacher-training establishments and extending schooling to all children came from the churches. In the UK the teaching of religion was always a feature of the curriculum, and until 1988 was the one subject legally required. The Government has given assurances that the subject is important and is not about to be replaced by citizenship education. But the fact that in the late 1990s many in the

RE profession were seriously worried about the retention of RE shows that it is not the key subject that it once was thought to be.

That the subject is in fact normally accorded Cinderella status matters little to the many who object to its being there at all. In his book *Better Schools: a Values Perspective*, Clive Beck[25] devotes a chapter to religious bias alongside chapters on racism, ethnic bias, sexism and class bias. There is no mention at all of secularist bias. The omission is significant: the danger is perceived as entirely pertaining to religious believers, and illustrates very well the hold which a secular view has on him and on the educational world in the West generally.

Indoctrination into secularism

Most people do not recognize the secularist bias precisely because it *is* ubiquitous and so forcefully put across. It has often and justly been observed that real indoctrination goes undetected except by those who for other reasons have cause to question the content of the beliefs and values into which they are being pushed. Most people in our society have no cause to question the truth of what is put across in the teaching of science, English or history, for example, and therefore the indoctrination which can go on there is largely unheeded. The fear and suspicion of religious indoctrination is a most powerful indicator of the opposite trend being uppermost. Most people have not been indoctrinated into religious faith but into a questioning or ignoring of religion as basically superseded if not actually false.

David Hay has called for a 'de-indoctrination' from secularism.[26] Copley also makes clear that 'education should embrace the possibility of God'. He points out that 'That is not the same as embracing the certainty of God or teaching . . . that God is a "fact" that cannot be challenged or denied . . . But what is happening at present in education and in wider British society is tending to eliminate or deny the possibility of God.'[27] Regarding the truth-claims of religion and of atheism, he notes

> If education ignores the question . . . it also commits indoctrination by virtue of not providing children with the tools and skills with which to enter the debate, or of teaching them that the question is of no importance. They are then left prey to media impressions of religion or doorstep vendors or to the unbalanced preaching from secular pulpits of some journalists. The only role for education in this apparent impasse, therefore, and one which is truly educational rather than indoctrinatory, is to induct children into the debate.

Copley asks 'Is the surrender of mind to an uncritical secular world-view inevitable?' We believe it is not, and the next chapter seeks to equip the reader with that critique which, as Copley notes on the last page of his book, can liberate and embrace emotional as well as mental intelligence.[28]

TO THINK ABOUT

If we start from a basic assumption that there is more to life than meets the eye, and if we think that this is justified, then what follows?
- does this entail a secularist view of the universe and of life as a whole?
- does it leave the options open for religion?
- does it maybe lead more naturally to a religious view of the world?

Do the same for these assumptions.
   Human rights are absolute.
   I believe that my life/human life in general has meaning.

NOTES

 1 Copley, T. (2005), p. xvi.
 2 Williams, R. (2004).
 3 Hassan, N. (2005) in *Times* article 'Are you ready? Tomorrow you will be in paradise', 14 July.
 4 Marsden, G. (1997), p. 7.
 5 Ibid., p. 20.
 6 Webster, J. (1998), esp. pp. 2–4.
 7 Copley, T. (2005), p. 139.
 8 Jackson, R. (1997).
 9 Hookway, S.R. (2004).
10 See e.g. O'Hear, A. (2001) and Furedi, F. (2004).
11 Ipgrave, J. (1999), pp. 137–45.
12 See e.g. Carroll, J. (2001) and Ludemann, G. (1997).
13 Hay, D. in Hammond, J. et al. (1990), p. 205.
14 See a lecture given by Harry Blamires © The Christian Institute, 1990, 'The Christian in a Secular Age'.
15 Macquarrie, J. (1968), p. 20f.
16 Polanyi, M. (1964a), p. 76; see also (1964b).
17 Fuller, P. (1990), p. 297.
18 The Religious Education Council is an umbrella organization which has a large and impressive membership of bodies with an active interest in RE. These include faith groups and professional organizations: www.religiouseducationcouncil.org
19 Copley, T. (2005), p. 148.
20 Or 'fake RS' as was put to one of us by a 15-year-old pupil about RS lessons in her school which do not involve writing or tests.
21 Harris, M. (1988), pp. 20–1.
22 See e.g. Morris, R.W. (1994).
23 Halstead, J.M. and Reiss, M.J. (2003), p. 3.

24 Pike, M. (2006). A chapter 'Citizenship and Moral Education through RE and PSHE' in a book to be published by Routledge/Falmer. But see John Marks (2001), pp. 5–36. Marks questions any simplistic connection between church schools and good exam results.
25 Beck, C. (1990).
26 Hay, D. (1990), p. 109.
27 Copley, T. (2005), pp. 139–41.
28 Ibid., p. 150.

CHAPTER 3

GIVING RELIGION A CHANCE

'The crucial question is always not what we think, but whether what we think is right. It is not whether we can produce an explanation that for some reason appeals to us, but whether we can discover an explanation which is grounded in the way that things actually are.' (Roger Trigg)[1]

We set out the intellectual case against secularism. Presenting this to pupils in a variety of appropriate ways is a major task for RE. We begin by showing that human beings live on the basis of assumptions which they cannot prove. It is important to acknowledge assumptions and to revise them where they are suspected of being faulty. We argue that the assumptions behind three major arguments for secularism – positivism, relativism/ post-modernism and hatred of religious intolerance – are defective. The case for a serious and open-ended study of religion is strong.

As the previous chapter showed, many aspects of growing up in today's world encourage a dismissive attitude to religion. If RE is to help pupils towards an under-standing of religion it must therefore challenge those attitudes. Pupils cannot be expected to reflect on religion in an informed way if their minds and emotions are already sealed tight against it, that is, if they assume that religion is outdated and not worth studying.

In order, therefore, to teach RE effectively we need to be very clear about how shaky the secularist stance actually is, and how strong is the case for an openness towards religion. RE is on a much stronger wicket than it is usually given credit for, provided it exhibits such openness. We shall return to this point at the end of the chapter.

It is a matter of practical importance that teachers can argue this case. Specific work on it in secondary schools is often essential in order to break down resistance to the subject. Many awkward classes become much less so if some exploration in depth is attempted of the kind of points discussed in this chapter.

It is important also that awareness of this argument informs what primary school teachers do concerning RE. In all sorts of situations it is called for, not only with children, but with other staff, parents and governors. Even very young children make remarks and ask questions which call for quite sophisticated understanding of such issues.

THE NATURE OF ASSUMPTIONS

Two preliminary points need to be made before setting out the argument against secularism.

First, we all have to live and act *as if* we were sure and *as if* we had reliable knowledge. We have to stand somewhere as we decide the next step forward. Yet whether we think of ourselves as secularist or as religious, we cannot be absolutely certain in such a way that our views cannot be challenged by other people. Delusion is possible for everyone: *feeling* certain does not mean that therefore the world is as we think it is. All of us can make mistakes. The unavoidable fact of the matter is that both religion and secularism are stances. To vary the analogy, not to be religious is already to have invested money in what is as high a risk venture as an investment in religion.[2]

Second, it is impossible to prove assumptions, but this does not mean that we are just locked into a position for ever. Experience of life, and genuine discussion with people of other views, can enable us to add to and revise, and even occasionally to give up, aspects of the stance which we have adopted so far. What is needed is a willingness to be open to fresh possibilities and to be prepared for a constant voyage of exploration.

We need to look at assumptions, seeing whether we think they really are justified, and if so, do they really lead to the positions which we at the moment think they lead to. For example, if we think that a basic assumption is that people matter as persons, and that this is justified, then what follows?
• does this entail a secularist view of the universe and of life as a whole?
• does it leave the options open for religion?
• does it maybe lead more naturally to a religious view of the world?

THE CASE AGAINST SECULARISM

At this point we can move to the case against secularism. RE needs to sow seeds of doubt into the current widespread acceptability of secularism. Suggestions are made on the website as to how this can be done in practical terms. Here we outline the intellectual arguments which it is important for the teacher to appreciate and share with pupils as appropriate.

In Chapter 2, twelve aspects of contemporary society which can cause trouble for religion were outlined. Three of these are of major significance regarding basic beliefs: (A) positivism, (B) relativism (with its close relative post-modernism) and (C) religious intolerance. The others are largely dependent on them.

(A) Secularism based on a mistaken view of science

Science has for many people ruled out religion. The root problem here is the question of how we can arrive at absolutely certain and reliable knowledge. Scientific method, using experiment and reasoning, has led to a marvellous extension of knowledge. But it has also led to assumptions which cause religion to be ignored, doubted and re-interpreted.

This is because of the significance of the little word *only*. If this word is added to the justified claim that 'scientific method can lead to reliable knowledge', it becomes an exclusivist claim which purports to deride all other ways to knowledge. *Positivism* is the name given to the philosophy based on the principle that all claims to knowledge must be scientifically provable and there must be positive proof. This philosophy was developed first in the seventeenth century and it has become increasingly influential ever since. Another term used to describe it is *naturalism* – the assumption that only the natural world exists. A popular word sometimes used is *scientism*.

This leads to an attitude of scepticism towards anything not amenable to scientific investigation. This in turn leaves beliefs and values out in the cold regarding what is considered to be knowledge, for they appear to be simply subjective. Facts are regarded as objective, reliable and unbiased, whilst values, principles and beliefs are subjective, unreliable and probably biased. On the doubtful side of this line come most of the things which people care most about, including matters associated with personal relationships, the arts, moral issues and religion. What may be called a fact/belief divide is set up.

To appreciate what this fact/belief divide is, see Figure 3.1. Here a number of statements are shown which many people may be inclined to put into one box or the other. Someone who believes that facts are quite different from beliefs, reliable in the way that beliefs are just opinions, would divide these statements into the two boxes quite easily. Which would be put in which box?

A number of other questions suggest themselves, such as:
- Can the statements in the fact box actually be proved?
- Is it true that there is no evidence to be considered regarding the statements in the belief box?
- Which box would you say tends to have the more interesting and important statements?
- Can you think why the fact/belief divide might be considered damaging in its effect?

Figure 3.1 *The fact/belief divide*

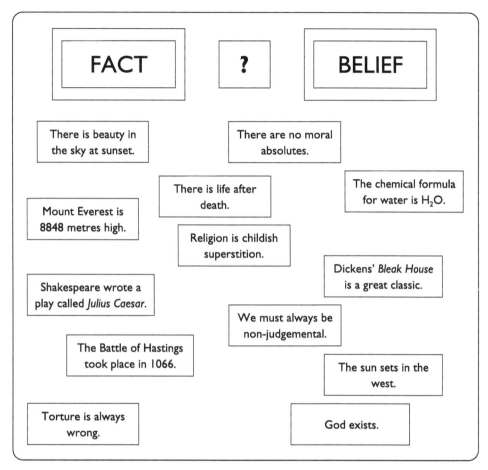

Impact of the fact/belief divide

Relativism is in many ways dependent on this fact/belief divide (see Figure 3.2). The simplest way to explain the variety of opinions which cannot be tested scientifically is to see them as wholly *relative* to the particular context giving rise to them, to cultural upbringing and different individual and group experience. Relativism has been powerfully strengthened by its near-relative, post-modernism, which has had the effect of vastly augmenting the area of intellectual activity deemed not to be objective in any meaningful way.

The fact/belief divide is powerfully at work today in education. Priorities in curriculum planning, resources, staffing and research clearly indicate that subjects most capable of yielding precise measurable, scientifically-sound knowledge are the top

Figure 3.2 *Dislocation of the creative circle between science and beliefs*

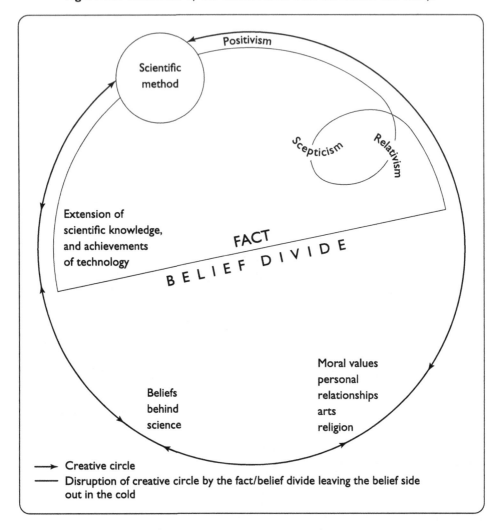

priority in schools, whilst subjects deemed to be subjective and vague lead an uneasy life on the periphery of official schooling. This occurs despite some verbal acknowledgement of how important they are.

The obsession with assessment as the best way to achieve standards has been a marked feature of the British educational scene in recent decades. This is a clear indicator of the presence of positivism. For it is presumed that:

- there are clear-cut provable 'facts';
- such 'facts' constitute the heart of education;
- objective testing of how far pupils have learnt these 'facts' is possible.

This has affected how the teaching of subjects like history and geography are seen. Many consider they should predominantly teach 'facts'. Matters which relate to 'mere opinion', such as environmental and moral concerns, are normally starved of time and attention in practice. In RE the teacher is expected to tell the pupils 'the facts' which are held to be neutral and uncontroversial but when it comes to 'values' they must insist that pupils make 'their own' judgements. For most people remain unaware that there is any problem with regard to the reliability of the (selected) facts. And they take it for granted that beliefs and values are not the sorts of things that can be held to account.

Mark Chater has suggested that there are dangerous political overtones in all this. He writes:

> Teachers receive very little encouragement to engage in values discourse in public or political contexts. Instead, curriculum and inspection values, and codes of profession-alism, encourage them to maintain modes of vocation and value as personal devotions. Rather than turning their evolving sense of vocation outwards towards critical dialogue with the system, teachers tend to turn it inwards, and thus allow the system to con-tradict their impulses. Thus, brutally put, the technicist curriculum is implemented termly by teachers who comfort themselves with a private, personal sense of values.[3]

More will be said about the technicist utilitarian curriculum in Chapter 4.

Here the fact/belief divide is dangerously at work promoting inauthentic teaching and a hypocrisy which requires pupils to exercise judgement on their own whilst teach-ers outwardly adopt the values required of them by the system. Yet the positivism which is ultimately responsible for this fact/belief divide is deeply flawed in three ways: it is *illogical, unscientific* and *exclusivist.*

1   It is illogical. It contradicts itself. It claims that proof is necessary for knowledge, yet cannot prove itself to be true. It appeals to reason, but in order to reason we have to take something for granted as a starting point and this cannot be proved.

In playing a game, pre-determined rules can be applied because it is a game. But claims about reality do not have such rules to which appeal can be made: they are neces-sarily themselves controversial. Furthermore, even in a game the exact direction for kicking the ball depends on the players' awareness and skills. Understanding of reality equally depends on people's awareness, intelligence and sensitivity.

Another way of expressing the same idea is that logic is like kicking a ball and it may go in a straight line, but if the direction is wrong it will not help the team to win the game. But how do we know in which direction to head? There is no proof on which to draw reliably for that. It rests on what is bound to be, to some extent, subjective assessment. Even in playing a game where there are rules and communal experience to draw on, success ultimately depends on the players' awareness and skill.

2   It is unscientific. Positivism contradicts actual scientific experience and findings. Many leading scientists do not consider that science can give absolutely reliable and unchallengeable knowledge. Increasingly today, they are accepting that scientific pronouncements have an unavoidable element, not only of subjectivity, but also of informed guesswork about them. This is because of the nature of the world which is so complex and has what appears to be an inbuilt indeterminism or chance.

An anecdote told by a scientist well summarizes this element of randomness: 'When I visited the European Medium Range Weather Forecasting Centre they told me, "We can predict the weather accurately provided it doesn't do anything unexpected".'[4] To insist therefore that science provides cast-iron knowledge is to *believe* in a mirage. Science cannot provide that kind of certainty.

Furthermore, it is often overlooked that we can only apply scientific method to a tiny fraction of the impressions upon which we act. This very selectivity of what the scientist chooses to notice and work upon is another reason for saying that science is to some extent subjective.

Besides this, the whole process of scientific investigation is based on a series of assumptions which the scientist makes, very often at an unconscious level. If those assumptions were seriously challenged the scientist would not be able to operate. A substantial article by Nicholas Maxwell in *The Philosophers' Magazine* points out: 'Scientists don't know that the universe is comprehensible. This metaphysical assumption – which must be made if science is to proceed at all – is a pure article of faith.'[5] (See the website for material on how science is based on such beliefs as order in the universe.)

3   It is exclusivist. A positivist view of science excludes an enormous area of life. Scientific method is obviously extremely valuable for finding out about things amenable to observation, experiment and logical progression of thought. To say, however, that this route supplies the *only* reliable way to knowledge is grossly to overstep its boundaries. It is in fact to be very dogmatic and to try to say something about every other way of knowledge, and every other thing to be known. For by insisting it is the *only* way to knowledge it is dismissing other ways as unimportant, irrelevant and probably misleading.

This is a wide agenda. Where is the scientific evidence to support so wide an onslaught? The intrusion of the single word *only* is a serious fault.

This challenge of scientific method to ways of knowing is probably more significant today than the well-publicized clashes between religion and science associated with Galileo and with Darwin. It was indeed Darwin's wife, Emma, herself a scientist, who pointed out the real danger in the use of scientific method when she asked him: 'May not the habit in scientific pursuits of believing nothing till it is proved, influence your mind too much in other things which cannot be proved in the same way and which, if true, are likely to be above our comprehension?'[6]

Doubt can play a very useful role in resisting credulity and naïvety, but to argue that only if you doubt can you arrive at the truth (a position of scepticism) is to disregard the question of what is to be known. In getting to know a person for example, to insist on doubting everything he or she does and says all the time will soon put an end to any effective relationship! We get to know people by accepting them, by trusting them and not entertaining doubt unless there is strong evidence for it.

Exclusivism frequently occurs unintentionally but nevertheless effectively through the teaching of separate subject areas which tends to give the impression that they offer a complete explanation of something.

(B) Secularism based on relativism
The fact that religion won't just go away has led those influenced by positivism to explain religion as entirely a matter of social and cultural conditioning and outward show: basically religion is a kind of cultural dressing-up game. This is a view of religion which is seen as primarily like fashion and what people 'put on'. Such 'sartorial' religion is taken seriously indeed, because it deals with deep human needs, desires and questions, and the level of conditioning can be deeply internalized. It can nevertheless be seen as a kind of charade whereby societies have in the past been held together but which, as a charade, is replaceable by something not involving the pretence element. For there is no truth to be found in a religion; it is all a matter of cultural focusing.

Relativism draws attention to what Aristotle noticed long ago: 'Fire burns both in Hellas and in Persia; but men's ideas of right and wrong vary from place to place.'[7] People brought up in different places and having different life experiences will come up with different opinions. If they had been born into a different culture they would have believed something quite different.

Before responding to this objection against religion it is important first to acknowledge the insights which relativism brings – insights often neglected in earlier centuries. Just as Figure 3.2 draws attention to the proper use of science, so does the relativist approach preserve important insights. These include awareness of:

1 an amazing diversity of views even within one society, and more so on a global scale;
2 the importance of context in understanding why people are as they are, and believe as they do, and assume what they do;
3 the possibility of self-delusion: we *could* be conditioned into mistaken views;
4 learning to take seriously what people believe before making a judgement upon that belief;
5 a style of education which encourages individual learning rather than teacher-dominated presentation of content. As such it seems particularly appropriate for a time of rapid change and the need to unlearn dogmatism.

These insights are muddled, however, if the little word *only* creeps in to the way in which they are expressed: 'What you believe is *only* a matter of where you were born, and what people around you believe.' The short maxim, 'It's *all* relative', expresses the same exclusivism. In this way beliefs and values are denied their claim to be real knowledge.

There are at least three strong arguments against relativism as a stance which it is important that we help pupils to understand.

1   It is illogical. Relativism is 'self-defeating'. For if all opinions are relative, then the view that all opinions are relative is itself relative and therefore not true in itself. So if it is true it is false.

This is like the puzzle which can quite infuriate children as well as adults: one side of the paper has written on it: 'The sentence on the other side of this piece of paper is not correct', and the other side has this sentence, 'The sentence on the other side is correct'. Which side is right? The point is of course that the puzzle itself is false in setting up an impossible situation. Similarly, the relativist stance does not work unless it makes an exception of itself which denies its own principle.

As in the case of positivism, we have found that children in primary schools as well as older pupils not only can see this point, but also enjoy doing so and they find it intriguing.

2   It is reductionist. Relativism as a stance ignores what is central to religion and its truth-claims. It assumes that there can be no evidence worth discussing concerning the truth of religious beliefs.

This is to misrepresent religion. Religious faith is practised because it is believed to be true. Within Judaism, Christianity and Islam, faith is a response to what is claimed as revelation about the nature of reality. Within religions of Indian origin, such as Hinduism, Buddhism and Sikhism, certain views of reality are taken for granted, such as *dharma* and the existence of a moral law, and *karma* and the impact of this on individuals according to how much they fulfil or fail to fulfil *dharma*, and *samsara* and the process of reincarnation. These are not regarded as just ideas in the mind, or a figment of the collective imagination, but as true; they demand to be taken seriously, and evidence for them discussed.

The attractiveness of the cultural explanation of religion is that it appears to account for the diversity in religious practices and beliefs without the necessity to get involved in controversy. Cultures are like colours and we can have any number on our palette without any problems. We don't need to enter the troubled waters of religious truth-claims. Yet as the sociologist Peter Berger[8] has pointed out, while a sociological perspective on religion is extremely illuminating, fascinating and insightful, it can be misread as an argument against religion. It can seem to offer a completely adequate explanation of religion which bypasses what religious believers have always insisted upon as the truth. Such matters become safely and clinically bracketed away into the equation: knowledge = understanding of religious people (who believe x, y, or z). The possibility that knowledge = understanding of x, y or z is ruled out.

This is to be just as dogmatic as relativists accuse religious people of being. It is to risk leaving out what religion is really about. The claim to be neutral regarding religion has a way of neutering religious claims, rather like music without sound, or mathematics without numbers.

3 It could be destructive in its consequences. The pervasiveness of a version of religion as culturally cosmetic subtly does a lot of harm to people; it can be very dismissive and hurtful, marginalizing what makes a religious person tick. This can have the effect of isolating that person and creating the ghetto mentality. A conversation reported by Niall Ferguson between one of the would-be Islamikaze bombers, Muktar Said-Ibrahim, and a former neighbour of his in Stanmore who told him she didn't believe in anything, pinpoints as Ferguson put it 'the gulf that now exists in this country between a minority of fanatics and a majority of atheists'. Writing as an atheist himself, he finished the article with this comment relating to the threat to 'our way of life' from such extremists: 'How far has our own loss of religious faith turned this country into a soft target . . . for the fanaticism of others?'[9]

Relativism can also cause self-crisis in which the mainspring of a person's belief system is called into doubt and inwardly crumbles without anything strong and important to take its place. Fear of this happening is a prime reason for some religious people's failure to relate to other people's views; they therefore take refuge in intransigent attitudes often referred to by other people as fundamentalist, religionist (to use John

Hull's term[10]) or extremist. Often therefore relativism produces, through reaction to it, precisely what it sets out to destroy: increased dogmatism.

More often the impact of dogmatically held relativism on other people is to cause them to waver, feel uncertain and drift into what they feel they can be sure about. This is mostly in Western society a materialist attitude to life, or perhaps pursuing a life-stance which thinks it has avoided value judgements. Of course it has not; for example, with regard to moral issues, the typically relativist view that there are no absolutes is itself a stance based on assumptions which it is possible to challenge.

Put in a nutshell, this puts the whole concept of justice into jeopardy. If all is relative, then protest against racism, sexism and other evils is at root an arbitrary subjective one and why shouldn't somebody be racist if all is a matter of mere opinion or expediency? If there are no absolutes or eternal values, then the moral imperative behind such movements evaporates into thin air. The concept of social responsibility is too weak because interpretation of it can vary so much and because it becomes ultimately a matter of negotiation.

The appeal to human rights, which has provided the primary motive power behind freedom movements throughout the world, has a non-discardable moral aspect to it which denies the relativist stance. This moral underlay even shows itself in the fervour and intensity with which relativists dismiss those who disagree with them as 'dogmatic'.

Values are necessarily grounded in belief. The relativism of values seems so sensible and convincing until we reflect on what this implies, namely that what we feel passionately about with regard to truth or justice or purpose of life has no justification apart from the fact that we happen to think like this.

Note on the impact of post-modernism

Post-modernism has done something powerful and important in helping to free people to some extent from positivism, although, as already discussed, positivism continues to be a powerful presence in our society. Post-modernism has also done much to reinforce the insights of relativism enumerated above. Post-modernism has not, however, much helped to challenge the weaknesses of the relativist stance. Indeed it has had the effect of intensifying them because of its dogmatic denial of the possibility of any absolute, universal meta-narrative. The intellectual world is, according to this theory, necessarily fragmented and reflecting purely local interests. Equally, universalist language which locally-conditioned people frequently use is in reality a claim to power.

As a philosophy it is open to the same objections as relativism. Like relativism post-modernism is self-contradictory in that it claims to be telling us the truth yet cannot substantiate its claim. Furthermore it is manifestly not true that all forms of belief are driven by power-hungry people, nor that people come to hold particular scientific theories because of the power they yield to their creators. May we not ask whether, if anyone is illegitimately exerting power, it is not the postmodernists who pull the carpet from under everyone else's position without troubling to show where this or that position is faulty?

The key to the problem concerning post-modernism is that it has not rebelled sufficiently against positivism! It still operates with the notion of *truth* which positivism holds: that to talk of truth means to speak of what can be proved beyond doubt or challengeability. Post-modernists are correct in seeing that such truth is impossible for us. But what needed challenging is not simply positivism but this idea of truth. The impasse can then be avoided of self-contradictorily denying that anything can be true. The way can be open to admit that rational discourse concerning reality is possible because there are criteria for judging truth in a provisional way.

A further point is that post-modernism could be destructive in its consequences because it can lead to a serious lack of confidence in the values necessary for civilized society. If all the old certainties are so no longer, value-pluralism is a real threat to us all. Why should we care more for a human embryo than a fish? What right do we have to cut down living trees? Why should we experiment upon animals of any sort? Where are the safeguards against unsavoury attitudes to life becoming a matter first of preference and then of right? Peter Berger in a chapter entitled 'From the Crisis of Religion to the Crisis of Secularity'[11] worries that society simply cannot survive in this situation.

(C) Secularism based on hatred of religious intolerance

A major reason why people decide to have nothing to do with religion is that, in the name of *religion*, much injustice, violence and bigotry has been perpetrated. An example of such thinking is the writer, A.N. Wilson, whose rejection of religion was on account of its encouragement of so much evil. An extract from his booklet, printed in *The Observer*, caused it to receive a record mailing from readers, many of whom supported his 'boo-ing' of all religious leaders as so many cackling geese.[12]

That this criticism of religion is taken seriously by at least some religious leaders is evidenced in a vivid phrase conjured up by Bishop David Jenkins: 'to hell with religion, to heaven with God'.[13]

This is so widespread a reason for rejecting religion, present in all strata of society and amongst all types of people, young and old, that any RE which fails to help pupils think clearly about it must be seen as deficient. Even whilst writing this chapter, the second of two TV programmes on the *Root of All Evil?* was broadcast at prime viewing time in which Richard Dawkins lambasted religion as the 'The Virus of Faith'.[14] Unless RE equips pupils to see the fallacies in such arguing, it is obvious that they will not take religion seriously at all.

We want to express this point very strongly. The sentimentality conveyed by the careful selection of only 'nice' aspects of religion to present to pupils causes them to see it (and perhaps believe in it) as just a fairy story unrelated to the real world. For in the real world there is a nasty side to religion, and religious people can become ogres. Religion is responsible for much injustice affecting ordinary everyday life as well as newspaper-headline material. Religious people often too easily run away from this, but school RE must not.

Various considerations however undermine the force of this objection to religion. To dismiss religion because of its potential for evil is to risk being one-sided and exclusivist, committing a logical error, failing to appreciate the nature of religion, and mistaking the real culprit responsible for such unedifying behaviour.

We discuss each of these considerations in turn.

1 A one-sided and exclusivist view. This objection to religion is highly selective in what it chooses to notice about religion; it ignores all its beneficial aspects. Religion has been, and is, capable of sustaining some of the finest civilizations the world has seen, and it has attracted many of the most brilliant and high-minded people who have ever lived. To ignore what has been regarded as central by such civilizations and persons can hardly claim to be a fair and objective approach.

If religion has produced its hypocrites and bigots, it has also produced people like St Francis and Sri Ramana (see Chapter 12). To notice only the bad, when there is so much good, may be seen as a jaundiced view.

2 A logical error. There is no necessary connection between evil and religion, either a logical one or on factual grounds. To argue that religion *can* go wrong, and therefore should be rejected, is like saying that because surgery *can* go wrong, therefore all surgeons should be pensioned off. Eggs can become poisoned, therefore eggs should no longer form part of a staple diet!

To blame religion for what could be people's failure to live up to it is not logical. Just because the vicar down the road is selfish and insensitive, we are not justified in concluding that therefore religion is bad. Another explanation of the vicar's selfishness is possible, namely that he does not live up to his religion and is therefore a poor representative of it. In fact this is the case because Christianity does not teach, 'Thou shalt put thyself first'. If the vicar thinks it does he is mistaken.

3   Appreciating the nature of religion. If the risk of eating eggs being poisoned is extremely high, then we should be justified in rejecting eating them. People who oppose religion on the grounds of its intolerance and bigotry think that the risks are very high. This is where we need to turn to the factual evidence.

This indicates clearly that religion has no monopoly of evil. The blatant example of dictators like Stalin has vividly shown the world this. It suggests therefore that there is another explanation for such behaviour. The diagnosis is misleading if it gives the impression that there is a straight connection between the expression of religious belief and bigotry.

It is essential to appreciate that when religious people show bigotry, intolerance, narrow-mindedness, violence and all other such forms of evil, they are in fact betraying the religion which they say they uphold. A marked example of this, mentioned in Chapter 2, is the association of Christianity with anti-semitism. Yet to find anti-semitism in the gospels is to misread them. Such anti-semitism is based on a 'falsification of scripture'.[15] (See Chapter 5 pp. 85–6 and Chapter 9 passim for detailed discussion of the need to sort out the complexities of this.)

Religious people stand condemned by the very tenets of their religions unless that religion is in itself a perverse and cancerous development which will in time kill what gave it birth in any case. All the great world religions have very high moral codes which reach out towards a quality of authentic selflessness and love for all others which is the antithesis of selfishness and hatred (see Figure 6.1, p. 95 on this).

The sternest critics of religion have often been found within religions. Religious people themselves, because of the strength and depth of their religious convictions, have appreciated most thoroughly the extent of the abuse of religion. This is because such bigotry and violence are the result not of being too religious, but of not being religious enough, of superficiality, of mistaken ideas about what religion is about. As Edward Hulmes has noted:

> The great teachers of religion have always had to get rid of the useless lumber which accumulates in its progress and the rigid dogmatism, the narrow legalism, the mechanical rites, the silly superstitions which may become a substitute for religious life.[16]

Many religious people are as worried as non-religious people about the abuse of religion. Speaking about the resurgence of interest in religion which many people see in the world today, the Chief Rabbi, Jonathan Sacks, asks 'Whether religious revival might be not a refreshing breeze but a destructive hurricane.' He goes on to note how 'revolutionary leaders have enlisted religious passion . . . it is an explosive combination. War becomes a holy struggle against the demonic other. Terror is sanctified. Hatred becomes a form of piety.'[17]

4   *The real culprit?* The distinction between religion and exclusivism is crucial. Often it is not religion, nor its truth-claims, that is the trouble, but rather attitudes of selfishness and possessiveness and of thinking of religion or of truth as an entity which we have and somebody else does not have. Dogmatism is dangerous in considering that one has possession of the truth oneself, and that anyone who fails to agree is simply wrong. Of course there are many instances in which beliefs are contradictory in which case both views cannot be right. It may also be the case that some beliefs are wrong such as, for example, the belief that Allah hates the infidel and sanctions terror against all such. But very many more beliefs may be different but not contradictory. Apparent contradictions often turn out to be paradoxes and insight relating to different circumstances and experiences. See Chapter 6 for further discussion of this.

What never fails to harm is pride in being right. People may actually be right but that is not an excuse for smugness and lack of interest in what anybody else thinks except to knock them down and force them to acknowledge the superiority of one's own views.

When this happens, the rightness of the belief or action is not infrequently forgotten altogether and ignored. The nineteenth-century head teacher who knew he was right that God loved everyone, and would therefore thrash any boy who did not acknowledge that, had in fact paid almost no attention whatever to the content of his belief. A moment's reflection would have helped him to see the folly, cruelty, and hypocrisy of trying to force someone to acknowledge this.

Many people suffer from the same disease of thinking they must be right all the time, and they must push their rightness onto other people. This is what does the damage and not religion, for it can be seen in all walks of life wherever people are emotionally involved. Because religion appeals so strongly to the emotions and to life commitment, it is a special temptation for religious people.

The need is for the quality of openness discussed in Chapter 1. Figure 3.3 shows the possibility of a creative circle of both openness and commitment, and how dogmatism leaves that circle to become a dead end. Openness and commitment should not be enemies:
   A denotes a basic attitude of respect for a person;
   B an initial presumption that the person has insight;
   C is the place for criticism and relating what the other person believes with one's own experience;

Figure 3.3 *Openness and non-dogmatic commitment*

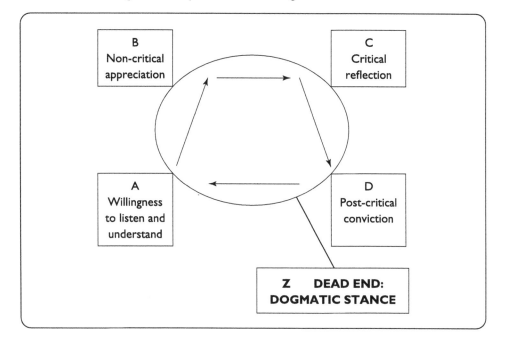

D is the place for provisional certainty which should move again to openness towards fresh understanding and insight.

Failure to move again from D to A breaks the circle and results in Z, dogmatism.

CONCLUSION: GIVING RELIGION A FAIR HEARING

The argument developed in this chapter is of vital importance for the teaching of RE because it concerns deep-seated anxieties with religion which people have today. We think that it is important to share with pupils some understanding of these -isms for religion. Common remarks which people make can help to explain what they are about, and tasks such as that in Figure 3.4 might be useful.

These must be addressed in such a way as to help pupils to see that the questions are open ones, worthy of their attention throughout life. Religion deserves a fair hearing, and effective RE will see that it gets that. It deserves it because:

1 Unlike positivism and relativism, it is not based on an illogical position. It does not assume any proof demonstrating its validity, and therefore it cannot be knocked down for not offering it. Of course religion can be challenged, but there are plenty of sound reasons *for* religion.

Figure 3.4 *Positivism, relativism and post-modernism*

Here are some common expressions illustrating one of these -isms. Which belongs to which?
1 That's just your opinion.
2 There's no such thing as truth – we each just have our own stories to tell.
3 I'm only interested in facts – keep your theories to yourself.
4 You shouldn't claim to know what you can't prove.
5 Of course you *would* say that coming from your background.
6 Statistics show that anti-social behaviour is caused by economic factors.
7 There are no right answers.
8 There are no historical facts – only interpretation.

2 To consider religion carefully is not to be dogmatic and exclusivist, but actually the opposite, for it allows an important area of both communal and private experience to be explored instead of being ignored or reinterpreted in terms inappropriate to it. Religion is thus allowed to speak for itself.
3 Religion *can* be creative. It can afford motivation as hardly anything else can, and its influence can help both society and individuals to a fuller and more satisfying form of life.

Whether school RE reflects the obvious case for it depends upon the openness with which it is approached and the style of teaching adopted. On this basis we may go forward to the next chapter on the purpose of RE.

TO THINK ABOUT

Jacques Beneveniste was arguably the most controversial scientist of the last 50 years. His 'crime' was the discovery of a mechanism for homeopathy, the popular but currently inexplicable alternative medical therapy . . . homeopathy is, according to conventional medical science, nothing but water. . . . The French scientific establishment demanded his resignation . . . [his comment] 'As a scientist, it was my duty to explore the truth without fear of the consequences. If a scientist like me can be branded as a heretic, it's because modern science has adopted a quasi-religious set of dogmas.' (Obituary in *The Independent*, 11 October 2004)
1 Explain how this is an example of the fact/belief divide at work.
2 Think of other examples.
3 Do you agree that the fact/belief divide is damaging? Why/why not?

NOTES

1 Roger Trigg from Farmington paper *What is an explanation?* Oxford.
2 See e.g. Watson, B.G. (2006), pp. 43–8.

3 Chater, M. (2005), p. 254f.

4 Stewart, I. (1989), p. 131.

5 Maxwell, N. (2005), p. 38.

6 Darwin, E., quoted from Stone, I. (1986), p. 33.

7 Aristotle, *The Nicomachean Ethics* V (vii), 2.

8 Berger, P. (1969), p. 9.

9 Ferguson, N. (2005), 'Heaven knows how we'll rekindle our religion, but I believe we must', *The Sunday Telegraph*, 31 July.

10 Hull, J.M. (1996).

11 Berger, P. in Douglas, M. and Tipton, S. (eds) (1983), pp. 14–24.

12 Wilson, A.N. (1991) discussed in the *Observer* on 2 June 1991.

13 Jenkins, D., correspondence with Watson January 2005.

14 Dawkins, R., *The Root of All Evil?*, 2/2 'The Virus of faith', 16.1.06, 8.0–9.0 pm, Channel 4.

15 Jones, G.L. (1999), p. 18.

16 Hulmes, E. (1989), p. 150.

17 Sacks, J. (1991), p. 79.

PART II

WHAT DO WE MEAN
BY RELIGION?

CHAPTER 4

THE PURPOSE OF RE

> C.S. Lewis noted in his meditation on heaven and hell, *The Great Divorce*, that in the end there are only two sorts of people: those who say to God 'Your will be done', and those to whom God says 'Your will be done'.[1]

What should the focal-point for RE be? We consider current theory and practice and show how RE has been profoundly influenced by cultural pressures, not always to its advantage. Three major agendas which have tended to drive education are discussed, and their impact on RE. We argue for an approach of critical affirmation which focuses on God/the Transcendent and an understanding of religion that helps pupils to be open to all that is insightful in religious discourse. We end the chapter with a six-fold task for RE.

Is it possible to agree on a purpose for RE? And would such a purpose be untroubled by any particular agenda and therefore free from causing offence to fellow citizens? Daniel Hardy analysed the ground-breaking 1975 Birmingham agreed syllabus and declared it to be an exercise in personal idealism,[2] yet to those responsible for it, the syllabus seemed quite free of partisan bias. It is of course quite possible (and highly likely) that a form of words will be agreed upon which legitimizes a variety of approaches to the subject. The very phrase 'agreed syllabus' implies something of the difficulty of the task and the likelihood of compromise. So does this mean that spending time thinking about and stating the purpose of RE is not worth the effort?

On one level RE exists because there are people who think it is important and write books and campaign about it. It is interesting that the non-statutory national framework puts, not the purpose, but the importance of the subject centre stage.[3] Indeed, when it comes to setting out the aims of RE the strategy of the national framework is to show how the subject supports the general aims of the curriculum rather then to propose specific aims.[4] There is a sense in which this is surely correct. No subject stands in isolation and it is particularly important perhaps for RE to demonstrate this. But RE should be able to set out what it is there to teach and why such teaching is a necessary (not just helpful) part of education.

There has probably never been a 'golden age' in RE since the 1870 Forster Act introduced publicly funded education in a systematic (and probably irreversible) way.[5]

Provision for religious instruction was written into the Forster Act but it was touch and go as to whether Parliament was going to agree to it, and fears that legislation might remove it have emerged at several points in subsequent history. In fact RE is probably as secure now as it has ever been.

So why RE? The 1931 Hadow Report on the Primary school declared: 'The teaching of religion is at the heart of all teaching.'[6] Rather more cautious was the statement of the 1938 Spens Report on secondary education: '. . . no boy or girl can be counted as properly educated unless he or she has been made aware of the fact of the existence of a religious interpretation of life.'[7] The 1931 report reflects the fact that religion in Britain has always been closely linked with education. The 1938 report, with its less 'confessional' language, nonetheless finds it difficult to envisage education without an understanding of religion. Historically, as Spens goes on to state, the form which that interpretation has taken in this country has been Christian, with the Bible taking centre stage as the basis of the structure of Christian faith and worship. But even in 1944 it was recognized that a syllabus of religious instruction might be needed which was appropriate for children from Jewish families.[8] From this we might derive two principles:
1 Schools in this country should give an important place to Christianity.
2 RE should, as far as possible, respond to the needs of the children receiving it.

It is fair to say that current legislation has accepted these two principles, particularly following the 1988 Education Reform Act which states that an agreed syllabus of religious education should 'reflect the fact the religious traditions of Great Britain are, in the main, Christian, whilst taking account of the other principal religions represented in Great Britain.'[9]

LEARNING ABOUT AND LEARNING FROM RELIGION

Students in training will not attend many sessions at university before being introduced to the phrases *learning about* and *learning from* religion. Indeed, expressed as attainment targets, they are fundamental to the non-statutory national framework for RE and are found in many agreed syllabuses. The framework describes *learning about* religion in terms of enquiry into the nature of religion.[10] Pupils are to gain knowledge and understanding of beliefs, teachings, practices and forms of expression. They are to learn to interpret, analyse and explain these matters using specialist vocabulary. Ultimate questions and ethical issues are to be identified and understood. *Learning from* religion, on the other hand, emphasizes the role of personal reflection and response to religious teaching, ethical ideas and questions of meaning. We now examine these two important aspects of RE today.

LEARNING ABOUT RELIGION

So, what reasons are given today as to why children should learn about religion, and what is involved in such learning?

It is often stated that children should learn about religions because this will help to bring about social cohesion.[11] Learning about what others believe and do, it is hoped, will bring people together and enable respect to grow. The events of July 2005 in London (see pp. 14–16) have caused us all to be concerned about threats to the fabric of society. It is surely right that RE and all other areas of the curriculum pay attention to the need for good relations between citizens. If learning about religion does increase a sense of common humanity and respect for others we should make sure that it is given the full attention of pupils. It rather depends what aspects of religion are taught. It is possible, however, that social cohesion arguments gain their force from the sense that religions are the cause of problems in society and that RE is needed to counteract a certain tribalism that religions may promote. If this is the case, pity the poor teacher who finds herself in the position of a biology teacher instructing children so enthusiastically about poisonous mushrooms that they learn to avoid mushrooms altogether. In practice, it is difficult to find any who argue for the inclusion of RE on social grounds alone,[12] and in the absence of evidence to prove that RE does contribute to social cohesion this is perhaps just as well.

The 'all religions on a par' approach

An example of the sort of approach which is thought to contribute to social cohesion is described in *RE News*, the journal of the Welsh National RE Centre. *RE News* reported on a faith festival held in Wrexham. The festival was called The Tapestry of Life and Faith Festival, a biennial event for schools that celebrates religious, linguistic and cultural diversity. It is an opportunity for pupils to experience at first hand many different religious and cultural practices such as storytelling from India, Indian dance, bible stories, Buddhist meditation, Islamic music, visits to churches and many other participatory activities. One very successful activity was the Labyrinth which takes the theme of life as a journey and invites pupils to enter a 'Holy Space' where they could let go of a worry and put it into God's hands. Cultural issues are explored through circle time, circus skills, traveller exhibitions and workshops, puppet theatre, African drumming and food exhibitions. The editor commented: '[the organizers] are to be congratulated on establishing such a fine model for the role of RE in contemporary Wales. Understood and presented in this way the real importance of RE is seen for promoting the wellbeing of local society and for generating the social capital on which future sustainability depends.'[13] The approach represented here mirrors many RE departments where the purpose of RE is to learn about the principal religions present in society in a positive and upbeat frame of mind.

It is difficult to fault an approach which clearly excited and motivated pupils to learn and enquire. But can we be sure that all children and all teachers were happy about what went on? Clearly we are meant to applaud this form of RE. It is presented as self-evidently correct and therefore the danger is that dissent goes unreported. But certain truth-claims are being advanced which should at least be examined. In particular it seems to be taken for granted that all religions offer experiences of the Divine. Furthermore it is presumed acceptable to practise Buddhist meditation whether or not one is a Buddhist. No entrance qualification is needed and no preparation to take part in (or be present at) the holy rites is required. Within a religious community it is usual for experienced guides to take charge of the 'mysteries'. The seriousness of religious initiation and practice may be subtly, although unintentionally, undermined.

After the festival children were asked to write about what they liked and what affected them personally. We are not told if teachers raised the issue of what was true and good in what they encountered. Of course we can expect that such matters would be raised after the event by teachers in class. If children are *only* asked to say what they liked and found significant there is the danger that they learn that what matters is what is personally significant to them, not what accords with the reality of what is good and true. But if one starts from a position of celebrating diversity it becomes very difficult to make negative judgements about any form of religious expression. Religion must be presented as an unmitigated and undifferentiated good. Difference is banished to the realms of the insignificant, such as matters of food, dress and habits of worship.

Further problems

There is much that is good about the multi-faith approach and our own approach relies heavily on engaging with plurality. A basic level of respect for people who think differently is essential for any civilized society. The approach allows differences to be expressed thus acknowledging the pluralism which is a fact today. But there can be problems with it. Here we list some further problems to be avoided:

1 The requirement to celebrate diversity means that there is no justification for excluding anything. More and more religious points of view will have to be accommodated. Such a pressure was clearly felt by those responsible for the national framework. As well as the study of Christianity at all key stages, it is suggested that pupils should learn another five named principal religions. In addition (and 'where appropriate') pupils may study other named religions and secular philosophies such as humanism. Everyone wants to be on board, including the secular humanists. This means that serious study of anything is increasingly difficult.

2 A further not unrelated problem is that it is difficult to generate coherence and progression when so many religions and non-religions jostle for their time and space in the classroom. This was one of the reasons given for the development of the national framework. Yet the framework failed to deliver along these lines.

3 We are in a weak position when it comes to warning pupils of religious cults, extremism and the like which may be damaging to society. We have, after all, taught them not only to accept, but to celebrate diversity. This is an extremely important point. To assume that all religions are good is as bad as assuming they are all bad, as did, for example, Richard Dawkins in his 'The Root of All Evil' television programme referred to above on pages 43–4.[14] Skills of discernment are essential.

4 This approach is in fact divisive in that it separates what religion actually is from how it is presented in the classroom. This is both false and unhelpful. Even the social cohesion argument is undermined by this approach. Not only might parents disapprove of it – which is also disorientating for their children[15] – but also those most urgently needing to learn tolerance are those most likely not to be engaged by this approach. Young, extremely devout extremists will simply see this as further fodder for their own views about the evils of current society.

LEARNING FROM RELIGION

The Hampshire Agreed Syllabus (2004) gives a useful explanation of what is generally understood by 'learning from religion'[16]: 'to support students in developing their own coherent patterns of values and principles, and to support their spiritual, moral, social and cultural development.'[17]

In contrast to the 'all religions on a par' approach, this way of doing RE places great emphasis on evaluation and interpretation in the context of coherence. The adjective 'coherent' is chosen to describe patterns of values and principles. This would appear to be a reference to the coherence theory of truth. In order to achieve a coherent set of values pupils must 'develop the capacities to interpret, evaluate and respond to differing values and beliefs'.[18] This equates with the definition of learning from religion given by the national framework (see p. 54). Coherence is important to this syllabus in more ways than one. A model of teaching is provided (to be used at all stages) that lends coherence to the teaching. The model takes the form of a hermeneutic circle. At the centre of the circle is the student who is encouraged to enquire into the matter in hand, contextualize it, evaluate it, communicate his or her response and apply the response to situations in her own and others' lives. In a sense what gives coherence to the syllabus is the student himself who is actively engaged in evaluating and developing his own stance.

So far so good to the extent that education should revolve round the student; he or she is the only one who can make sense of the curriculum offered. But the point of education is to enable this to happen in as sound and constructive and enthralling a way as possible. Does the Hampshire Agreed Syllabus help here? Hampshire states that pupils are to develop their beliefs and values 'in relation to those values that society prizes'.[19] But this aspect is not developed in any way. What really matters for Hampshire is that pupils are put under no pressure to choose one particular set of values. This is the value-free ideal which has become so pervasive and controlling of what happens in education generally and therefore in RE that we need to look at why this has happened. This can then alert us to a possible way out of the dilemma it causes. We can challenge the assumptions which underlie it and which are causing the trouble (see Figure 4.1, p. 61).

This means that like the 'all religions on a par' approach it commends nothing in particular. And by the same token there is little that it forbids. Yet this approach undermines all religions, since the implication is that nothing of their vision of the good life may be commended to pupils who must live by a religion of their own creation. And if children are to 'think and feel what they want' why should they be forced into developing *coherent* thinking and feeling? There is an element of compulsion here which we discuss shortly.

Underlying the Hampshire syllabus is a particular view of religion which is foundational and not the subject of critical evaluation by pupils. Religions are presented as responses to human experience of the world. The syllabus is:

> based upon understanding and responding to the key concepts within the major religious traditions and non-religious beliefs represented in Great Britain. It aims to inform pupils . . . of *how these concepts present differing understandings of human experience and ways in which religions view the purpose of life.* In response, pupils and students are encouraged to develop their own concepts to interpret their own experiences and explain the experiences of others in the wider world.[20]

Religion is presented here as the human activity of meaning-making. Certain experiences are singled out and said to be common to all human beings. But it is not difficult to identify the privileging of Western, secular culture here. Thus when the syllabus identifies common experiences there is no mention of conscience, awe, infinity, awareness of God, guilt, obeisance, prayer. A practical example is that when studying pilgrimage pupils are to think about a journey to a revered football ground or the house where Dad was born. It may not be the intention that pupils are assumed to be non-religious but this is how it comes across. It would be quite possible (and empirically well-grounded) to assert that religious experience is primary rather than secondary. The irony is that Western religions see themselves as responses to the action of God rather than human constructs which make sense of life. A religion like Islam makes demands upon followers. Islam patently is not in the business of inviting 'any kind of response'.[21] Nor do the revealed religions accept that human experience is foundational, a view which effectively denies the claim to Divine action in the world. Indeed religious life may require the believer to accept that meaning is beyond our grasp. We see through a glass darkly. We simply do not know the mind of God. We believe even though, at times, life may seem absurd.[22]

OUR 'TAKE' ON LEARNING ABOUT AND FROM RELIGION

There is much that is the same in the two targets as set out in the non-statutory national framework. Both stress interpretation and analysis of religion and the place of ultimate questions. Learning about religion may require 'explanation' while learning from requires 'evaluation', but can a proper distinction be made between the two activities? There may be more than one explanation of the life of Jesus (for example) but no satisfying explanation can avoid evaluation of who He (or he) was (or is). It is stated that learning from religion requires application and the communication of pupils' own responses, but such activities are to be conducted in the context of the 'skills' which are to be deployed in learning about religion. The only way any sense can be made of the distinction between the two activities is if one advocates the view that learning about religion can take place in a neutral, objective fashion whereas learning from religion is a subjective activity. This is yet another example of the fact/belief divide at work – already challenged in Chapter 3 (see pp. 34–6). Yet the same criteria are to be deployed in both areas and the framework itself states that the two targets are closely related. The framework looks both ways. Yet it is essential to take on board the fact that all genuine *learning about* religion enters the intellectual and emotional bloodstream of a person, and *learning from* is based on understanding – or misunderstanding – what religion is. We therefore favour an approach which, like Hampshire, sees the point of RE as being an engagement with religion *per se*, although we try to avoid what we see as the value-free ideal behind this syllabus.

Learning about and *learning from* are phrases that have become institutionalized in the profession. Why? In a society where religious ideas are considered controversial the idea of learning from religion is going to be problematic. Yet the majority of us involved in RE instinctively want pupils to learn and experience something of what it is to be a religious believer. Education cannot help but influence pupils. That is its function. But it is difficult to agree on what pupils should learn and experience. Either, it seems, we have to accept all forms of religious belief and not make distinctions between the differing religious claims (the 'all-religions-on-a-par' approach) or we reduce religion to what is acceptable in society, in all likelihood some form of lowest common denominator religion with its comfort zone firmly within secularism. In UK society the latter is likely to rely on Western categories rather than Eastern.

Feeling that this is somehow unsatisfactory and does not do religion justice, we insist that pupils make the choice. We sense that the task is important but to introduce a scale of values and ways of coming to grips with religious claims is fraught with difficulty and likely to be challenged at every turn. The level descriptions in the national framework, designed to help teachers assess how well their pupils are doing, are a clear indication of our difficulty. No attempt is made to introduce pupils to what is of value (or to warn them about what is not). Rather it is assumed, perhaps optimistically, that they already know.[23] In a 'value-free' environment pupils are required, ironically, to clarify their values. No pupil can escape this. But can we always give highly reasoned insights for our most cherished beliefs? And can it be right for pupils to have to expose their feelings after truth in this way? If pupils already know what to believe and value what is the point of RE lessons?

It is safe to assume that RE teachers like all teachers want their pupils to adopt particular values and, in their teaching, do what they can to emphasize and illustrate them. But we fail to see that we have already weighted the odds against ourselves. To the extent that we are reluctant to commend particular theological or moral truths we teach children that it is a matter of no great consequence what they choose. Other subjects in the meantime are not shy of showing where truth may be found. It is one reason why citizenship has been brought in to the curriculum to try to instil value and purpose. We take refuge in the phrase 'learning from' because, although we may have given up the aim of teaching them anything in particular, we hope that they will learn from our 'teaching'.

It is a striking fact that the national framework pays little attention to content. A wide range of religions are specified, Christianity at all key stages and secular philosophies 'where appropriate', but nothing at all about what it is important to include and why. This is left to the relevant bodies to decide. The heavy emphasis on including as many religions and world-views as possible to give breadth of study, without any balancing emphasis on depth, serves to direct attention to the mere fact that people believe different things rather than the content of what they believe being weighed and discussed. It may be that tolerance requires knowledge and understanding of a wide range of points of view but 'knowledge, skills and understanding' do not necessarily guard against egoism which, if allowed to run rife, will make any civilized society unworkable. It is of crucial importance that the language of pupil choice of values be put alongside the reality of what is appropriate, positive and true.

CULTURAL PRESSURES

The problem is not confined to RE.[24] Society today is afraid to *value* anything for itself, and we need to ask how this situation has come about. On what fallacies does this fallacy depend? Education, both in universities and schools, has seen a marriage between two dominant agendas over the last 200 years which has profoundly influenced us today (see Figure 4.1).

Figure 4.1 *The agendas driving education in the West*

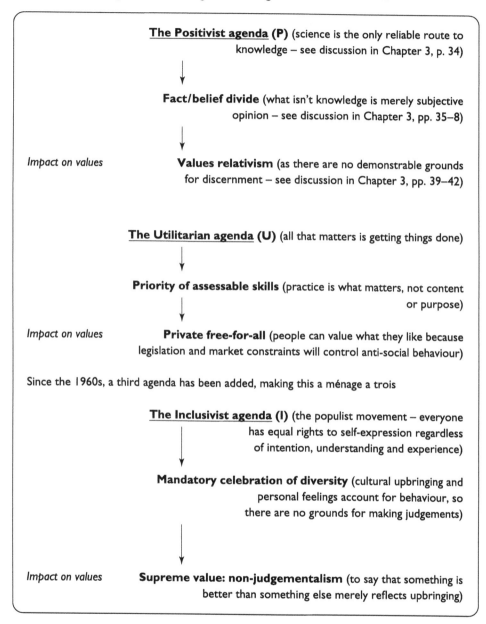

The **Positivist agenda** (**P**) (science is the only reliable route to knowledge – see discussion in Chapter 3, p. 34)

Fact/belief divide (what isn't knowledge is merely subjective opinion – see discussion in Chapter 3, pp. 35–8)

Impact on values **Values relativism** (as there are no demonstrable grounds for discernment – see discussion in Chapter 3, pp. 39–42)

The **Utilitarian agenda** (**U**) (all that matters is getting things done)

Priority of assessable skills (practice is what matters, not content or purpose)

Impact on values **Private free-for-all** (people can value what they like because legislation and market constraints will control anti-social behaviour)

Since the 1960s, a third agenda has been added, making this a ménage a trois

The **Inclusivist agenda** (**I**) (the populist movement – everyone has equal rights to self-expression regardless of intention, understanding and experience)

Mandatory celebration of diversity (cultural upbringing and personal feelings account for behaviour, so there are no grounds for making judgements)

Impact on values **Supreme value: non-judgementalism** (to say that something is better than something else merely reflects upbringing)

Table 4.1 *The impact of these agendas on RE*

Positivist agenda (P)	Utilitarian agenda (U)	Inclusivist agenda (I)

If people are brought up to believe that,

*there is no hard evidence for anything outside science	* life is a matter of skills not knowledge and understanding	* cultural diversity must be tolerated and never critiqued

they are almost programmed to regard RE in schools as

really a non-subject suitable only if people happen to believe in it, for religion just concerns emotions and opinions and cultural nurture.	teaching skills which can be assessed – e.g. facts about world religions.	private search for meaning. RE must be driven by what pupils themselves want and choose to believe – any attempt to encourage them to believe something else is unacceptably judgemental and authoritarian.

and the perception of religion is bound to suffer

Agenda P will ensure that there is little time, resources or status accorded to RE in school.	**Agenda U** will keep appreciation of its subject-matter, its challenge and integrity well below the horizon for most pupils.	**Agenda I** regards any criticism of what pupils believe as judgemental.

The impact of these agendas on RE can be tabulated as shown in Table 4.1.

In such a situation, the perception of religion is bound to suffer. Such fallacies need exposing and challenging if there is to be any significant change. What is happening to RE is an example of these deep-seated agendas at work. This maps out a purpose for RE:

1 To challenge the false fact/belief divide caused by positivism. See Chapter 12, for example, on ways in which dialogue between science and religion can be encouraged.
2 To make available for pupils serious consideration of values beyond the utilitarian and pragmatic.

3 To discuss truth-claims, criteria for discernment and evidence for religious belief which, whilst retaining the openness and provisionality to which relativism and post-modernism correctly point, nevertheless engages with questions concerning the reality of the world.

CRITICAL REALISM

The line of thinking we take is close to that of critical realism, a position adopted by Andrew Wright.[25] Critical realism accepts that reality exists outside of the perception of the knower. Reality therefore demands to be understood in certain ways rather than others. Anti-realism, by contrast, states that the world is infinitely pliable and open to interpretation. Critical realism (as opposed to naïve realism) emphasizes the ambiguous nature of our understanding which is always partial and open to revision. We agree. Our position has much in common with that of Wright. Our core values are wider: compare those set out in Figure 1.1 (see p. 5) with Wright's list of 'honesty, receptivity, wisdom and truthfulness'. Moreover, our attitude to post-modernism is somewhat different. Whilst Wright opposes dogmatic post-modernism he proposes 'post-modern alterity' (otherness). We prefer to acknowledge the provisionality of knowledge and emphasize critical affirmation. We see this as a more rounded approach which also avoids the dangers to which Cooling draws attention.[26]

We consider that the philosophy of critical realism is the only one which avoids
- simplistic dogmatic faith;
- the reductionism of positivism; and
- the incoherence and self-contradictoriness of post-modernism.

To critical realism we add the warmer, more comprehensive qualities of critical affirmation. This denotes a willingness to trust all ways of knowing including experience and intuition, and is not so dependent on prioritizing reasoning. We argue that this better reflects both the nature of reality and of our necessarily imperfect and limited understanding of it. Descartes was troubled about how one could be certain about anything and went back to the one thing he could be certain of, that he was thinking. The fact that he was thinking assured him that he could be certain of his existence ('cogito, ergo sum'). But even so, this did not allow him to conclude that his thinking processes could be trusted to give accurate knowledge. Radical doubt may be the end result and the narrowing of knowledge to what may be empirically proven or mathematically demonstrated. To an extent the problem is caused by the drive to have exact and complete knowledge.

An earlier theologian, Nicholas de Cusa,[27] based his (very detailed) theory of know-ledge on quite a different foundation. Cusa argued that the first step to knowledge is the acceptance that we are finite beings, unable to perceive fully to the heart of things. Hence *not knowing* is a kind of knowledge ('docta ignorantia'). He argued that human knowledge is perspectival and, to an extent, constructed. Only God really knows the world that He has created and we can never attain to what God knows. But this did not mean that Cusa thought that knowledge was beyond our grasp, rather that we can never claim that our knowledge is complete and that we should adopt an attitude of humility and be willing to change our views. There is always something more to be known. Cusa taught that knowledge begins with wonder and a desire to affectionately embrace that knowledge which God has given us the ability to grasp, a knowledge which requires us to employ all our capacities, including the moral. Knowledge is a possibility for all human beings and not just the most gifted. It allows for precise use of reason where appropriate, but acknowledges the unavoidability of moving beyond reason. What we claim to know wears a provisional character and it is appropriate to accumulate ever-fresh insights as we move through life on the basis that other people do also have insight which, if we are prepared patiently to look for it, we too can access.

Critical affirmation is a kind of gloss on critical realism which accepts Cusa's insight and therefore perhaps does need to be distinguished from it. As an example of these -isms at work, let us take a topic not directly related to RE: the theory of morphic resonance.[28] Pieces of evidence such as that in Figure 4.2 have led to such a theory. Attitudes to the evidence are governed by underlying assumptions.

THE GOAL OF RE

If schooling is to be truly educative, and not collapsed into something wholly taken over by the three agendas outlined in Figure 4.1, then it needs to teach the young to live well, be reflective about this and seek to realize the highest good in life. It involves teaching the young how to exercise critical judgements that are based on what is true, what is good and what is of great worth. All subjects should aim at this so the focus for RE must be upon what it is that religion uniquely offers. Enquiry into what it means to believe in God and take faith seriously is at the heart of RE. Religion must be taught for its own sake, and not as an interesting (or otherwise) cultural artefact. The 'sheer deep-down loveliness' of it all must not be missed. The openness to tran-scendence and mystery must be preserved and hinted at in all that goes on, or at least this must be the intention.

The way to do this is not to give pupils the impression that they are the judges of what life is all about or that religion is a commodity that they can understand rather

Figure 4.2 *Does your pet have a sixth sense?*

Of course it's true – animals are so lovely and intelligent!

NAÏVE REALISM

Of course it's not true: it can't be scientifically proved.

POSTIVISM OR NATURALISM

'Though my husband comes home at very different times each day, I always know when to put the potatoes on, because our dog goes and waits near the gate the moment he leaves work.'

No point in saying whether it's true or not – everyone has their own story.

POST-MODERNISM

There could be something in it, so we'll look further into it.

CRITICAL REALISM

It's likely to be true unless contrary evidence is forthcoming.

CRITICAL AFFIRMATION

as they might understand the structure of a blood cell in order to have power over it. Rather it is to open up the challenge and the seriousness of being born into a world which is rich in mystery, grace and risk. A world which calls them to live their lives in certain ways rather than others and where the hard and narrow road may sometimes be the right way to take. We must avoid giving the impression that religion is something out there that (other) people do and they need to 'know about' rather than a reality which challenges them to understand themselves and act in certain ways. The idea of religion as a mirror reflecting back to children something of who they are is an excellent one.[29]

BUT WHAT DO WE MEAN BY 'RELIGION'?

A recent textbook,[30] based on the national framework, attempts to answer this question for pupils. Unit 1 introduces the topic 'What is religion?' Pupils are taught that religion involves: stories; belief; right and wrong; community; buildings; ritual; feelings. Having matched pictures to these words pupils are told that they now know what religion is about and are introduced to the fact that the word religion means to join up or link. Religion links people together. Its function is to help people work out answers to important questions such as: Why is there a universe? Is there any point in being alive? What happens when we die? Pupils are taught that the way to tell if someone is religious is to identify such things as buildings, prayers, clothing, rules, scriptures, eating, beliefs etc.

The text is very clear and well presented with excellent pictures. But faults include:

1 Positivist assumption that religion is quite straight-forward – easy definition and can be observed from the outside i.e. the externals indicate the presence of religion in a naïve way;
2 God is nowhere mentioned;
3 Ultimate questions of profound significance casually brought in, and even worse the impression is given that religion is useful for giving answers to these instead of the other way round, namely that religion actually opens up these questions for people.
4 Teaches pupils to think that now they understand about religion!

At an academic level the notion of religion is highly contested.[31] Ninian Smart did not 'crack it' and admitted that the best we could do was to use the word in its ordinary sense.[32] It may be that Smart underestimated his own influence in determining what ordinary sense is however! His six (later seven) dimensions of a religion have been very influential, as witnessed by the textbook described above.[33] God, for example, does not feature as one of the dimensions of religion. Grant Maple has argued that the modern concept of a religion distorts certain religions and that the widespread adoption of Smart's model has contributed to the problem. He writes: 'In contrast, it can be argued that Christianity is primarily about God calling humans into relationship with himself, thereby restoring right relationships with others (Matthew 22:34–40) rather than a set of beliefs or a code of practice.'[34] We agree and this is why we think that the heart of RE should be an enquiry into what it means to believe in God and take faith seriously.

The non-statutory national framework does not attempt to define religion and expects religion to be studied through discrete religions. Religion, however defined, is found at depth in the lived experience of particular individuals and communities, in their history and varied practices. Suffice it to say that we do not use the word to mean that all religions are saying the same thing, that differences do not matter, that they all have basically the same origins or fulfil the same functions. Diversity, controversy and possible contradictions have to be taken seriously. Pupils need to be introduced to the complexity of it, rather than told what 'it' is. The question *What is religion?* IS an excellent starting-point. It should open up a really exploratory enquiry characterized by growing awareness of just how complex that question and any presumed answers to it are.

The externals of religion do bear a relationship to why and how people are religious, but the links are by no means able to be just read off the surface. Superstition, pure routine, subservience to authority, etc. have little in common with genuine and deep religion, and yet the outward practice appears the same. Brenda Watson remembers a first visit to a Hindu temple in Varanasi: 'I was nearly thrown off balance by the (to me as I then was) dreadful and obscene images which seemed to me to be idols. But as I watched the worshippers I was very struck with one woman who somehow, by the light in her face and her so reverent posture, conveyed to me a little of the depth of her belief. I thought at the time that somehow I'm sure God is close to her – she's not worshipping an idol. What she's doing is worshipping God through her offering to the image symbolizing God for her and for her whole culture. But it seemed to me that many of the others may have been just doing their duty or indulging in a bit of superstition.'

There is a need to separate genuine religion from just cultural upbringing, outward practices etc. And of course by even daring to mention the word genuine, this is suggesting that religion can be engaged in wrongly. So it forces us back again to ask what is religion? Here the concept of God is crucial. For genuine religion, as opposed to inadequate or even evil forms of religion, seeks to worship God as He is, not just God made in man's image as the famous quip by Voltaire put it: 'God made man in his own image. Man has returned the compliment.'[35]

SO WHAT IS THE PURPOSE OF RE?

The central purpose of RE is understanding of religion in as great a depth as possible, so that pupils can think about it sensitively and intelligently for themselves based on some knowledge rather than on ignorance or prejudice.

At the heart of religion is belief in God or the Transcendent. By focusing RE on this as the core fundamental concept around which the rest of religion revolves we can both give RE coherence and be properly inclusive.

1   Such God-focusing is that to which secularists fundamentally object – because they believe that God is non-existent. To the outsider in the modern world, the phenomenon of religion waltzes round a non-existent Spiritual Reality. We argue this not in the sense of assuming that everyone believes in God or ought to, but in the sense that the concept of God is crucial in coming to any understanding of religion and intelligent acceptance or denial of it. Focus on God doesn't mean whitewashing religion or failing to take seriously abuse of religion. Indeed, by inviting consideration of what is at the heart of religion it will enable far more in-depth criticism.

2   *Such God-focusing is what holds religions together thus enabling us to use the word of such disparate phenomena.* In fact there can be no understanding of religion without refinement and awareness of the concept of God or the Transcendent – that Spiritual Reality with capitals S and R – which in most religions is given the name of God: Brahman, Allah, Yahweh etc. That is the real defining attribute of religion, and justification for using the term across so wide a spectrum. To the objection that some forms of Buddhism and Hinduism are non-theistic, it must be remembered that they are not a-theistic in the Western sense of the word. They do not see God in personal terms as in any sense Personal Being, but they do acknowledge the primacy of a Spiritual Reality which transcends, even as it is immanent in, this world of time and space.

3   *Such God-focusing is what lies at the heart of religion.* Saints and scholars in all the major religions insist on this, as does the content of the religious language and ritual to which all the religions give priority. For they constantly reiterate the centrality of the Divine, and the need for humans to dispose themselves appropriately towards the presence of the Divine. The very word Islam e.g. means submission to Allah.

4   *Such God-focusing is also the best way in which to help pupils towards what is important about the social cohesion and personal meaning goals discussed earlier in this chapter.* Here is an extract from an address given by Rabbi David Goldberg at a service attended by three faiths following the London bombings.

> Today's service brings Jew, Christian and Muslim together in shared grief and con-demnation of the carnage inflicted on London a fortnight ago. If it is to be more than a one-off gesture, soon forgotten, we must pledge that church, synagogue and mosque will revive the initiative begun twenty seven years ago and work together to create a just society in which those of every faith and none can live in peace, tolerance and mutual respect.

May that be the will of the One God whom we all worship. AMEN.[36]

A six-fold task for RE
We suggest that RE should be: concerned with the following:
1 Response to secularism
2 Teaching thinking skills
3 Definition of religion
4 Knowledge of religions
5 Imagination and links with other areas of the curriculum
6 Spirituality and RE

1 Response to secularism. RE should aim to help pupils to challenge secularism in an open, non-dogmatic way. This involves at least the following:

(a) RE should enable pupils to appreciate the complexity of the issues involved and be aware that even the most fundamental belief, that is belief in God, is controversial and cannot be *proved* correct.

(b) Pupils need also to understand that what is sauce for the goose is sauce for the gander too. Secularist belief, namely that there is no God, cannot be proved either.

(c) Our understanding, whether we call ourselves religious or secularist, is bound to be partial and provisional so that, although we have to act as though we are certain – indeed we can do no other – we need to be open always to the possibility of fresh evidence and fresh ideas.

(d) Rowan Williams[37] has argued that Philip Pullman's atheistic fiction should be included in RE because understanding of truth gains from a dialogue between opposing positions. This is intellectually stimulating, and can encourage pupils' own reflection, on the basis of understanding rather than of possible prejudice. Open-mindedness must include openness to religious truth-claims as well as to secularist truth-claims, and both need to be approached in a sensitive and intelligent way.

2 Teaching thinking skills. RE should aim to teach pupils thinking skills understood as far more than just logical reasoning and problem-solving. Three particular points are relevant:

(a) We advocate an RE which can hold up its head intellectually in the modern secularist world and encourage RE teachers not to be afraid of challenge and debate – an RE which therefore has a good chance of being really interesting and important for pupils. This is not arguing for a mainly cerebral approach – far from it because one of the damaging assumptions RE should challenge is the false notion that mind and emotions are in separate compartments (i.e. the fact/belief divide – see Chapter 3, pp. 34–9). Both are needed for understanding in a constantly on-going correcting and inspiring polarity.

(b) RE needs to show that this divide is based on the interference of fundamental assumptions which are themselves challengeable and unnecessary.

(c) There is an urgent need to make thinking skills an integral part of RE right from the beginning, from Key Stage 1 upwards. Faulty thinking needs exposing, and pupils need help to think straight. It should promote openness without loss of integrity. In particular, it should develop the capacity to discern authentic religion from its many subterfuges.

3 Definition of religion. RE should aim to enable pupils to discuss what is meant by religion, and how that relates to religions, appreciating that this is an on-going question. It should never be presumed that this is an easy straight-forward matter to understand what really, if anything, holds different religions together.

Essential for such discernment is a focusing on the key/fundamental/core concept of God or the Transcendent by which religions can be distinguished from other socio-logical phenomena.

4   *Knowledge of religions.* RE should aim to inform pupils about a variety of religious and non-religious world-views through depth of study – clearly the number will have to be limited in order that superficial coverage which is either irrelevant or damaging may be avoided. Wrestling with questions of content is crucial not optional. Attitudes to scripture, for example, play a leading part in creating serious dispute between religions and within religions. RE should therefore have much to offer as a way of helping overcome what is unnecessary and damaging in such attitudes.

5   *Imagination and links with other areas of the curriculum.* RE should aim to invite pupils to practise critical affirmation rather than tolerance towards the beliefs and value-positions of others. The global perspective is indeed crucial, and learning how to live peaceably in a world full of controversial beliefs is a major concern for RE. But teaching tolerance without the capacity for critical affirmation can easily become patronizing, superficial and irrelevant for many of those who most urgently stand in need of learning tolerance.

6   *Spirituality and RE.* RE should aim to promote the spiritual development of pupils through access to holistic ways of learning and knowing. Spirituality concerns the whole of life. It is therefore most important that the fact/belief divide is force-fully challenged. See Chapter 12 for detailed discussion on this.

Additional note on Wright's concept of critical realism

Wright is concerned not to fall foul of a knowledge–power dynamic. In non-realist approaches to RE this is avoided by a rejection of the 'big' narratives which religions tell and adoption of the 'small' narratives that the individual child is thus enabled to tell. Religions are viewed as power-hungry oppressors. Critical realism wants to avoid the imposition of naïve truth on children too and Wright's tactic here is to argue for an 'interim ethic' or provisional certainty. We agree with this and believe that teachers should utilize a sense of provisionality in their teaching and underline the need for personal engagement in order to find the truth. Wright, however, goes further than this, as shown by Trevor Cooling.[38] Wright worries about the adoption of critical realism and wants teachers to bring in 'postmodern alterity' as a debating partner of equal standing. Yet relativism in all its forms denies the possibility of truth (however provisional and uncertain). This undermines his whole project, argues Cooling. Secondly, Wright wants to assert, if only for the practical purpose of reducing religious tensions, the equality of all cultures. Thus, Cooling argues, 'the utilitarian agenda of peaceful harmony seems to have prevailed over the realist agenda of the uncovering of ultimate truth'.[39] We do not think it necessary for

Wright to flirt with post-modernist alterity which leads to relativist sentiments. Where he presumes that cultures are equal, what we say about critical affirmation goes a good way beyond this, arguing for initial respect which can then be the proper subject of critical reflection before being assimilated if true. We need to hold on to the idea of truth while maintaining a certain humility and willingness to change our views when the evidence warrants it.

TO THINK ABOUT

What would be lost if RE was missing from the school curriculum?

Would it matter?

Why?

Construct an appeal to launch RE in a school which has tended to ignore it.

NOTES

1 Lewis, C.S. (1945), p. 66f.
2 Hardy, D., *Learning for Living* (Autumn 1975), vol. 15, no. 1, p. 14.
3 QCA (2004), p. 7.
4 The county of Cornwall (2005) follows a similar strategy. The aim of this syllabus, taken from the Children Act (2004), is to help pupils to 'be healthy, to stay safe, to enjoy and achieve, to make a positive contribution and to achieve economic well being', p. 8.
5 For a brief history of RE up until the 1960s, see Hilliard. F. (1963), ch. 1.
6 Board of Education (1931), the Hadow Report.
7 Board of Education (1938), the Spens Report.
8 Hence the reference in the 1944 Education Act (still in current legislation) for a local authority to approve more than one syllabus for use in its schools.
9 Section 8, 3 of the 1988 Education Reform Act (ERA). This clause has been carried forward in subsequent Education Acts. See Copley, T. (1997), ch. 5 and, for a more controversial account, Thompson, P. (2004b), ch. 9.
10 This is, of course, not as straight-forward as it sounds. The definition of religion has been a long-debated topic and the framework, wisely perhaps, does not offer a definition. For an analysis of how the framework uses the word religion see Thompson, P. (2004c).
11 See, for example, Hampshire (2004) where the second of two aims for RE is 'to foster mutual understanding between students of differing religious and cultural backgrounds', p. 7.
12 Robert Jackson, for example, is an important advocate of the social cohesion argument but insists that this is only one of the grounds for RE. See Jackson (2004) and Jackson (1997).
13 *RE News* (Autumn 2005), no. 73, p. 2.
14 Dawkins R., *The Root of All Evil*, 2/2 'The Virus of faith', 16.01.06, Channel 4.

15 See Mott-Thornton, K. (1998) for a penetrating study of this matter.

16 Hampshire does not follow the usual attainment targets, bravely preferring to see religious education as a unitary enterprise consisting of one target only: 'interpreting religion in relation to human experience'. We have introduced it here because it is a sophisticated example of an agreed syllabus and, despite not using the language, a good example of what is understood by learning from religion.

17 Ibid., p. 7. A 'further purpose' for RE is to 'foster mutual understanding between students of differing religious and cultural backgrounds'. Social cohesion is an important by-product of the teaching.

18 Ibid., p. 7.

19 Ibid., p. 10.

20 Ibid. (italics added).

21 The phrase found in QCA (2000) on p. 16: 'to learn fully about religions pupils need to be involved in forming some kind of response to what is being taught'.

22 See Thompson (2004b), ch. 11 for a more detailed discussion of learning from religion.

23 This is the case whether a pupil is at the beginning of education or at the upper end. The only difference is that at the end of the process a pupil can give 'highly reasoned insights into their own and others' perspectives on religious issues' whereas at the beginning it is acceptable for a pupil to talk about 'what is of value and concern to themselves and others'. QCA (2004), pp. 36, 37.

24 See report of a conference on 'A Future for Classical Music in Britain?', held 21 September 2005 in London by the National Centre for English Music.

25 Wright, A. (1997a, 1997b).

26 Cooling, T. (2005).

27 For an excellent introduction to Cusa see Jasper Hopkins at www.cla.umn.edu/jhopkins

28 See e.g. article in *The Times* by Rupert Sheldrake, 'Does your pet have a sixth sense?', 4 April 1994.

29 Sue Hookway (2004).

30 Keast, A. and Keast, J. (2005) – the first of 3 books for Key stage 3.

31 See Jackson, R. (1997, 2004).

32 Smart, N. (1997), *Sophia*, vol. 36, no. 1, p. 4.

33 Schools Council (1971). The dimensions of religion in this work are almost identical to those found in the Keast textbook: doctrinal (beliefs), mythological (stories), ethical, ritual, experiential, social.

34 Maple, G. (2005), p. 47.

35 Voltaire, *Le sottisier* (xxxii).

36 Goldberg, D., 21 July 2005.

37 Conversation between Rowan Williams and Philip Pullman at the National Theatre, London, 15 March 2004, entitled 'The Dark Materials Debate: Life, God, the Universe . . .'. See also Williams, R. (2004).

38 Cooling, T. (2005).

39 Ibid., p. 92.

CHAPTER 5

CHRISTIANITY

> 'Our problem is ... that of making Christianity visible again, of making people see it as a really possible way of looking at things.' (H.A. Hodges)[1]

We begin by examining the case for prioritizing Christianity in RE in Britain. We argue that critical engagement with Christianity is crucial for a variety of reasons. We then consider the difficulty of agreeing on what Christianity is. We see a focus on Jesus as central, providing a criterion by which the performance of Christianity itself might be judged. We also argue that Christianity must be sited historically and in relation to other faiths. We give an example of how to engage with areas of commonality and difference with Islam. Finally we suggest that Christianity has an important contribution to make to education.

WHY CHRISTIANITY?

Why have a chapter just on Christianity and not on each of the other major religions? Isn't prioritizing Christianity in this way unacceptable in a pluralist society? Reasons may include:

1   Every teacher has to teach Christianity. There are several reasons for including this new chapter on Christianity. Agreed syllabuses specify the teaching of Christianity at every key stage and it would be unusual for any other religion to be taught throughout schooling. This has probably been the case for as long as religious education has been taught, but the 1988 Education Reform Act[2] has reinforced this practice. It is vital that teachers have a good grasp of all the religions that they teach. However, whereas teachers may find it possible to bypass religions they feel unsure of, they are not going to be able to bypass Christianity. Christianity must be taught as well and as effectively as possible since this is the religion that pupils are going to have most experience of. Poor lessons on the Christian faith may put pupils off religion altogether.

2   Pupils are being disadvantaged through lack of awareness of Christianity. A current research project undertaken by the Stapleford Centre[3] has found that there is widespread concern amongst those involved in the teaching of English literature about the lack of biblical literacy and understanding of Christian faith amongst many pupils and some teachers. Project co-ordinators have been told by academics, teachers and examiners that it is becoming increasingly difficult for pupils to grasp the real meaning of some English texts since pupils do not have the necessary biblical understanding to make sense of it.

3   *The need to challenge anti-Christian tendencies.* Despite, or because of, the marked influence of Christianity upon our common life pupils are growing up in a society with strong forces prejudicing them against Christianity. The release of the first of the Narnia stories in public cinemas before Christmas 2005 was met with a considerable degree of alarm in certain quarters of the media. Deborah Orr wrote in *The Independent* of liberal commentators warning parents that the film was a form of child abuse which innocent children should be spared at all costs.[4] According to Terence Copley,[5] large sections of the media are implacably biased against Christianity. Boris Johnson views the BBC as embarrassed and unable to cope with any serious expression of Christian faith.[6] Thomas Sutcliffe, following an excellent portrayal of life in a Benedictine monastery on BBC 2, felt it necessary to instruct his readers that 'proper' Christianity was far more sinister.[7] The widely read and influential *Independent* gave nil coverage to the religious aspect of Christmas on 24 December 2005. The *Daily Telegraph* and *The Times* did give thoughtful leaders but not much more. Protecting the rights of other religions is sometimes used as a convenient way of pushing Christians further to the periphery of public life and ridiculing them in public. The media fan this mood, giving trite presentations of Christianity and making the most of the admittedly serious divisions and reactionary attitudes of some Christians. Add to that the grave ignorance of Christianity in the population at large,[8] and we have a strong reason for promoting good teaching of Christianity in RE in schools.

4   *The link between Christianity and culture.* A fourth reason for giving a special place to Christianity in RE is the argument from culture based on such considerations as the following:
(a) Numbers. The fact that, for example, over 70 per cent of those ticking the religion box in the 2001 census said that they were Christian.
(b) The place of the Church of England as the established church, linked with the monarchy and a privileged place in Parliament and important days in the life of the nation.
(c) The influence of Christianity upon our language, way of life, educational system, law, music, art, architecture, literature and so on.
(d) Its unique role in our history and day-to-day customs.

The argument from culture has its weaknesses. It may minimize the contribution of other religions and belief systems. To teach a religion as the religion of *culture* may give it the feel of an ancient artefact rather than a living faith. A third objection is that it does not seem right to teach a religion in order, as it were, to undergird culture.[9] A fourth objection is that the argument from culture sees culture as something static, capable of being packaged up neatly and handed on to the next generation. A fifth is that culture can no longer accurately be described as Christian.

Nonetheless there is no doubting that Christianity *is* taught in schools for some or all of the reasons listed above. No one doubts that the Christian traditions are the principal religious traditions of the country, a fact that should warn against teaching the faith as an ancient artefact. As Jackson put it:

> Christianity will generally warrant more space on the timetable than the other traditions because of its historical and contemporary presence in British society, together with its significance as a global religion.[10]

However, it does seem as though there is something not quite right in teachers' eyes with the cultural argument. When one of us was writing a syllabus for a Year 7 group recently it was virtually impossible to find a textbook which explored the relationship between Christianity and British culture. The only text that could be found, suitable for Key Stage 3, was a publication issued by the Lord's Day Observance Society to mark the Millennium.[11] Is the cultural argument at heart an embarrassing fact to be got over with as soon as possible in order to let the real teaching begin? Or is it an argument to encourage teachers to teach the faith boldly, even, perhaps to 'wear the badge with pride'?

To put the same question another way. Should Christianity be taught on the same basis as other religions? The quotation above from Jackson continues: 'It [Christianity] stands open to academic scrutiny, however, on the same terms as any other religious tradition.'[12] We entirely agree but academic scrutiny is not incompatible with according a special place to Christianity as the religion most closely associated with culture. However, it is important to examine the criticisms that lead to this sense of unease.

OBJECTIONS FACED

1 It minimizes the contribution of other religions and belief systems to our sense of societal identity. It is possible to teach as if the only important influence upon our common life is that of Christianity, although it would not (in our experience) seem to be a line that is taken by many teachers today. Equally a superficial treatment may give the impression that Christianity is devoid of influences from sources such as Judaism, Hellenism and Islam. But in the concern to acknowledge the contribution to cultural life that derives from other sources, it is important not to minimize the impact of Christianity. It is a question of balance and preserving an attitude of openness to all sources of cultural enrichment. Provided this is done, we think it important to share with the young the ways in which our identity as citizens of this country has been forged by living according to biblical norms. The welcome to the stranger and the notion that all human beings have something to offer are themselves insights that are rooted in the Bible.

2   *Teaching Christianity as the religion of culture risks giving the impression that the faith is an ancient artefact.* It is not a good idea to take children on visits to churches mid-week when the building is cold, the lights don't work and the only person around is a retired person brought in to open up. A visit to a cathedral may turn out to be a disaster when conducted by a guide who, careful not to offend, concentrates on dates, obscure architectural features, who built what and when. It is also possible for children to be told correct facts about the worship that goes on in the building but in a way that makes it seem as though this is all something that 'other' people do and has nothing to challenge them. In fact cathedral staff are generally alive to these dangers and many are adept at giving children an inspirational and truly edu-cational visit that leaves the children with an abiding sense that Christianity is a faith that matters today.

3   *It is wrong to use a religion to undergird aspects of culture.* Governments have, in the past, attempted to use churches to further their own policies. The Dutch Reformed Church justified apartheid by means of biblical texts, Kierkegaard railed against the church of his day for passivity in relation to the political powers. But Thomas More stood up against the political powers of his day. There is the danger that children brought up to respect Christianity may end up subverting authority rather than sub-mitting to it! The RE profession is being asked to lay emphasis on Christianity, not to make children into either societal conformists or religious fanatics, but because it is felt that much that is good in our society and that we want to preserve has its roots in the Christian vision of life. Teachers should not be embarrassed about this.

4   *The argument from culture tends to see culture as something static which can be pack-aged up neatly and handed on to the next generation.* Human beings have a natural tend-ency to make lists (according to the sociologist Mary Douglas). We do this in order to impose order on chaos and set about changing things. Yet, as Jackson powerfully argues, culture is dynamic, constantly changing and difficult to get a handle on. Yet human beings are not without imagination and discernment. We can describe and identify different cultures, if only provisionally. We can and must discriminate between values we want to promote and practices we want to avoid. The important thing, when helping the young to understand Christianity (and its relation to cul-ture), is to help them see that the Christian tradition is internally diverse, dynamic and constantly in revision.

5   *Society is no longer accurately described as Christian*. Such an objection invites the riposte 'but it never has been' (note the distinction made by Jenkins on p. 43). Accepted without question today is the notion that the state is not a theocracy and that human beings must engage in political debate as to how the good is to be realized in society. Yet it was the Christian sense that this world is imperfect and looks towards an end-time that led Western civilization to desacralize the state and open the door to debates about how the state might best bring about justice and human flourishing. In many respects Christianity has given birth to the secular.[13] It has become problematic to describe society as Christian but this may be because people have an inadequate understanding of both Christianity and society. It depends, in both cases, what the measure is and the results are ambiguous. A good discussion of this may be found in Copley's *Indoctrination, Education and God*.[14]

THE POSITIVE CASE

Examples of the influence of Christianity exist in architecture, art, sculpture, music, literature, language and ways of life. A teacher of younger pupils might begin by suggesting that pupils look up organizations named after saints in the business pages of the telephone directory. Such a study is likely to show how much social work is done by Christian organizations, in itself a telling lesson. Or get them to find out how many schools and roads are named after saints. One Muslim girl one of us taught in Liverpool, on doing this, pronounced 'There are millions of them, Miss'. There are excellent resources nowadays which introduce pupils to works of art inspired by the Bible.[15] Visits to cathedrals and churches are obvious examples as are introducing pupils to some of our most cherished music, hymns, oratorios and so on. One of us introduced a topic of favourite hymns into a Year 11 class. Year 11 were quite happy to hear what 'Miss' liked and offered their suggestions.

Three other areas are particularly important:

The impact of Christianity on ethical understanding

Pupils should know that many charitable organizations were started out of a sense of Christian mission.[16] Years of being told in school that you should love your neighbour has certainly contributed to the fact that charity is central to our British way of life. A recent survey of the motivation of teachers revealed that many embarked on the profession out of a sense of vocation. Mark Chater remarked: 'It is likely that the biblically influenced idea of vocation performs a hidden task of cultural osmosis, by invisibly and gradually suggesting something of the person's feelings and assumptions about themselves and what makes them different from their fellows.'[17]

But we cannot take even our strongest moral convictions for granted. Soviet law proceeded on the basis that the State was responsible for its citizens and would, god-like, take care of everything. As a result the tradition of charity began to die out and in some cases was forbidden by the state. Churches, for example, were forced to hand over their charitable work to state organizations. By contrast individual acts of charity under the Third Reich were advocated, but only on behalf of those considered 'worthy of life'. The biblical doctrine of the uniqueness and worth of every individual person, created in the image of God, underwrites human rights as well as acts of charity. The example of Jesus in the gospels, a powerful figure who was on the side of the oppressed and marginalized of his day, as were the prophets before him, is a further incentive not to neglect the weak and vulnerable.

But it will not be enough to inform children in a vague sort of way about 'what Christians believe'. David Kettle wrote: 'Will the BBC limit itself to echoing these beliefs, their prevalence and their vagueness, all unexplored, to its viewers and listeners?'[18] He goes on to say that the BBC needs to open up the 'positive Christian revelation which lies deep below their vague beliefs, their values (including the value of "service") and their cultural landscape.' The same is true of religious education. The reaction to the Narnia film[19] is significant. Ideas and values which really matter take centuries to become really absorbed in a civilization – consider e.g. attitudes to slavery, to women, to the disabled. The notion of disinterested pure love capable of sacrificing itself for others is one which, nurtured for centuries through Christian doctrine, is now becoming almost completely below the horizon for many who are in danger precisely of becoming like the White Witch, incapable of perceiving that such a thing can exist, let alone be desirable.

Many more examples could be given. The point is not to question the decline in religious belief or the fact that many people live without conscious reference to religion. It is rather to acknowledge with A.N. Wilson that 'Christianity invented a way of looking at human nature and the inner life which is part and parcel of our very civilisation'.[20] The fact that modernity has turned against Christianity is itself testimony to the continuing effect of the faith. Sometimes modernity is right to turn against Christianity since the Church and the churches have not always got it right. But if Wilson is right, then pupils are being short-changed if they are not given insight into the way in which they are already living as those influenced by Jesus.

The importance of tradition

The quest for shared values is essential for a society that is multi-cultural. And here it is necessary to relate to the historical matrix of the society in question. Celebration of diversity is only possible on the basis of certain really shared values. If we ask the question how is society in the West to welcome ethnic minorities in their midst, society can't do this by abandoning the roots of the tradition which has prompted the desire to play fair with people in the first place, but by understanding, appreciating and strengthening those roots. This involves criticism of tradition necessarily – see below regarding anti-semitism – but the criticism has to be based on what is true and worthwhile in the tradition. In relation to the Christian tradition, the doctrine of the equality of all people as persons loved by God is immensely important – however little society has ever actually lived up to that ideal. Failure to live values doesn't disprove the values but calls for far greater vigilance concerning them. That is what the criticism of tradition should be about. Basil Mitchell put it like this:

> To be religiously educated is not a matter of being led to accept in an uncritical and unreflective way, a set of beliefs and values, which are themselves so neatly parcelled that they can properly be handed over in this way, but of being encouraged to share in a tradition which is continuously being rethought and reapplied.[21]

Adrian Thatcher makes the same point in stark fashion by linking the frailty of human knowledge to the fact of the Atonement. Self-criticism, for any Christian theory of education, is necessary because 'its understanding of Christ's death is a "No" to the adequacy or self-sufficiency of any human endeavour before God.'[22]

Not only does the knowledge and experience we have accumulated affect how we see Jesus and his significance, but also it has to be translated into terms which people in each generation can understand. Thus John and Charles Wesley spoke a message of salvation to the largely unchurched in the eighteenth century, clothed it in hymns and songs, powerful sermons often delivered out-of-doors etc. C.S. Lewis' meditation on the meaning of the gospel led him into an entirely different way of communicating – via myth. So he invented Narnia which can be understood as an exciting story or one expressing profound theological meaning. In all this a sense of history is very important. G.K. Chesterton wrote: 'Tradition is the democracy of the dead. It means giving votes to that remotest and obscurest of classes, our ancestors. It refuses to submit to the arrogant oligarchy of those who simply happen to be walking around.'[23]

Christianity worldwide

Equally Christianity is not a domestic product that may or may not please UK citizens who happen to be walking around today. It is important that, at some point, pupils begin to understand the spread of Christianity throughout the world and the wide variety of ways in which the tradition has developed. Links can be made with schools in Europe, Africa and anywhere where computers have been installed! This sharing of experience can be very fruitful. This may require some judicious teaching of church history. But pupils love stories and much useful church history can be done this way. There are good resources available to help teachers.[24]

WHAT IS CHRISTIANITY?

We have assumed up to this point that it is a straight-forward matter to say what Christianity is. An article in the *British Journal of Religious Education* entitled 'Will the Real Christianity Please Stand Up?' warns of difficulties.[25] The Pope, together with the Curia, might speak for the Roman Catholic Church. In so doing he would call upon centuries of thinking and speaking by his predecessors and, ready to hand, he would have the authoritative Catechism of the Catholic Church. The Westminster Confession will help the non-conformist. Even the Society of Friends, a group which dislikes precise definitions, has its website and 'take' on what the society stands for. Each group will have its own particular definition and shades of meaning. Some of these shades of meaning are met commonly in the classroom. 'There's Catholics and Christians, Miss!' 'My religion's Protestant and his is Catholic!' The modern ecumenist may go pale in response to such 'prejudice' but taking an appropriately pious stance in protest at such uncouth sentiments is unlikely to make them go away.

Answers from the man or woman in the street are likely to evince puzzlement or a wide variety of suggestions. Syllabus conferences may point to the historic creeds present in the liturgies of Anglican, Catholic and other churches. But even the historic creeds are easily shown to be products of their time and place. Even to write of 'other churches' betrays a particular stance. A Catholic following *Dominus Iesus* would, when referring to any grouping other than RC or Orthodox, write of 'ecclesial communities'. And must Christianity be perceived as only in relation to the Church, however understood, or can it, and does it, exist apart from the Church? Is there a real possibility of a de-churched Christianity as Dietrich Bonhoeffer claimed to have discovered in a Nazi prison? Reflection on this question can produce another: did Jesus actually intend to found a brand new religion put into watertight compartments from the Judaism which was its matrix?

Time and space raise further problems. Is Christianity the same through time and across space? Clearly not. We know that the Roman Catholic church has changed over the years. In reacting to this some seek out a primitive form of Christianity such as did the great Cardinal J.H. Newman in his years as an Anglican, reading through the early church fathers in order to discover the note of apostolicity that he felt should mark the authentic (Anglican) Church of Christ. Present writers may follow suit. Doble writes of a 'much older Gospels' tradition'.[26] To teach only what may be discerned in the gospels and the fathers as authentic Christianity appears attractive, but such teaching bypasses developments that have taken place in both doctrine and practice and may bring about yet more division and argument. It runs counter to Christian faith in the Holy Spirit[27] to imagine that fresh truths have not been revealed over the years. The doctrine of the Trinity, for example, does not appear fully developed in the Scriptures. And what would this 'Gospels' tradition' look like? The words of

Luther ring true: 'There will be great confusion. Nobody will conform with another man's opinions or submit to his authority. Everybody will want to be his own rabbi ... and the greatest offences and divisions will arise from this.'[28]

Even the apportioning of a name introduces problems. It treats Christianity as static and easily identifiable. Robert Jackson warns that we should not view any faith as a homogeneous whole, neatly wrapped and insulated from outside influences. Rather we should see a 'faith tradition' (Jackson's favoured term) as having fluid boundaries and subject to constant change and growth, more like an organism than a concrete block. Furthermore we need to take care that we do not give the impression that Christian faith is just an object of knowledge rather than something which *is* and which calls for a response from us. However, even an organism has a structure and we need to have some idea of what it is we are teaching if we are not to fall foul of the fashionable fallacy of which G.K. Chesterton spoke.[29]

And would the end result of any agreement about what Christianity is be worth very much? Benjamin Disraeli spoke disparagingly of 'county council creeds' springing up and down all over the country as each local board prescribed what form of religious teaching should take place in its schools.[30] Peter Doble has written of 'that "Christianity" known to no Christian community, an abstract construction fashioned from what local talent takes to be important'.[31] In fact syllabus conferences have had no great difficulty setting out basic beliefs and practices that characterize the faith. There is a remarkable commonality to them. These are the basic tools which teachers must use to make their teaching come alive. Yet 'local talent' is important and can be of great help in showing the nuts and bolts of faith as it is practised 'on the ground'. A good example of this is the 2004 Cornwall Agreed Syllabus which covers basic beliefs *and* local practices and traditions. A local authority syllabus (which may not be based on a particular denominational understanding) will always have its limitations as compared with a diocesan syllabus, but much can surely be achieved.

At this point the reader may like to consider the following statements about Christianity:

(A) If asked to define Christianity would any of these be helpful? Why/Why not?
1 Church attendance
2 Level of political and economic power
3 A genuine and informed following of Jesus
4 A being-nice-to people morality
5 Upholding old-fashioned notions of sexual behaviour
6 Believing in God in some vague way
7 Appreciation of and participation in Christian-inspired arts e.g. the music of Bach, cathedrals and concerts

8 Attachment to Christian-inspired ideas such as that all human beings are equal because they are all loved uniquely by God.

(B) Here is a modern summary of Christianity:[32]

> The Christian faith assumes God. God is Creator, and the universe and everything in it depends on God for its origination and being. God the creator or father of all is revealed decisively in Jesus Christ, the human face of God. God is revealed elsewhere. The 'Word made flesh' (Jn 1:14) is also the Word without whom 'no created thing came to be' (Jn 1:3), and who is already life and light for all humankind (Jn 1:4). God is Father, Son and Spirit, whose being is a loving communion of persons. By his life, death and resurrection, Jesus Christ has reconciled the world to Godself (2 Cor. 5:18). Estrangement from God (to use Tillich's synonym for sin[33]) is manifest everywhere in human selfishness, greed and failure to live in love. But salvation from sin is available partially, now, and is yet to be realised in the final purposes of God. God the Spirit is the inspirer of all that is good in human culture, science, religion and society. The divine love, out of which the universe flows, seeks union with all that has been made.[34]

Which, if any, of the characteristics listed under (A) emanate from this summary of faith?

THE CENTRALITY OF JESUS FOR CHRISTIANITY

It is not our intention to set out a comprehensive manual on Christianity. However, we do wish to highlight some aspects of the faith that we feel are central. It is important to understand that at root Christianity is neither church-centred nor doctrine-centred but Person-centred.

We argue this on at least the following grounds:
1 because without Jesus there would be no Christianity anyway – the argument from history;
2 the Church (or churches) points towards Jesus all the time;
3 it's what all kinds of forms of Christianity have in common – the very word itself;
4 Jesus is an inspirational figure, 'too dynamic to be safe', in the words of Dorothy Sayers (see website for more on this).[35]

Christianity revolves around Jesus – or should! Many Christians today, for example, speak of new ways of 'being church'. This is an odd phrase, but it is trying to get away from the notion of church as just a building or just an institution with hierarchy etc. It sees the purpose of the buildings and the institutions as helping Christians actually to live a Christian life – to be like Jesus in the world today.

Similarly, doctrine is the attempt by Christians to put into words what they see as Jesus' experience and their own (see Figure 5.1). Chapter 9 will discuss further the question of what happened to Jesus, and Chapter 12 will give examples of the experience of Christians such as Anthony of Sourozh and Hugh Montefiore.

Further comment on some aspects of doctrine

Trinity stands opposed to the view of persons (the word itself deriving from early theological understanding of the three persons of the Trinity) as self-regulating, independent centres having no need of others and relating to God, if at all, on a one-to-one basis. By contrast, in biblical understanding, there is no true humanity without relatedness and mutual interdependence. Dignity is to be found, not in standing apart from others, but in surrendering autonomy. The model for all this is God, already existing in community, who enters into a covenant of faithfulness with men and women who are called to mirror divine faithfulness by their faithful relatedness to one another.[36]

Creation raises the question as to how far human beings have the 'right' to do what they like. Psalm 8 expresses the paradox that persons are both creatures like other

Figure 5.1 *Christianity centres on Jesus*

TRINITY		CREATION
The belief that God is three persons in one God matches Christian experience.		The world matters and Christians are called to follow Jesus in his teaching and example of love.
CROSS AND ATONEMENT		RESURRECTION AND ETERNAL LIFE
Jesus allowed sin to do its worst without diminishing his message of love. Christians came to find in contemplating his death forgiveness and renewal.	**JESUS**	Christians believe that Jesus was raised from the dead – the victory of life over death and good over evil that is extended to the whole of creation.

CHURCH
The communion of those who seek to follow Jesus. In its long history many different churches have been formed.

creatures yet called to greatness. Identity as the 'sons of God' opens up vistas of car-rying on the work of creation as well as the calling to develop the moral and spiri-tual qualities that this might require. God, we might say, is uniquely unlimited, unbound and 'at liberty'. To the extent that persons are made in the image of God, they too experience, if at lower power, this sense of freedom and expansion. Yet the doctrine of creation also calls human beings to service of God and all that God has made.

Sin carries overtones of particular types of wrongdoing (often to do with sex) and seems to cast humanity in the role of perpetual under-achiever or hopeless cause. Yet it is fundamental to Christian understanding and needs to be taught in a posit-ive light. The idea that sin is a 'falling short' of what it means to be human/divine (as a son of God) points forward to the taking hold of something yet to be revealed because 'God in his being is an infinity of promise for man'.[37] Jesus is not ashamed, as the writer of the book of Hebrews says, to call his followers brothers. The doc-trine of sin is a reminder of what it is human beings are called to. It should not be taught separately from the doctrine of grace (God's limitless reaching out to persons).

Salvation or redemption is the idea that human beings are called to participate in the life of God both here and hereafter. It is a call to individuals but includes the whole of creation. It is something that creation itself may be said to look forward to eagerly. The goodness of creation calls out for deliverance from all that is evil and destructive. The power of the cross is, to use mythical language, the power that breaks the spell that binds us, and, at the same time, shows forth the love which, as the hymn-writer put it, 'will not let us go'.

Teaching Jesus

The centrality of Jesus leads on to two major considerations – what we can know of the historical Jesus and how to understand the claim that he is the Son of God.

One of us did a short stint of teaching at a girls' school in Liverpool when an RE teacher was off work. She introduced the topic of what we know about the life of Jesus and how reliable are the accounts we have in the gospels. 'Oh', said one pupil, 'the gospels are all myths made up by a granny'. All the class agreed. On investigation it was discovered that this had been told them by their teacher. He had not troubled them with the evidence since, in his view, there was no evidence worth taking seriously.

It is very important that pupils know that the evidence for the existence of Jesus is strong and that the gospel accounts cannot just be written off as fabrications. We have suggestions for this on the website accompanying this book. See also Chapter 9 for further discussion (pp. 152–9). We give an example of how to handle the issue of the claim that Jesus is Son of God.

It is important to know that Jesus is worshipped as God, but serious thinking about this topic cannot take place if pupils misunderstand what is meant by the phrase 'Son of God'. Indeed to know the fact that Christians believe that Jesus was the Son of God can indeed be damaging if it is interpreted by someone in a misleading way. Here are some examples:

1 A literalistic interpretation: that God is a male person who has children or that there are two gods. This is false and positively damaging.

2 In a more sophisticated way there can be misunderstanding along these lines, that there's nothing special about the title Jesus the Son of God. There were lots of *sons of God* in the Ancient World, the ancient religions and mythologies were full of such stories.

3 Or another sophisticated misunderstanding centres on the view that this means that Christianity is the best religion and others are either wrong or subsidiary to this one. This then can be interpreted in a way which sees Christianity as simply arrogant to claim a unique relation of God.

The consequences of these blunders in understanding are serious. They can make Christians seem naïve and smug, stupid and/or imperialistic, and it would be better that such people did not know of the Christian belief in the Son of God.

At its simplest level the term indicates relatedness to God and, in the gospels, describes the closeness to God that Jesus experienced. The term, when used of Jesus, indicates (in addition) the fact that Jesus bears a unique relationship to God. It points to his eternal being with the Father. As John's gospel puts it: 'No one has ever seen God; the only son, who is in the bosom of the father, he has made him known' (John 1:18). The wording in the Greek indicates the closest possible communion between persons. The metaphor of sonship points to what transcends it.

True and false Christianity?

The difficulty of agreeing on what is essential to Christianity must not detract from the importance of asking the question. Without a firm grasp on this it will not be possible to criticize many false turns that have been taken over history and still are around today. Secularists generally stereotype religion, and especially Christianity, and many Christians stereotype non-Christians. The strongest criterion for judging Christians is by asking whether what they do and say is in direct line with what we know of Jesus. Thus e.g. anti-semitism with which unfortunately many Christians have been involved in the past shows itself up as anti-Christian if tested by what we know of Jesus:

1 Jesus and all his early followers were Jews.

2 Jesus taught love even for enemies, so there can be no Christian place for racial hatred.

3 Jesus accepted death at the hands of his enemies, transforming it into victory. Therefore those who purport to be his followers have no business to be bothered

about revenge or justice on behalf of Jesus. Christian anti-semitism is therefore illogical and anti-historical. It constitutes abuse of what Christianity is meant to be, because anti-semitism does not reflect the character of Jesus.

This leads us to ask how Christianity relates to other religions.

CHRISTIANITY AND OTHER RELIGIONS

Christianity cannot be taught without reference to the influence of Judaism and Islam. Without denying that what are sometimes known as the Western or Abrahamic religions are separate religions with traditions and histories that need to be understood in their own terms, it is also true that they have interacted in history and continue to do so. Just as the early Christians were sometimes understood as a Jewish sect[38] so Mohammed was seen by John Damascene as one of many preachers of heresy.[39] A recent travel-writer, William Dalrymple, came across an obscure Christian group in Syria who prostrated themselves in prayer in a way very similar to the way Muslims still do today. It may be that Muslims are preserving an early Christian practice! The idea of pushing Christianity at the expense of other religions is a mistaken way of looking at the question of inter-relationship between religions. This is because:

1 Christianity properly understood and practised should provide the safeguard for the freedom and dignity of other religions in our midst.
2 Christianity properly understood shows them respect – indeed sees them as allies in the struggle against secularist indoctrination/conditioning.
3 Christianity has taken much initiative in dialogue between religions.
4 Christianity, in seeking to make disciples of Jesus must be faithful to the teaching of its founder, treating others with respect and not as conversion material.

Introducing debate on inter-faith issues into the classroom

Good RE will not ignore or pass over differences but debate them courteously and generously. Disagreements must be voiced in an affirming manner. This of course is also sheer good teaching. We can understand why teachers are tempted to avoid this kind of discussion. It is so easy to offend people in a world where deep emotional and political rifts between religions and within religions are constantly inflamed by extremists, propaganda and intensive media coverage. We write this as the Danish cartoon controversy is taking its course.[40] So it's easier for teachers to say simply about controversial beliefs 'this is what Christians believe', 'this is what Muslims believe' etc. and leave it at that. Nevertheless this explosive situation actually makes it more important, not less, that teachers engage with and teach dialogue about conflicting truth-claims in a place where it *can* happen. The RE classroom offers such a space. Pupils can feel safe and respected as people there – or they ought to so feel.

It should be stated that Muslims have a great respect for Jesus, known as the prophet Isa, and indeed, that the Qur'ān contains miracle stories occurring in his infancy. Modern textbooks often introduce different understandings of who Jesus is. But Muslims do not accept that Jesus was in any sense God on earth. Such a notion is seriously wrong from a Muslim point of view, bordering on the blasphemous as it puts a human on the same level as God. The Qur'ān firmly counters the Christian claim: 'He, Allah, is one, Allah is he on whom all depend. He begets not, nor is he begotten. And none is like him' (sura 112). Here is a specific area of disagreement. How can it be handled?

A way of handling disagreement

The above quotation from the Qur'ān indicates an awareness of and reaction to Christian claims. As we have already mentioned, it was possible for a Christian theologian to understand Islam as a heretical form of Christianity. In fact Christians and Muslims were occupied (and still are) in trying to resolve similar theological conundrums such as the interplay of providence and free will. The following imaginary dialogue attempts to highlight some similarities and differences:

Christian: I guess we've got lots in common – believing in the One God for example. But how do you see Jesus?

Muslim: Jesus was a holy man – one of the prophets. But I think you Christians see Jesus as another God, don't you? So you don't believe in One God but in three. Indeed, don't you talk about a Trinity? Can you explain that to me?

Christian: We don't believe in three Gods at all. There is only One God, but we believe that God came down to earth in the person of Jesus, and that after his return to heaven God sent His Holy Spirit to be with us. So the doctrine of the Trinity – worked out painfully and slowly is an attempt to find language for this great Mystery of One God but three distinct ways in which He is revealed to us.

Muslim: I guess I don't understand very well. You talk of Jesus being God's Son, don't you? Well doesn't that mean you see God as like a sexual human person? That to us is blasphemous.

Christian: When we talk about Jesus as God's Son we are using metaphor to indicate close relationship – indeed identity between Jesus and God. In fact our scriptures use a variety of metaphors and titles to speak of Jesus. One important title is the Word of God. Am I right in thinking that your holy book is understood to be the Word of God and that the Spirit of God is mentioned there?

Muslim: This is true but we believe that the Word of God is uncreated and has always existed as it is part of God's attribute of speech.

Christian: What about God's spirit? He must be uncreated too?

Muslim: Yes, you are right but we don't think of God's Spirit as existing independently as I think you do.

Christian: Still; there would seem to be a great deal in common between us here. You also seem to be seeing God in different aspects. I expect you would agree with the eleventh century saint and scholar St Anselm who said that God is infinitely greater than anything we can possibly think or imagine?

Muslim: Yes, and I understand that our theologians and yours debated several such matters in the years after the death of our holy prophet. But I can't see how you can believe that Jesus was God. That seems to deny the transcendence of God.

Christian: The followers of Jesus – all devout Jews who believed in only One God – came to believe that Jesus had some unique relationship to God because of what they experienced and what they saw happen to Jesus – especially the cross and resurrection of Jesus. I have heard that the Qur'ān has a different version of these events?

Muslim: There is a strong tradition that someone else was substituted for him although some scholars question this interpretation of the Qur'ān. But in any case our view is that it is impossible for God to take on human nature, because this would make Him less than God. And He cannot become what He is not.

Christian: For me that's the great thing about God. He was willing to take on human nature and become just like us. The gulf is bridged and something of the divine nature is imparted to us.

Muslim: Well we believe that God is very close to us, but that every Muslim is his own redeemer.

This dialogue is, of course, a theological debate concerning the nature of God and whether or not God could become man.[41] It is as much a Christian debate as a Muslim one, which is why John Damascene could write as he did. Other examples of how to handle areas of disagreement appear on the website.

The contribution of Christianity to education

Christianity cannot of course be confined in a box called religious education. The contribution of Christianity, and of other important religions, is discussed by Edward Hulmes in his book *Education and Cultural Diversity*.[42] We would like to end this chapter with two quotations; one ancient and one modern:

The great seventeenth-century Comenius (c.1660) argued that the young should be taught from the beginning that human beings are born not for themselves alone, but for God and the human race. To live for God and the human race is to maximize happiness and delight, a happiness which is put in jeopardy when human beings harbour hatred, envy or bias against others. This quote from Comenius could be shared with pupils:

> Bias towards persons, nations, languages and religious sects must be totally eliminated if we are to prevent love or hatred, envy or contempt, or any other emotion from inter-fering with our plans for happiness . . . How utterly thoughtless – to hate your neigh-bour because he was born in another country or speaks a different language.[43]

Pupils might be asked to think why Comenius included the word love in this list of emotions that might interfere with happiness.

Marius Felderhof put it like this:

> If the Christian religious voice could once more speak in the world of education it would be a voice which beckons to vocation. It would entice the youth to love the transcendent, to love the world which forever issues from the creative power of transcendence, and to love their neighbour as themselves. It would invite ministry rather than mastery as the true prize of education.[44]

There is further discussion of the possible contribution of Christianity to education in Chapters 10 and 11.

TO THINK ABOUT

In *A Short History of Christianity*, Stephen Tomkins who spares no punches regarding the corruption, failure, sin and weakness of the Christian Church writes:

> Modern humanism is the child of a Christian family. It may oppose and criticise its parents, and it may often be right; it may uphold values like equality and freedom more consistently than the church; but where did it get those values from, if not from its Christian upbringing? The Enlightenment did not create them *ex nihilo*, or learn them from non-Christian societies. It took Christian ideas that had originally been scandalous, like the equal value of every person, and made them scandalous again. When Western society censures the church for being slow to accept new liberations, it is right; but it is turning our own truths on us, which is often the way with kids. (quoted in 'Sins of the Fathers' *Third Way* p. 15 Summer 2005)

How far do you agree with this comment?

NOTES

1 Hodges, H.A., quoted in *Christendom Awake* by Aidan Nicholls (1999), p. 83.
2 Section 8:3 of the 1988 ERA states that an agreed syllabus 'shall reflect the fact that the religious traditions in Great Britain are in the main Christian whilst taking account of the teaching and practices of the other principal religious traditions represented in Great Britain'.
3 www.stapleford-centre.org. We are grateful to Alison Farnell for this information.
4 Orr, D. (2005), *The Independent*, 17 December.
5 Copley, T. (2005).
6 Johnson, B. (2005), *The Daily Telegraph*, 26 May, p. 24.
7 Sutcliffe, T. (2005), *The Independent*, 26 May.
8 For examples see Copley, T. (2005) introduction et passim.
9 See Jackson, R. (1997), p. 77.
10 Ibid., p. 79.
11 It is an excellent production although it (inevitably) reflects a Protestant view: www.dayone.co.uk/ad. For pupils aged 8–14 there is a useful CD which introduces links between Christianity and culture. See www.culham.ac.uk/Curric/lstones.html

12 Jackson, R. (1997), p. 79.

13 See Rowan Williams' (2005) speech to the Forum Debate: *Is Europe at its end?* Palais de Congress, Lyons. 12 September. www.archbishopofcanterbury.org

14 Copley, T. (2005).

15 *Picturing Jesus*, available from www.christianeducation.org is excellent. Also good are *Images of Salvation*, the story of the Bible through medieval art (available from www.stapleford-centre.org) and, also available from the Stapleford Centre, *Bible through Art, Jesus through Art*.

16 The RSPCA, NSPCC, Dr Barnardo's, YMCA to name but a few.

17 Chater, M. (2005), p. 252.

18 Kettle, D. (2005), p. 2.

19 A film adaptation of C.S. Lewis' *The Lion, the Witch and the Wardrobe* was released at Christmas 2005.

20 Quoted in Thompson, P. (2004b), p. 168. More examples of the effect of Christianity may be found in this book. More recently Wilson has written of the 'commonality of the inner life' which he likens to a 'hidden stream running beneath the surface of national life'. *Daily Telegraph*, 30 January 2006, p. 21.

21 Mitchell, B. (1994), p. 139.

22 Thatcher, A. (2004), p. 180.

23 Chesterton, G.K. (1995 [1904]), ch. 4.

24 For example, *Global Perspectives on Christianity*, which comes with a CD with pictures and music from around the world, available from www.stapleford-centre.org.uk

25 Astley, J. (1992).

26 Doble, P. (2005), p. 153.

27 John 16:13: 'When the Spirit of truth comes, he will guide you into all the truth.'

28 *Luther Table-talk*, 27 June 1538, no. 3900.

29 'The fashionable fallacy is that by education we can give people something that we have not got'. Chesterton, G.K. (1912), p. 198.

30 The precursor of the local education authority.

31 Doble, P. (2005), p. 152.

32 Summaries will always be contentious; for example there is no mention of the church in Thatcher's definition.

33 Tillich, P. (1957), p. 51.

34 Thatcher, A. (2004), p. 177.

35 Sayers, D.L. (1949), pp. 5–6.

36 See Newbigin, L. (1983), p. 56.

37 Milbank, J. (1997), p. 135.

38 The Roman historian Suetonius (c.75–160 AD) wrote: 'Since the Jews were continually making disturbances at the instigation of Chrestus, he [Claudius] expelled them from Rome.'

39 Born in Damascus of a Christian family in the latter part of the seventh century he worked for the Caliph of Damascus until the latter's hostility to Christians led him to become a monk in the monastery of Saint Sabbas near Jerusalem. Writing of

Muhammad: 'having chanced upon the Old and New Testaments and likewise, it seems, having conversed with an Arian monk, devised his own heresy . . . he gave out that a certain book had been sent down to him from heaven. He had set down some ridiculous composition in this book of his . . .'. It is interesting that John felt free, despite living under the caliphate, to pen such a frank assessment of the claims of Muhammad! It is also significant that, living outside the Byzantine Empire, he was able to challenge iconoclasm; a case of Christian insights being preserved under Islamic patronage!

40 In February 2006 a Danish newspaper printed cartoons representing Muhammad. This aroused controversy which was widely reported.

41 It is also a debate about human nature. Muslims tend to see humans as basically good and therefore able to redeem themselves through living a good life and observing the Qur'ānic ordinances etc. This debate has been important for Christians too. The Pelagian heresy is close to the Islamic view.

42 Hulmes, E. (1989).

43 Comenius, J.A. (1990), p. 70. We are indebted to Professor David Smith for this quotation from Comenius.

44 Felderhof, M.C. (1995).

CHAPTER 6

OTHER WORLD RELIGIONS

'My goal is to transform contradictory statements into different but not contradictory ones. My assumption is that what is positively intended by those who have lived, thought and felt deeply is likely to be true, whereas their formulations are likely to exclude other truths that should not be excluded.' (John Cobb)[1]

We begin by considering the relationship between religions and invite readers to locate the approach which we develop with the help of seven figures. We argue that teachers should consider areas of commonality across religions with children from a young age. Areas of controversy should be tackled head-on but in a spirit of critical affirmation which refuses to dismiss other views too easily. The role of symbol and ritual is considered, along with the dark side of religion and the crucial part played by reform. We see the role of RE as potentially trail-blazing in enabling pupils to appreciate how world religions can relate to each other with integrity.

Criticism of approaches to RE based on social cohesion was given in Chapter 4, particularly on the grounds that in practice they tend to lose touch with much of the religion they set out to understand and include. Yet it remains important to take on board the intentions behind such approaches: the global vision, the search for harmony, and the emphasis upon fairness to all religions, has never more been needed in the world than today.

RELATIONSHIP BETWEEN RELIGIONS

In recent years it has become common to posit three ways of thinking about the relationship between religions. This typology was first suggested by Alan Race in his book *Christians and Religious Pluralism* (1983). The first is exclusivism which holds that one single religion is true and all other religions are false. The second is inclusivism, which holds that while one religion is true, other religions also contain truth but are to be measured against the one true religion. The third is pluralism which holds that all the major religions have true revelations in part, but that no single religion can claim definitive truth.

The moral high ground in religious education in recent years has seemed to lie with the third position, the pluralist option. It is argued (by John Hull and others) that religions should no longer see themselves as competitors but as partners in the search for truth.[2] Geoff Teece, in a recent article, argued that RE should adopt John Hick's pluralist view as the foundation for religious education.[3] In essence this view claims that there are many equally valid and authentic ways of coming to God, known as 'the Real', who calls all human beings into a life of compassionate living.

There are two important criticisms of this view. The first is that of Gavin D'Costa who has argued that the pluralist option is a disguised version of exclusivism. In fact, he says, there is no such thing as a pluralist option. He holds that Hick's pluralism is dependent on a particular (Christian) truth-claim which is privileged as against other truth-claims. So, the claim is made that an all-loving God has created the world to bring all women and men to eternal fellowship with Him. Such a claim must exclude all claims to the contrary and is therefore really exclusivist.[4] The second criticism is made by Philip Barnes. He has argued that modern RE has disguised the radically conflicting nature of religious truth-claims by promoting a liberal Protestant creed of the unity of religions. This works to eradicate difference since religions are 'smoothed over' to present them as really saying the same thing. And eradicating difference is not a good way of promoting respect and tolerance.[5]

D'Costa suggests that the really important thing is to examine what truth-claims are being made and examine how they differ from other truth-claims. This being so, the reader is invited to examine what truth-claims are being made in this book! We hope that what we write in this chapter will be found to be helpful across a wide spectrum of views about the relationship between religions.

In this chapter we try to apply the principle of critical affirmation to world religions. This approach does not prioritize one religion, but assumes that there is truth to be found in all. At the same time it takes the quest for truth seriously, neither assuming that all religions are really saying the same thing, nor seeing them in watertight compartments each selling quite different wares.

It is an approach which is essentially God- or Transcendent-centred as that around which religions gravitate. We think it important that the different traditions are studied and discussed in a way which is affirming of members of the traditions without succumbing to naïvety or blandness; in other words to be both affirming and critical.

To share this approach with pupils certain introductory points about it are important:

Introductory points relevant to our approach
1 It assumes cultivating those attitudes and skills associated with education as discussed in Chapter 1 (see pp. 4–7).

2 It acknowledges that controversy is unavoidable. What is needed are ways of expressing controversy courteously. Even very young children are aware that people think
differently, and as they get older they need a model of how to discuss differences
honestly without papering over the cracks.

3 It makes no claims for quick results; rather it is to embark upon a lifetime's exploration. All religions stress the need for preparation in depth for any understanding
of their religion.

4 It appreciates the 'pointing towards' quality of religious language, gesture, behaviour and ritual. It is crucial not to take everything in either a literal sense or in
a humanistic, re-interpretative sense. The meaning of symbol in religion can be undermined not just by literalism, but by evacuating the content of the symbol, making it 'just symbolism'.

5 It searches first for what can be seen to cohere and fit together before attending
to what does not fit. It is rather like doing a jigsaw puzzle where one might never
get started if insisting first on finding the exact home for this one particular piece
before trying with the rest. We cannot expect to arrive at consensus easily but we
can at least *want* to find out what is in common before worrying about what appears
to contradict.

Sharing these points with pupils will help to build up the appropriate attitudes and
skills in a relatively safe way, as well as increasing understanding of the great world
religions.

Something of this should be attempted with all children, including those who are
quite young, using appropriate examples and language. To delay the attempt to begin
to understand religion in these ways is to risk making it very difficult for people ever
to understand.

The kind of descriptive approach already widespread in schools – and for which there
is plenty of published material available – needs from an early stage to be supplemented in an important way. The following series of seven figures gives some
suggestions on a possible order. The six world religions specified are those recom-
mended in the non-statutory national framework for RE, but there is scope for
others, as well as for work on distinct traditions within each religion. Depending on
the age and aptitude of pupils, as well as on local circumstances, work on just two
or three religions may be appropriate. OFSTED, commenting on standards of RE in
primary schools, stated: 'Generally, where few religions are taught in depth, pupils
are more likely to have retained an understanding of what elements – such as
beliefs, festivals, forms of worship, people and books – belonged to which religion,
while their understanding of religions as coherent yet diverse and complex entities
is enhanced. In these cases, pupils are more likely to build on existing knowledge,
understanding and skills when they reach secondary school.'

WHAT MAJOR WORLD RELIGIONS HOLD IN COMMON

Figure 6.1, using the shape of a circle containing equal segments, gives an example of what religions have in common: they all teach very high ethical standards and ideals which are seen as intimately related to the metaphysical reality behind the world – a reality which in most religions is called 'God'. Morality, for religious people, is not something invented by people to keep community life sweet; it is for them an obligation arising out of the nature of the way things are.

Morality may not be the same as religion – although in many of the great religions this distinction is not clearly perceived – but sincerity in pursuing religion is normally expected to carry with it sincerity in pursuing a high moral code. The reverse also holds, that failure to live morally betrays and invalidates religious devotion unless there is genuine penitence.

Figure 6.1 *The Golden Rule: an example of what major world religions hold in common*

BUDDHISM
'Hurt not others
with that which
pains yourself'
(Samyutta Nikaya
V. 353)

CHRISTIANITY
'Always treat others
as you would like
them to treat you'
(Matthew 7:12)

HINDUISM
'Do not to others what
if done to you would
cause you pain'
(Mahabharata, Anusasana
Parva 113.8)

SIKHISM
'As thou deemest thyself,
so deem others'
(Kabir)

JUDAISM
'What is hateful to
you, do not do to
your fellow man'
(Talmud: Shabbat
31a)

ISLAM
'No one of you is a
believer until he loves
for his brother what
he loves for himself'
(Forty Hadith of
an-Nawawi 13)

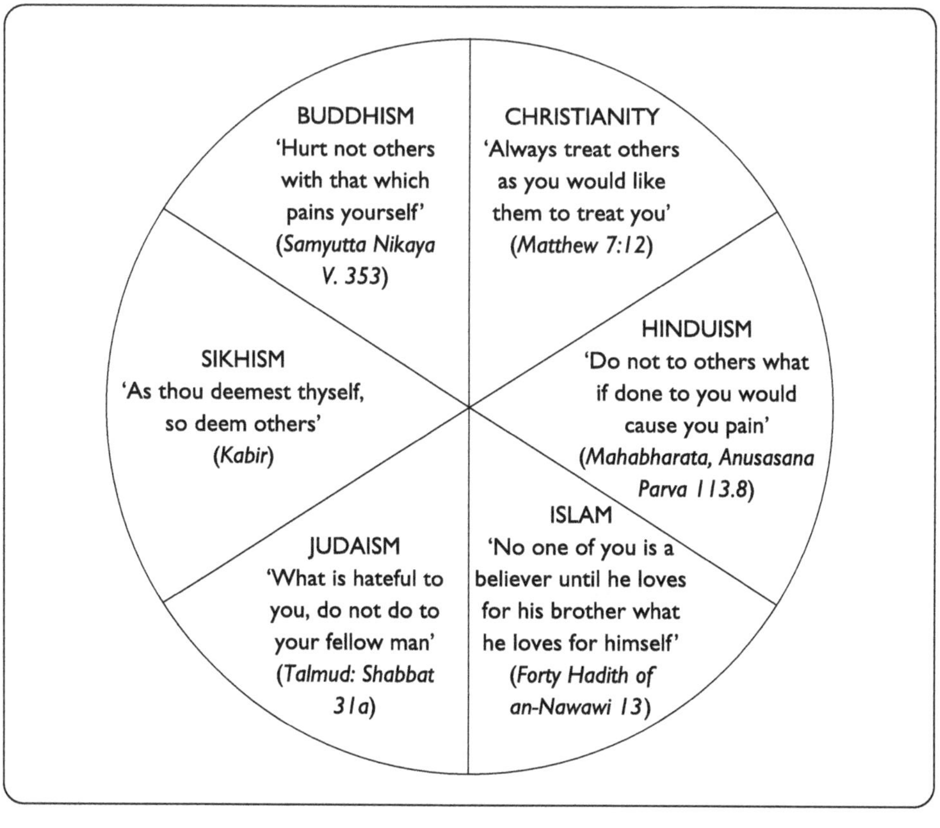

A clear example of the degree of common ground is what has been called the Golden Rule in the different religions. This is developed in almost all religions into a requirement to love even enemies. The degree of emphasis given in each religion may vary considerably – some may not give it the prominence which another does. But yet it should not be regarded as a quirky development, but as part of that to which the other more familiar aspects of the religion are pointing. Many other themes concerned with moral education could be given.

POINTING TOWARDS THE MYSTERY AT THE HEART OF REALITY

Figure 6.2, starting at the centre of a circle and pointing out towards an indefinitely increasing circle, relates to the way in which all religions point towards Mystery. Mystery

Figure 6.2 *Pointing towards the Mystery at the heart of reality*

'The Teacher has taught the abandonment of the concepts of being and non-being. Nirvana is properly neither existence nor non-existence' (*Nagarjuna, Mulamadhyamaka Karika 25*)

BUDDHISM

'To speak of God we should be at once poets, musicians and saints' (*a Russian Orthodox Christian; see p. 97*)

CHRISTIANITY

'Only Thou who made it all can speak, For knowledge is Thine alone' (*Japji 21*)

SIKHISM

HINDUISM

'Brahman is *neti, neti*; not this, not this' (*Brihadaranyaka Upanishad 4.5.15*)

JUDAISM

ISLAM

'As the heavens are high above the earth, so are my thoughts higher than your thoughts, saith the Lord' (*Isaiah 55 8f*)

'None knows the Unseen in the heavens and earth except God' (*Qūr'ān XXVII. 67*)

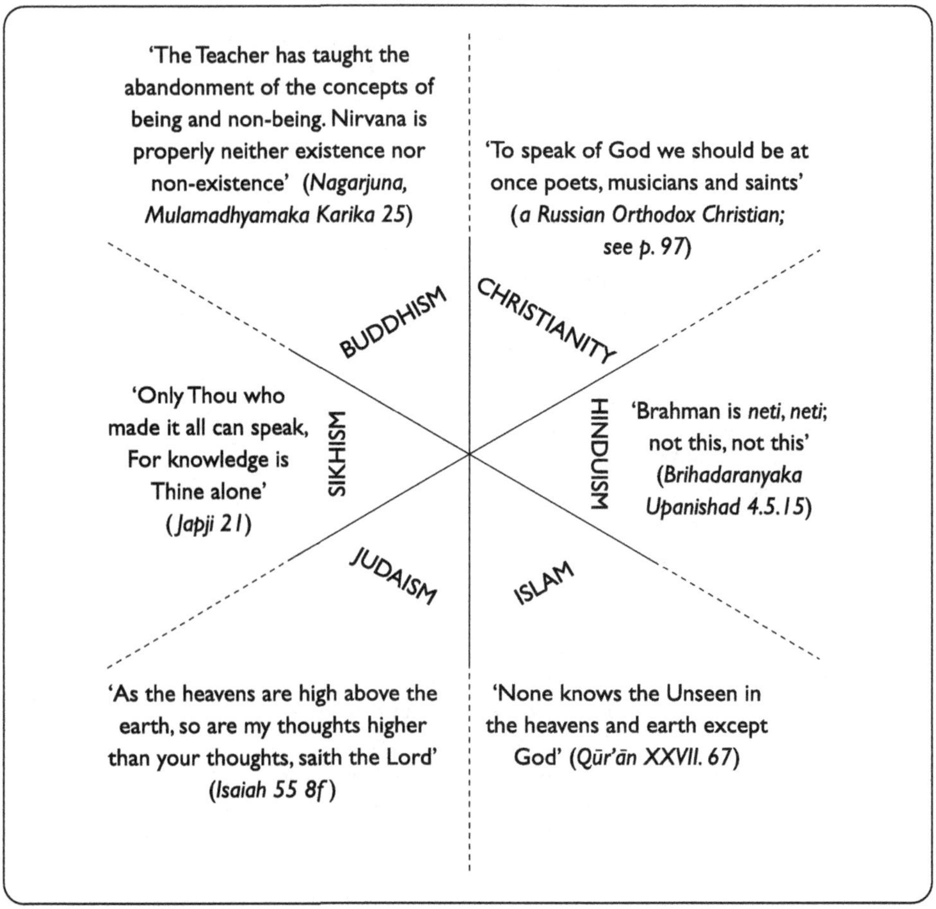

has nothing to do with a 'who-dun-it'. There is a profound difference between the kind of problem-solving which encourages us to use reason in order to reach a solution and the awareness of Mystery which leads to feelings of wonder and awe and worship in the light of what is being contemplated. This is how a modern scientist, John Cole, has put it: Mysteries 'are not the product of thought, but of experience. We can think about them, but not explain them, only know them. We must never attempt to reduce Mysteries to problems.' He then summarizes what Mystery means to religious people of many faiths as 'an intense awareness of the Presence abiding with and within themselves and the world', and he then quotes from Hindu and Muslim as well as Christian sources.[6]

This has profound implications for the way in which religions talk about God. As a Russian Orthodox Christian has expressed it: 'To speak of God we should be at once poets, musicians and saints.'[7] There are innumerable passages in both the Jewish and Christian scriptures which speak of the ineffable greatness and holiness of God.

Sikhism sees this Mystery at the heart of religion in the same way. The scriptures of the Sikh faith, the Granth, are full of such hymns as this:

> Saith Nanak: a million weights of paper, written over with learning and devotion,
> With ink in unending stream, with the motion of wind to scribe –
> Even thus might Thy greatness be not expressed!
> What measure might I give of Thy Name?[8]

Muslims emphasize the greatness and transcendence of Allah, and this informs their attitude of 'Islam' or submission to the will of Allah. The Sufi tradition in particular stresses that only through the use of symbols can any understanding be reached:

> It is through symbols that one is awakened; it is through symbols that one is transformed; and it is through symbols that one expresses. Symbols are realities contained within the nature of things. The entire journey in God is a journey in symbols, in which one is constantly aware of the higher reality within things.[9]

All religions use what in classical theology is known as the *via negativa* – the negative way of speaking about the centre of religious worship or meditation. Within Hinduism a classical reply to what or who is Brahman is *neti-neti* – 'not this, not this'. It is interesting to note (cf point 4, p. 94 above) that this is a seemingly negative phrase which is actually affirming something positive. The phrase does not indicate that Brahman does not exist, or that we know nothing about Brahman, but that we know that Brahman is so far beyond our understanding that anything we say will be misleading and therefore we must content ourselves with saying *neti-neti.* Christians too use the *via negativa.* They speak of God as immortal, invisible, infinite, incomprehensible, ineffable, and so forth.

This approach is most obviously to the fore in Buddhism which emphasizes the necessity for getting beyond concepts by the use of words like *anatta*, *anicca*, and *nirvana*. Indeed most Buddhists are unhappy even to refer to 'God' at all. The point is worth making that historically it was out of a background of theological wrangling by Brahmin priests over the nature of 'Brahman' that the young prince, Gautama, rebelled exasperated and went on to seek – and to find – enlightenment elsewhere thus becoming the Buddha. Knowledge concerning that enlightenment was what he passed on to his disciples, and this – the positive content of the Four Noble Truths and the teaching of the Middle Way – is what has made Buddhism live down the ages and still today.

Yet reluctance to use the word 'God' does not mean that Buddhists deny the reality of Mystery with a capital M. For they believe in 'Nirvana' as not literally referring to nothingness but to the enlightenment attendant upon the laying aside of barriers to it. It is greater than any concepts we can have to such a degree that they hold that any concept at all prevents our seeing it.

The word 'God' in all the explicitly theistic religions refers to that Mystery which is at once transcendent and immanent. It does not refer to naïve anthropomorphism, to childish notions of a kind of finite Person resident somewhere. The language of person which is applied to God is metaphorical, as discussed in Chapter 5, regarding the designation of Jesus as *Son of God* (see p. 85).

OUTWARD FORMS OF EXPRESSION AND INNER MEANING

Figure 6.3 offers a way of bringing the phenomenological perspective on one religion into relationship with other religions. What they each have in common is the use of various signs and symbols concerning both behaviour and belief. The diagram has one segment filled in; pupils could fill in the others themselves, working either in groups or individually.

The arrangement of the signs and symbols is designed to encourage a deepening awareness of their 'pointing-towards' character; the deeper we penetrate behind the scenes as it were of the various words and actions, the closer can they be seen to become, because all alike are pointing towards that Mystery which is beyond straight-forward conceptual understanding.

Farid Panjwani writes about the relationship between outward forms and inner meaning in this way:

> In Muslim tradition there is a deep-rooted reverence for the Prophet Muhammad. This inner relationship between the Prophet and his followers is articulated in culturally

Figure 6.3 *Outward forms of expression and inner meaning*

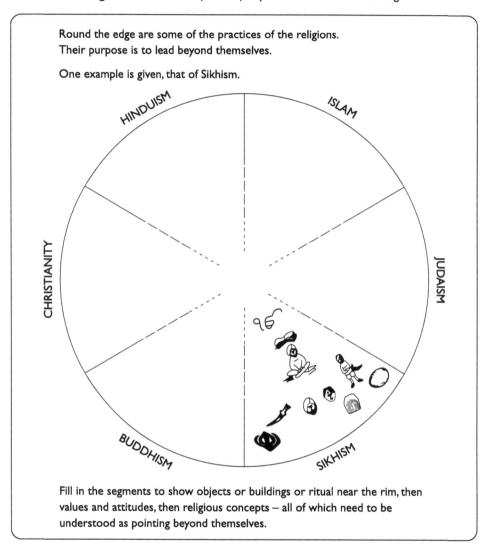

Round the edge are some of the practices of the religions.
Their purpose is to lead beyond themselves.

One example is given, that of Sikhism.

HINDUISM ISLAM JUDAISM SIKHISM BUDDHISM CHRISTIANITY

Fill in the segments to show objects or buildings or ritual near the rim, then values and attitudes, then religious concepts – all of which need to be understood as pointing beyond themselves.

different manners. In the Indian context for example the poetic expression of love for the Prophet draws upon the local symbols and metaphors and often one finds great resonance between the idioms in Muslim and other Indian religious traditions. This is because they all draw upon a common stock of symbols.[10]

Rituals, creeds and so forth are important, for they can help people to reach a state of awareness of what is beyond understanding. By the same token, teaching them in RE is important, but only if it is constantly related to their purpose within religions.

For they are not the goal, but a means to something else, and any understanding of the religion concerned must acknowledge this. Thus if the first purpose of a particular religion is to help people to a sense of the presence of God and express a response to God, then the study of the ritual which helps them towards this goal must constantly draw attention to this significance. A short section on the teaching of ritual may be helpful.

Teaching about ritual

The warning concerning how we teach about ritual is necessary. It is easy to make this colourful and fascinating, with varied activities. But what will pupils take away with them? Will they equate being religious with performing ritual? Will they see this as largely superstitious – the invocation of a kind of magic? Will they assume that people engage in this ritual because they have always done so and have been conditioned into it? Will the details of the ritual mean anything to them? Will the experience of studying the ritual bear any creative relationship to their own lives?

In order for work on ritual to become really educational, it is necessary to share with pupils what the functions of ritual are. Thus, for example, it enables expression of religious conviction in more than intellectual terms: the appeal to the senses, the performance of actions and so forth. These become vehicles by which an idea is conveyed with immediacy – the power of the symbol for evoking an emotional and emotive response. Another important feature is that it helps to overcome distractability so that people can focus attentively in prayer or meditation. Dissipation of energy through lack of concentration is one of the chief sources of non-awareness.

The difference between routine and ritual needs to be discussed. Superstition occurs when the distinction between the outer action or words and the inner meaning or purpose is forgotten. This is a great temptation facing the religious believer. But failure to appreciate the force of this distinction can also shipwreck attempts by observers to understand religion – to read correctly what is going on as a person performs a religious ritual or speaks religious words.

A story which can help pupils to discuss the role of ritual, and the way in which other people can misconstrue it, is that of the little fox in the Legends of Moses.

> Moses finds a shepherd in the desert. He spends the day with the shepherd and helps him milk his ewes, and at the end of the day he sees that the shepherd puts the best milk he has in a wooden bowl, which he places on a flat stone some distance away. So Moses asks him what it is for, and the shepherd replies, 'This is God's milk.' Moses is puzzled and asks him what he means. The shepherd says, 'I always take the best milk I possess, and I bring it as an offering to God.' Moses, who is far more sophisticated than the shepherd with his naive faith, asks, 'And does God drink it?' 'Yes', replies the

shepherd, 'He does.' Then Moses feels compelled to enlighten the poor shepherd and he explains that God, being pure spirit, does not drink milk. Yet the shepherd is sure that he does, and so they have a short argument, which ends with Moses telling the shepherd to hide behind the bushes to find out whether in fact God does come to drink the milk. Moses then goes out to pray in the desert. The shepherd hides, the night comes, and in the moonlight the shepherd sees a little fox that comes trotting from the desert, looks right, looks left and heads straight towards the milk, which he laps up, and disappears into the desert again. The next morning Moses finds the shepherd quite depressed and downcast. 'What's the matter?' he asks. The shepherd says, 'You were right, God is pure spirit and he doesn't want my milk.' Moses is surprised. He says, 'You should be happy. You know more about God than you did before.' 'Yes, I do,' says the shepherd, 'but the only thing I could do to express my love for Him has been taken away from me.' Moses sees the point. He retires into the desert and prays hard. In the night in a vision, God speaks to him and says, 'Moses, you were wrong. It is true that I am pure spirit. Nevertheless I always accepted with gratitude the milk which the shepherd offered me, as the expression of his love, but since, being pure spirit, I do not need the milk, I shared it with this little fox, who is very fond of milk.'[11]

(Discussion of this story occurs in Chapter 7 on p. 119.)

It is interesting that in Islam a similar message is found in a dialogue between Moses and a shepherd. This is in a poem by Rumi which suggests inter-mingling of stories and traditions. Here is another example from Islam.

Allah sent the angel Gabriel to search for a pious man in a certain place. Gabriel saw a man praying before an idol, lying prostrate. He reported back to Allah that he could find only an idol worshipper. He was asked to go and look again. This time he heard the idol speak, saying: 'I forgive you your sins, go in peace.' He returned and told Allah the curious story, and Allah replied: 'That was not really the idol speaking my word, that was me!'

This story was told by a Muslim in the course of some Christian/Muslim conversations held in Birmingham.[12]

POINTS OF CONVERGENCE

Figure 6.4 refers to the way in which, whilst all religions emphasize many particular understandings, ideas, beliefs, and practices not found in other religions yet many of these are not contradictory to those found in other traditions: they are different not contradictory. Mostly indeed such 'insights' are also present in other traditions but not stressed to the same degree. Sometimes this is because they are actually taken for granted.

Figure 6.4 Points of convergence

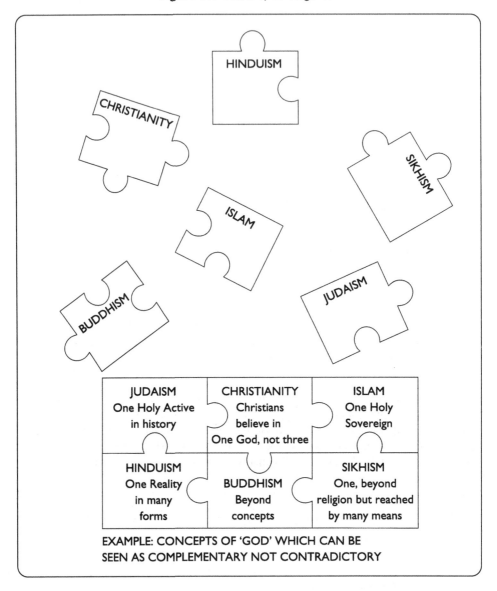

JUDAISM One Holy Active in history	CHRISTIANITY Christians believe in One God, not three	ISLAM One Holy Sovereign
HINDUISM One Reality in many forms	BUDDHISM Beyond concepts	SIKHISM One, beyond religion but reached by many means

EXAMPLE: CONCEPTS OF 'GOD' WHICH CAN BE
SEEN AS COMPLEMENTARY NOT CONTRADICTORY

By affirming these non-contradictory emphases, members of different religions can move closer together without fearing loss of integrity. Many themes can be explored in this way, like pieces of a jigsaw coming together. The diagram gives as an example the concept of God. Some may object that there are important differences in the way religions see this concept. We quote such a comment in Chapter 11 (p. 189) but there is more common ground than a superficial look might suggest.

In the story *Little Prince* by Antoine de Saint-Exupery, the Prince encounters a large bed of flowers and starts to disbelieve the boasting of the flower he had on his planet. He subsequently meets a fox who helps him see the uniqueness of his flower in a new way. Panjwani writes: 'By shifting the uniqueness from the content of a religion vis-à-vis other religions to the relationship between a tradition and its followers, the book, I think, provides a good way of both seeing the uniqueness of one's own religious tradition and acknowledging similar unique relationship between the other religious traditions and their adherents.'[13]

The reality of points of convergence should not, however, blind us to the fact that there are enormous divisions, not only between religions but within them. They are not the monolithic structures which they are often presented as being. Within Judaism for example there are Orthodox, Conservative and Reform Jews, or as Jews themselves often prefer to say Traditional and non-Traditional Jews (see Chapter 9, pp. 151–2, for further reference to this). In Islam the Sunnah-Shi'ah division is particularly significant.

THE DARK SIDE OF RELIGION

This draws attention to the ambiguity of religion. Differences do not, as we have seen with Figure 6.4, necessarily mean conflict, but they can easily lead to this if a spirit of possessiveness is also present (as discussed in Chapter 3, p. 46). Human nature can so easily become competitive and aggressive, fearful and defensive; and then bigotry, intolerance, bitterness and enmity are born, as unfortunately the history of *all* religions shows. Religions frequently fail to live up to their high moral standards. Religious wars and persecutions and the present use of terrorism by religious extremists have already been discussed (see Chapter 2, pp. 14–16).

Figure 6.5 shows a way of depicting how religions can present two quite different – and this time contradictory – faces: one of radiance and perfection, for which light is an appropriate symbol, and one of shadow, for which darkness is an appropriate symbol.

As discussed in Chapter 2, many people today are acutely conscious of the dark side of religion, and some see this failure as so colossal that they wish to have nothing more to do with it. All religions show how difficult the path is to embodying their high moral ideals – they acknowledge a high failure rate; the majority do not come anywhere near achieving what they should, and the more saintly or holy within the religions see this the most clearly. The fulminations of the Hebrew prophets such as Amos, Hosea and Jeremiah against the betrayal of religion are an example.

The story is told of Guru Nanak that even as a boy he argued that the ancient Hindu ceremony of tying on the sacred thread did not prevent men from acting wrongly.

Figure 6.5 The dark side of religion

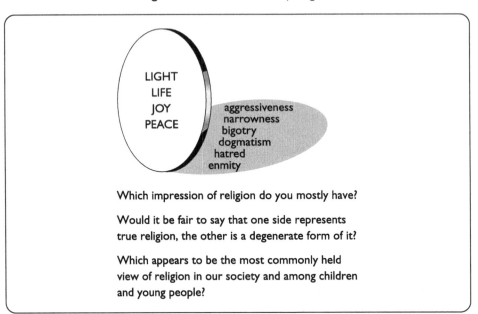

LIGHT
LIFE
JOY
PEACE

aggressiveness
narrowness
bigotry
dogmatism
hatred
enmity

Which impression of religion do you mostly have?

Would it be fair to say that one side represents
true religion, the other is a degenerate form of it?

Which appears to be the most commonly held
view of religion in our society and among children
and young people?

Centuries earlier the *Bhagavad Gita* had noted the same difficulty: 'Self-conceited, haughty, full of pride and arrogance of wealth, they do acts of religious worship in name alone.'

Because humans are fallible, the history of all religions has its dark side. The holy war can be terrible in its course and consequence, and is open to distortion and misuse for a variety of purposes.

The distinction between human fallibility and the goal of the religious quest is constantly referred to in all religions. Sigmund Sternberg, as chairman of the International Council of Christians and Jews, considered that: 'Many recent religious revivals experienced in particular by Jewish, Christian and Muslim communities . . . have assumed frightening forms of intolerance, exclusiveness, racism and fanaticism as well as nationalism, using religion as a weapon in defence of particular causes.[14] He then refers to the conference held in 1991 with some 300 theologians, historians, educators and lay leaders from 25 countries who endeavoured to disentangle what is considered legitimate use of religion from its apparent misuse. He concludes with this paragraph:

> If religion throughout the ages, and certainly in many parts of the world today, has been used as a weapon for destructive purposes, are we not called to demonstrate that as people of faith we can both live in passionate commitment to our respective

tradition and at the same time in compassionate respect for each other and to affirm that the faith commitment of each one is only truly realized when we live in that mutual respect accordingly?[15]

'WE KNOW WE ARE RIGHT': THE CAPACITY FOR CATEGORICAL ASSERTION WITHIN RELIGIONS

Figure 6.6 relates to one aspect which is often associated with the dark side of religion: the insistence within all religions that 'we know we are right'. Normally there is present a great deal of assurance and this finds expression usually in ways which are not too finely sensitive to the assurances of others. Of course none of us would take any action at all if we adopted too great an epistemological humility! We must believe that what we do is the right and proper course of action. What is damaging

Figure 6.6 *'We know we are right': the capacity for categorical assertion within religions*

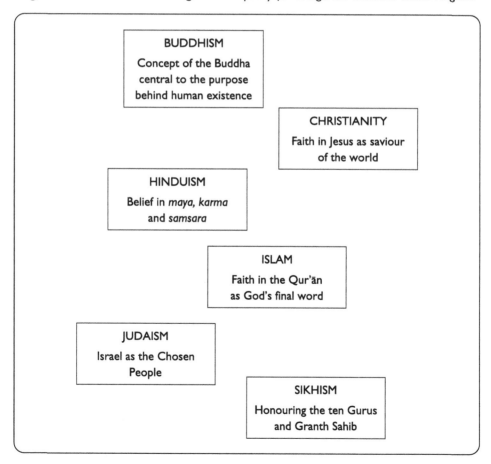

is to think that we can never be wrong or to fail to look for advice and correction along the way.

Each religion and religious tradition has been subject to geographical, historical and sociological factors which have influenced its vocabulary and the thought-forms enshrined within that vocabulary, and which have become unknowingly exclusive of the insights of others. To be open to the assurances of others and to seek relationship between assurances is an important way forward. Can our assurances be seen as pieces of a jigsaw which fit with others? Or is each to remain stubbornly not a piece of a jigsaw puzzle, but in its own watertight compartment, as shown in Figure 6.6?

The problem here is not just possessiveness and failure to live up to the high ethical ideals proclaimed by a religion. It is also confusion between a proper assurance based on experience and the insight deriving from it, and the dogmatism which so easily follows but is distinct from it, and which insists that what we happen to know is the *only* thing that matters – what others have discovered or had revealed to them is unimportant. This attitude can be unintentionally fostered through sheer repetition, through authoritarian methods of expression, and by reason of the default factor (i.e. what is *not* taught). These can be as much responsible as actual content of teaching for the development of dogmatism.

Yet as Keith Ward, writing as a Christian, notes: 'I can say "Jesus shows me what God is like, and makes the love of God available to me" without having to add, "Jesus is better than any other spiritual teacher, saint or prophet; so all other ways are inferior to mine".'[16] But it is a great temptation for people to say the latter, especially if they are ignorant of what others believe. And it is this spirit of competitiveness which can cause a link to be forged between the 'categorical assertions' of religions and the dark side of religion.

John Taylor has something extremely important to say about these potential sources of offence: 'We may learn to reformulate these irreducible convictions in the light of our dialogue. But we know that the reformulation may never reduce or dilute the content of experience which it interprets.'[17] Integrity must be retained.

There are two points to note here:
1 It is crucial to appreciate the distinction between an experience and how it is put into words. We need to ask what was the experience which gave rise to the beliefs and which they encapsulate, however inadequately.
2 Speaking of experience in this way does not mean that religions are merely the subjective products of human invention. Experience is always experience *of* something – something one comes up against as in communication from other people.

Religious people claim to be responding to communication from God – what in many religions is termed *revelation*.

FAULT-RESISTANT FEATURES IN RELIGIONS WHICH POINT TOWARDS THE TRANSCENDING OF RELIGION

Figure 6.7 looks at the way in which all religions have available within them certain fault-resistant features which is why their demise, so confidently predicted by many who see their grave faults and failures, rarely seems to happen! There is built in to these religions the requirement for self-criticism, a guarding against idolatry, against hypocrisy, against superstition, against injustice, against self-centredness, against self-satisfaction, and against taking refuge in particular rituals or concepts. A spiritual dimension is at work in all religions and constantly pushing and making uncomfortable the easy surrender to unspiritual and despiritualizing tendencies. All religions have a history of reform movements which operate from within and are not imposed from without.

This awareness of the need for reform, and the capacity for renewal, is linked to an increasing appreciation of the limitations of 'religion' itself.

There is a sense which is appreciated in almost all the religions that religion is itself unsatisfactory and has to be left behind. Such awareness is considerably to the fore today where people appreciate the need for a global concern – the need to relate in a non-violent, just, perceptive and generous way to the traditions of others.

It is worth noting that the word 'religion' either does not naturally feature in some religions, or is regarded by many religious people with considerable disapproval. For sociological grouping of religions has encouraged an attitude of defining each over against others. We need to consider the possible question with pupils, especially as so many are de-religionized anyway, of whether religion, in order to be true to itself, needs to transcend the 'religions'? If the latter are regarded as territory to be defended, as rallying cries for confrontation with others, perhaps we ought to be asking whether they need to be so territorial?

Many passages in the Jewish scriptures refer to the way in which religious observance itself can become an enormous obstacle and has constantly to be overcome. Thus Jeremiah speaks of a 'new covenant being written in the heart'. And Jesus, in his conversation with the Samaritan woman who asked him where true worship happened, answered that 'God is spirit and they who worship him must worship him in spirit and truth,' for 'the time will come when neither here nor in Jerusalem will men worship' (see pp. 190–91 for further discussion of this). It is debatable indeed

Figure 6.7 *Fault-resistant features in religions which point towards the transcending of religion*

whether or not Jesus came to found a new religion. It often seems to Christians that the Christianity which has wrapped itself round Jesus has served to obscure him.

The need to transcend religion has nowhere been more clearly expressed than within Sikhism. Was it really Guru Nanak's intention to found a *new* religion, or even a new religious community? It is true that just six months before his death he chose Lehna as his successor. Various stories about him, however, confirm how strongly he perceived that the outward forms of religion have to be internalized, and therefore could perhaps become redundant.

Hindus have long since seen that we have to transcend separateness. And for Buddhists this forms part of their central affirmation, to arrive at the point of 'emptiness' – the central doctrine of Mahayana Buddhism (*Shunyata*). On the question of religion, the Buddhist tends to think of it as a raft with which to cross the tempestuous seas of existence, and the Buddha once asked, 'What would you say to someone who carried his raft around with him when he had arrived?'

Of course this assumes that in this world we do arrive! Most religious people would consider that even the most saintly have a long way still to go. This is why religions and their varied practices remain important. They may only be stepping-stones towards a goal greater than themselves but this does not diminish their significance.

THE ROLE OF RE

In its approach to world religions, school RE may be able to be truly pioneering, blazing a trail whereby seemingly very different and rival groupings can meet with respect and even love. This will help us to get beyond the phase of advocacy of 'tolerance' which has never been adequate on its own. Only at a very basic level of respect for all persons as persons has this been so. It cannot be the ultimate value because it manifestly ignores so many other values such as those of justice, as well as ignoring the truth-claims which religions inevitably have to take seriously.

Chapter 11 on school worship will take up this point, and discuss the possibility of overcoming the unfortunate dichotomy between Christian or multi-faith at the practical point of assemblies (see especially pp. 189ff.).

TO THINK ABOUT

Andrew Wingate gives an account of Christian/Muslim conversations in Birmingham in which a Franciscan and a Sufi spoke about their ways of life and teaching.

> A Franciscan brother from the college is now part of the group and, wearing his habit, he held all of us spellbound with a simple but profound account of the calling of St Francis, his life and teaching, and of his own response to this. The message seemed to speak quite beyond the bounds of one religion. We then heard an exposition of what being a Sufi was about from Nazir's own brother – and he suggested that this was no more and no less than what being a truly spiritual Muslim was about.[18]

1 Why do you think the writer was so impressed by what these two religious people had to say?
2 What does the phrase 'a truly spiritual Muslim' mean to you?
3 Were the approach to religion of these two people common, what kind of changes world-wide in attitudes to religion might result?

NOTES

1 John Cobb (1990), p. 93.
2 Hull, J. (2000).
3 Teece, G. (2005).
4 D'Costa, G. (1996).
5 Barnes, L.P. (2006).
6 Cole, J. (1988), p. 13.
7 Bobrinskoy, B. (1986), p. 7.
8 Talib, G.S. (1975), p. 158.
9 Bakhtiar, L. (1976), p. 25.
10 Farid Panjwani in correspondence with Brenda Watson (14.2.06). A useful book illustrating how Muslim devotion to the prophet in varied cultural contexts is Asani and Kamal Abdel-Malik (1995).
11 Quoted in Anthony of Sourozh (1986), p. 150f.
12 Wingate, A. (1998).
13 Farid Panjwani – see note 10 above.
14 Sigmund Sternberg (1991), 'Use and misuse of religion' in *The Times*, 1 August.
15 Ibid.
16 Ward, K. (1991), p. 69.
17 Taylor, J.V. (1978), p. 12.
18 Wingate, A. (1998), p. 40.

PART III

SKILLS FOR UNDERSTANDING

CHAPTER 7

CONCEPTS AND IMAGINATION

> Cardinal Newman once remarked, 'It is not reason that is against us, but imagination.'

It is vital that imagination is developed in RE. We show how religious understanding is dependent on making imaginative connections, as indeed is learning in science. Imaginative insight should cause us to see links and wonder at the complexity of it all. But pupils' powers of imagination need developing and RE needs to pay close attention to how this relates to religious concepts. We give examples of how this may be done through story, art, and work on symbolism and metaphor. We end the chapter with discussion on how to teach about God.

Saying that imagination is essential for effective RE is perhaps like pubs advertising good food. No one in their right mind would consider one offering bad or indifferent food! Our society pays lip-service at least to the idea of imagination in that the word 'imaginative' is normally regarded as a compliment – the opposite of 'dull'.

Imaginative teaching does not necessarily produce the capacity for imagination in pupils. They can be overstimulated by variety, and often it is the teacher's ideas that are expressed and not the pupils'. Often, too, the teacher trammels the pupils too much within particular boundaries so that they are forced to go in the teacher's direction and not their own. Being an enabler of pupils' learning is an unselfish task and 'imaginative' teachers do not necessarily excel in qualities of humility and standing back and giving space to others.

THE IMPORTANCE OF IMAGINATION

Why, however, is it important that pupils' capacity for imagination is developed in order to understand religion?

Imagination is essential for getting on the wavelength of religious people
The importance of practising empathy, especially with what may appear strange and uncongenial, is a major aspect of RE. This is not at all an easy task.

H.G. Wells wrote a story about a traveller in South America coming across a community of people who had all been born blind. Imagine yourself as that traveller. How would you set about convincing these blind people about the blueness of sky, the greenness of grass, the beauty of painting? This kind of putting oneself in the place of another and attempting to portray and communicate something through a medium which is unsuitable to it is very essential for an understanding of religion.

The capacity for this use of imagination is closely related to attitudes of mind. Openness, and a spirit of generosity towards other people and what makes them tick, can enable very great barriers to be overcome. It is not easy, for example, for a modern Westerner to understand Eastern religion or the Semitic thought-forms at the root of Judaism, Christianity and Islam. An imaginative 'thinking what I would think, if I was in their place' is something which has to be worked at.

Imagination is essential for understanding religious language and other forms of expression

It is easy for people to misunderstand religious language and ritual. There is a very strong tendency to take literally what needs imaginative interpretation. All the great religions affirm that at the heart of religion lies Mystery which nothing can adequately express: all religious forms of expression have the character of pointing towards this Mystery, and not describing it.

We need to appreciate that, as used in religion, 'mystery' does not indicate a problem to be solved. The kind of response which it calls forth is not a factual wonder *why* but a wonder *at*. It does not question as such, but accepts the givenness of mystery which arouses awe and even adoration.

Much religious language is not primarily informational but inspirational in becoming more and more aware of the extraordinary ramifications of the few essential truths. This must be understood, really understood, for otherwise – whether or not we agree with the 'truths' – we are likely to misinterpret what religious people believe. For awareness of Mystery brings a paradox: at the same time that religious people claim to have knowledge of this Mystery they become more deeply aware that it is infinitely beyond any understanding. The function of religious language, ritual and art form is in fact to try to express the inexpressible as a way towards greater awareness.

Imagination is essential for gaining knowledge in religion

Imagination extends the possibilities of knowledge. Often people think of imagination as necessarily fantasy far removed from reality. Yet imagination can be the means by which we can come to understand reality. It enables us to envisage what is not immediately present to the senses. Imagination is the capacity to make links and to see links – it is not discontinuous with reality, but is a way of understanding what really is there if only we can see it.

Einstein noted that imagination is more important than knowledge. He used to conduct what came to be known among his fellow-scientists as his 'Gedanken' (thought) experiments. Russell Stannard explains how Einstein made his discoveries, not by finding new experimental results, but by drawing out the implications of what was already well-known:

> One of Einstein's ways of working things out was to take the laws of nature as they were understood at the time and imagine them in unusual fictitious situations – such as, for instance, trying to imagine what it would be like to catch up with a light beam. In this way he was led to discover that the old laws could not make sense of these situations. So this, in turn, led him to revise the laws of nature.[1]

Stannard commented that, though such 'thought'-experiments are open to everyone, 'not many people think hard enough to produce one'.

Hard thinking is indeed required because the kind of information which science is dealing with and seeking to extend is quite literally mind-boggling. That light travels at the speed of five times around the earth in the time it takes to say *rice pudding* is indeed an amazing matter. The potential truths of religion are even more staggering to the imagination than straightforward empirical matters.

A great deal of 'making links' is achieved through the use of metaphor and analogy, for word-pictures can help us to move forward into fresh insights. Colin Gunton has written,

> It is now widely accepted that almost all intellectual advance takes place by means of metaphor . . . Metaphor is not mere ornament, but an indispensible means of articulating the shape of reality . . . They are the means of interpreting one part of the world by another.[2]

A precise use of imagination with regard to religion is that without it a person can quite easily not even consider the possibility of there being truth in religion. For no one can believe anything unless they previously know it to be *believable*. 'We are obliged to believe only what we think is consistent, without having any real choice in the matter' as a textbook on Logic puts it.[3] Imagination does not lead necessarily to belief, but belief cannot happen without the ground being prepared by imagination.

THE DEVELOPMENT OF RELIGIOUS CONCEPTS

Imagination is, in all three aspects of its value for RE, intimately connected with the development of religious concepts. Inadequate concepts cause people:
1 to misinterpret religious people's behaviour and commitment;
2 to take literally what may have been intended metaphorically or symbolically;
3 not even to see the *possibility* of the truth of religious concepts.

Effective RE must therefore be concerned with the building-up of concepts which are worthy of a person's total development, emotional, experiential and intellectual, and which fairly represent what is at the heart of all great religious traditions. Only on this basis can people make the informed choice which is the hallmark of the educated person.

An enormous task faces the RE teacher here. Two well-known quips make an important point: Xenophanes' famous remark in the sixth century BC, 'If oxen had gods they would look like oxen',[4] and Voltaire's sarcastic remark already quoted on page 67, 'God made man in his own image. Man has returned the compliment.'[5]

It is not difficult to illustrate the insight these sayings convey. This is reflected in such comments as that of the Russian astronaut Gagarin who said, 'I didn't see God in space', or of the scientist who says, 'You can't prove God exists', or of the literalist churchgoer who says, 'If you don't go to church you are not worshipping God', or of the religious fanatic who says, 'God tells me what to do'. All these responses are based on a seriously inadequate concept of God as being literally like a man, best denoted by a small g: a god who is visible; a god who has physical properties like anything else in the world; a god who inhabits certain places and not others; a god who acts and behaves just like another person. Such concepts are unworthy of educated people and refer to anthropomorphism which has been misunderstood.

The picture of an old man in the sky is not taught by any of the great religions – yet this may come as a surprise to many people today. Many adults have grown up in an environment in which they have picked up extremely infantile notions – notions which have never been challenged directly, but which, because of their almost total inadequacy and failure to square with other knowledge and experience, cause religion itself to be rejected as people become more sophisticated in other departments of life and other areas of knowledge.

Reasons for immature conceptual development in religion
Important research carried out at Oxford University by Olivera Petrovich[6] suggests that such naïvety is something which children learn from adults rather than being innate. In carefully structured interviews on the concept of God with three- and

four-year-old children she found that if she began by asking them to distinguish between objects which were man-made and ones which were natural and then to speculate about origins in each case, a majority of the responses referred to the natural objects being made by God or an unknown power (almost half and half responses on this). When questioned further very few of them thought of this God or power as a man, but either as a person without a body or as something like air or gas, and a few said they did not know or that there was no God. The concepts therefore were for that age quite sophisticated, indeed quite sophisticated by many adults' standards.

Petrovich found that if she started off asking the children about 'God', as a word which they had learned, the majority of them said that God was a man. She therefore deduced that crude anthropomorphism is something which children are taught, not necessarily intentionally, but it is something which they pick up from the comments which they hear and the deductions which they make.

The possible distortions which people can pick up are numerous. In a famous book entitled *Your God is too Small* J.B. Phillips[7] drew up a list of twelve inadequate concepts of God which people tend to carry around with them. These include such images as Parental Hangover, Resident Policeman, and Managing Director. It would not be difficult to draw up a similar set of misunderstandings from a survey of pupils in the classroom.

In almost every other sphere of knowledge and learning, the young child's highest intuitions are developed and allowed to mature – in mathematics, science, art, language-work, and so forth. But as regards religion, there appears to be a conceptual descent from an age of enlightenment in early childhood to one of childish lack of awareness in adulthood. Why is this?

The responsibility of RE

There are many reasons for this, but a major one has been the impact of the theories of Piaget on RE mediated in this country through Goldman in the 1960s. This has effectively banished explicit work on religious concepts in most primary schools, because children in those age-groups are deemed unable to think in abstract terms, but only concretely.

Petrovich's conclusions, however, destroy the credibility of Goldman's research based upon Piaget's work. Her research shows that even pre-school children *are* capable of thinking in abstract terms.[8]

Extending her research to include Japanese children, Petrovich discovered remarkable similarities with British children in their capacity for abstract thinking. Quoting Kant's famous sense of awe at the sight of 'the starry heavens above . . . and the moral law within', she notes 'In my recent studies in Britain and Japan, virtually every child that I have tested could articulate this connection by the time they are 4 years old.' Her research findings are the more impressive given the fact that 'the Japanese culture excludes any concepts of transcendent causality'. So the Japanese children she tested arrived at this concept of God on their own – not because they were taught it or heard it.[9] She writes 'Psychological research suggests that human beings are born with mechanisms or "expectations" by means of which already in infancy we begin to learn about and understand how our universe works' and that this includes postulating a divine creator.

RE must encourage such maturing of this human cognitive capacity to infer the supernatural from the natural. In so doing, RE should not take away the freedom of pupils to go along with or to challenge such postulating of the Divine, but rather to generate sufficient space and interest for such development or such challenging.

Lack of sound education in building up more mature religious concepts leaves pupils a prey to chance forces, snatches of conversation and the effects of the implicit and null curriculum. Many today are not encouraged at all in the development of imagination. The snatch of conversation in the 'To think about' box on page 128 suggests the poverty of understanding which a child growing up in a religiously deprived background might have of one of the most evocative concepts in religious language, that of 'heaven'.

RE needs to address this situation. Crude anthropomorphism (i.e. *identifying* God with a human being, instead of realizing this is a metaphor *likening* God to a person in some respects) effectively closes the door to understanding of religion. Nor do any of the great world religions teach it. Literalistic interpretations of heaven such as a suicide bomber's belief that large numbers of virgins await him in paradise, indicate misunderstanding of the fundamental thrust of Islam. Whether or not there is a God, none of the great religious traditions can be saddled with intentionally fostering such anthropomorphism, for it goes against the fundamental tenets of their faith. (See Chapter 6 for further discussion on this. See also the website for detail on this.) How 'God' is understood at the deepest level in all religions, with the possible exception of certain forms of Buddhism, can be understood by Key Stage 1 pupils (see Table 7.1).

RE must endeavour to revive the natural awareness and sensitivity which most likely has been lost by the middle years of schooling, and apply this recovered awareness to the religious vocabulary which pupils need to understand in order to make sense of religion. Otherwise, the views which they have about religion are no more valid or meaningful in themselves than those, for example, of a beginner mathematician on advanced calculus about which he/she knows nothing.

Table 7.1 *Concept of God for under-8-year-olds*

Dora Ainsworth as an experienced primary school teacher and lecturer sums up what is readily understandable by under-8-year-olds:

1 That God is One not many and that God is known by many names.
2 That God is the creator and sustainer of all.
3 That God is love and desires our love, and our love for each other.
4 That God is spirit and that God is beyond description.
5 That religious people use language in a special way when they talk about God – 'pointing towards' language.
6 That God is good and just, and wants us to be too in the way we behave.

WHAT CAN RE DO TO ENCOURAGE THE IMAGINATION NECESSARY FOR UNDERSTANDING RELIGION?

The use of story

RE needs to introduce pupils to religious myth and story. These can incorporate religious truth in a far more effective way because they appeal directly to the imagination of the listener who can then re-create it anew.

An example of story is given in Chapter 6 on page 101: that of The Little Fox. The story makes some very profound points about the role of ritual in religion, the development of conceptual understanding, the meaning of the word 'spiritual' and how it is related to religion. Yet the story says simply what it may take many pages to explain in words.

Further points about the story are:
1 that it can be appreciated even by young children;
2 that it is memorable;
3 that it holds the attention.

Little wonder therefore that all religions have used story as a prime means of communicating and of inspiring people.

We need to remember, however, that story by itself will not do. The inadequacies of a diet of bible stories in RE has long been appreciated. Telling and re-enacting stories and myths is part of RE but dangerously not enough. There is the danger that using the term story may fictionalize what was intended as history. There may not be justification for this (see Chapter 9, pp. 152–3). It is also easy for the religious significance of the story to be missed.

Thus the story of the Good Samaritan which is intended as story not as history is often taught simply as a message of 'Be kind and helpful' or 'Don't be racist'. But there is so much more to it than that. The historical context shows Jesus told the parable in an exchange with a lawyer who was quizzing him on what it means to love God and how, quoting the Jewish scriptures, this involves loving one's neighbour. 'Who is my neighbour?' the lawyer asks. The response Jesus gave leads close to the heart of what Christianity is supposed to be about. Really to appreciate this incident and Jesus's response to it sheds a brilliant light on the nature of religion.

First, the parable is saying that the neighbour is everyone who is in need of whatever we can give. The neighbour is beyond race, colour, gender, economic status. Not to love the neighbour whose need is in your way is not to love God.

Second, Jesus expressed criticism of official religion in that those who held authority within it clearly failed on both humanitarian and religious grounds. The parable thus was quite a dangerous pronouncement, for the Levite and the priest 'who passed by on the other side' wielded power in society. The risk to Jesus was real and parallels the Samaritan's risk in the parable. The original listeners would have known that the Samaritan could himself have been attacked.

Third, the parable clearly indicates that it is not what we say that counts but what we do. The priority of how we actually live is what matters. 'By their fruits ye shall know them' is a major test of genuineness in loving. Hypocrisy is a major temptation.

A further reason for caution with regard to RE through story is that knowing a story does not by itself provide sufficient safeguard against serious misunderstandings which can have far-reaching effects on people. The Adam and Eve story, for example, has spawned some monstrous offspring which include such distortions as a dismissive attitude towards women, a view of pain and hardship as revealing personal guilt, a view of the earth as the property of homo sapiens who can choose what to do with it, and a view of God as an insensitive landlord demanding slavish obedience of the human beings he has created.

Teaching story is not enough. Misinterpretation is easy for children today growing up in an environment very different from those in which the stories were told originally. Within religious traditions myth and story have received overtones through many other factors which are not available to modern children (a total lifestyle, worship, theological language, above all a community of people to whom it is real). Most children today are religiously naked – they have none of these 'clothes' with which to adorn their perceptions. It is like expecting them to see distant stars without the help of any binoculars or telescopes but just with their own native eyesight. Some stars can be seen that way if the conditions happen to be appropriate, but children will not get very far as astronomers unless their own resources are supplemented by those accumulated by the tradition of astronomy built up over the centuries. For astronomy read religion.

The responsibility of the RE teacher is clear. How well most dereligionized pupils can come to an understanding of the profound significance of such stories for religious people depends on teaching which is both informative and inspiring. Chapter 9 draws attention to the importance of considering the context and overall thrust of the Bible, and suggests ways of sharing such skills with pupils (see pp. 154–9).

Work on symbolism

Some explicit work on symbolism is also crucial. Work on the external aspects of religion, such as putting on special clothes and going into special buildings, is likely to be seen by children as quite literally what religion is about. Even the most up-to-date methods and generously multi-faith context, which includes visits to temple, mosque, gurdwara, synagogue or church, may not overcome this hurdle but rather reinforce for children the cultural and sociological explanation of religion.

Many of the resources available for RE are likely to have this effect. Often they are well-produced and informative. From this point of view, teachers should have no difficulty in finding suitable material. Yet there is a problem with many of them. They mostly do not adequately safeguard pupils against a casual, almost literalist, understanding of symbol.

There is normally, for example, little discussion of the difference between idolatry or superstition on the one hand, and authentic religious devotion on the other. Symbol seems to be thought of just as standing in place for the real thing because that is absent. The idea that symbol denotes presence within the means appropriate for time and space is hardly anywhere mentioned. A specifically religious term, 'sacramental', probably needs to be introduced at this point.

It is illuminating to note the difference between the average response to an icon and that of a member of one of the orthodox churches. For the former it is a work of art reflecting a particular symbolic way of describing certain believed truths. For the orthodox, however, it is not so much an aid to devotion as a way of communicating with God. The icon mediates a presence not an absence.

Admittedly this is a very hard point to get across. If the secularist assumption is operating it becomes almost impossible. This is because the assumption is that the significance of the icon is based upon the faith of the believer and so the possibility of a meeting between the believer and that Reality is discounted from the start. Lucien Jenkins[10] in speaking about how the claim is made that classical music is characterized by its transcendence simply states – as though obvious to everyone – 'transcendence is in the listener, not the work'. It is like in a story such as the ballet *Giselle* when Alberic goes to her tomb and is caught up in a vision of her. The secularist looking on will see the act of his taking the flowers to her grave as symbolic, in the sense of a way of expressing his grief, which is rewarded by an imaginary visit from her. Similarly, the act of lighting candles or passing round the *arti*-lamp in a religious ceremony will be seen in the same way. The possibility of there being a real lover, and a real response 'from the other side, as it were', is not even considered.

Unless, however, such a possibility is considered, the onlooker is not really appreciating what the ritual means to the religious person. This does not necessarily involve affirming it. I may believe it is possible that the dead *Giselle* really did communicate with Alberic but that in fact she did not. But the difference needs to be grasped before I can venture an opinion usefully upon that.

In trying to teach such a distinction, it is helpful to discuss, as a kind of bridge or way in, such phenomena as ghost stories and other instances of paranormal experience. Fairy stories too, and at a more sophisticated level plays like Shakespeare's *A Midsummer Night's Dream*, can be helpful in raising the question of whether appearances are real or imaginary. The point is at least to raise the question.

Work on metaphor

Pupils are likely to be able to make more sense of symbolism if some work on metaphor is done from an early age. Here we need to encourage pupils to think and express themselves in vivid ways using word pictures. Contrasting proverbs with ponderous prose offers a way in: 'too many cooks spoil the broth' is a far more expressive way of saying: 'Over-maximization of the workforce is counter-productive because it inhibits the realization of a satisfactory outcome.'

From such word-pictures we can move on to simile and metaphor, found especially in poetry. At a simple level children can appreciate this. Here is a poem by a 10-year-old girl who had never before written any poetry.[11] The class had done some work explicitly on metaphor, and the poem was a voluntary outcome of a visit to a churchyard. The accompanying notes, given when her teacher asked for them, indicate a sophisticated grasp of metaphor, and a high level of imagination.

Lavender Lily

Lily was a flower girl,
Her house was in the air,
Sweet lavender she picked gladly
Without a single care.

Her shop it was the streets;
After noon and after morn
Wearing her shoes, tattered and torn,
She walked to see her mother yew
Who once, in olden days, she knew.
Her bed was the moorland grass
On mountainside or in the pass.
Her fingers were the summer breeze,
Her voice like rustling in the trees.
Her face was pretty, like the swan,
Her sparkling eyes, a lake.
Her old white dress and purple shawl
She bought once from an ancient stall.
Her soul, God rest it, it has left –
People say 'it was for the best'.
They found her in the lavender field
With her flowers as her final shield.

Her conscious understanding of how she was using language is clear from the explanations she gives for the expressions she uses in the poem: (on line 2) 'She lived outside in the open, so the air was like her house'; (on line 5) 'the streets were like a giant shop where she could pick and choose out of bins and gutters'; (on line 8) 'this means she was close to nature and she felt like the yew was her mother'.

From being able to recognize and use metaphor, we need to share with pupils how metaphor works. I.A. Richards has defined metaphor like this: 'In the simplest formulation, when we use a metaphor we have two thoughts of different things active together and supported by a single word, or phrase, whose meaning is a resultant of their interaction.'[12]

We can give simple examples such as, 'Lucy is a gem'. Here thoughts about Lucy and about gems are active together and cannot be given a satisfactory literal translation describing exactly the degree of similarity between Lucy and a gem. The metaphor of the gem here is like a filter or a screen through which Lucy can be seen in a fresh light, and as such the metaphor has the 'power to inform and enlighten' which a literal paraphrase would not have – it would fail 'to give the insight that the metaphor did'.[13]

This applies also to the religious use of metaphor. When, for example, God is thought of as like light, the metaphor is meant to bring into play all kinds of overtones and ideas which can help the user to a greater understanding of the word God: light shares some characteristics which can be applied to God – but ones which cannot be neatly packaged up in literal words.

It is important to help pupils to appreciate that metaphors require interpretation within a background of shared ideas. It is very easy to pick up a meaning from a metaphor which was perhaps not the one intended. If God is likened to a king, as in Islam especially, it indicates that God is in control, that we can trust God, and so forth. But it is possible for people growing up in a totally different culture to see kingship in terms of tyranny, in which case they would receive the statement that God is like a king as meaning that God is tyrannical, even some kind of dictator, so that religion resembles a prison rather than paradise. Thus the same metaphor can lead to diametrically opposite understandings.

Within Judaism and Christianity, Psalm 23 for instance has spawned many misunderstandings. Likening God to a shepherd has made many people assume that the point of the metaphor was to emphasize the sheep-like quality of people – that they have no mind of their own, that they are there to be told what to do and treated like sheep. In fact in its original Hebrew setting the shepherd referred to a totally different picture – one who actually cared for and was perhaps even prepared to give his life for the sheep, protecting them from very real danger from which they could not be expected to protect themselves. None of the overtones of subordination and all the rest of it would have been present to the Hebrew.

Another very telling metaphor used of God – supremely so within Christianity – is the metaphor of the father. This has run into very heavy water in the twentieth century, and not only because of Freud's onslaught on religion in the name of wish-fulfilment, where he portrayed the idea that people create an imaginary father in the skies to give them comfort. Other factors have been the break-up of family life, the prevalence of one-parent families, very often only a mother, and the whole feminist movement which sees such language as sexist. Attempts to rewrite the Lord's Prayer and the whole of Christian theology are now being seriously considered.

The problem here is the failure of very large numbers of people today, both religious and non-religious people, to appreciate the metaphorical nature of the language they are using. The term 'father' was never intended to be taken literally. The question of whether God is male or female is supremely bad theology. It is like saying that if Jim Bloggs is an ass it means he has got long ears and brays. In our society we would normally not interpret a phrase like that wrongly, because everyday usage confirms that when we say someone is an ass we mean they have been rather stupid. But in theology we commit enormous howlers. The point of the metaphor of father is to indicate the experience which religious people have of God as a loving parent. It has nothing whatever to do with gender.

Of course this does not mean that we should not be careful about the metaphors which we use. It is possible that if a metaphor ceases to mean what it used to mean in another society then we should abandon it. This is often seen with regard to metaphors like shepherd for example. Work with pupils can often translate these metaphors or similes into something more meaningful, like that in Carl Burke's book *God is for Real*[14] where the 23rd Psalm is given a quite different translation by one boy: 'The Lord is like my probation officer': the probation officer was the only person in his life who had ever shown any real love and care for him. We are not arguing therefore that metaphors should not change, but that it is impossible for us to change them organically unless we understand them in the first place. If 'father' today means for many people a non-existent person, a drunkard, someone unkind or hateful, or if it denotes for others an exclusion of women, then it needs to be appropriately translated in different terms.

Work on artistic representations

Artistic representations like metaphor, are powerful ways into understanding religion. But first it would be important to raise the question as to the legitimacy of representing the Divine in human form. The prohibition on the making of idols in the Ten Commandments, because of the ever-present danger of worshipping what is created rather than the Creator, lies behind both Muslim and Jewish nervousness about figurative art. Islam forbids any representation of the prophet Muhammad; hence the outcry over the cartoons published in Denmark in early 2006. Christians on the whole nowadays have few problems with art and (in the Eastern Church) with icons. But it was not always so. The eighth and ninth centuries saw outbreaks of iconoclasm and, nearer to home, Oliver Cromwell's armies saw little that was right in stained glass windows, chancel screens and painted walls.

Christians have defended the general use of art on the lines that all created matter is good and that God's glory is revealed through the material order that God has created ('Glory be to God for dappled things' as Hopkins put it). The imagination has to be trained and exercised in order to 'see' God and one important way to do this is to meditate on the material images all around us in the created order. The role of the image (and the imagination) in Christian theology was developed in a sophisticated way by St John Damascene at a time when iconoclasm was at a peak.[15] If one accepts the role of the image in revealing God then artistic representation of Jesus, the ultimate image of God, becomes particularly significant. The incarnation renders particular honour to the human form. Furthermore the artistic portrayal of Jesus in the early history of the Church was of particular importance in stressing his real humanity over against those who said his human appearance was a sham.

There are excellent resources available for teaching Jesus through art. Some have already been mentioned in Chapter 5. Of course any picture of Jesus is a very human creation and it is good to ask pupils what any work of art they study reveals about the artist. A particularly good set of pictures is produced by CEM, called *Picturing Jesus*.

Artists are from different parts of the world and portray Jesus from within their own cultures. Each picture is given a Biblical reference so that pupils can find out more about what the picture may be saying, and questions help pupils reflect on the meaning of the pictures. You can try getting one pupil to describe a picture to a partner who then attempts to draw it. Pupils enjoy this but it does have a practical point. To describe a picture requires that one understands it and means that great attention to detail has to be given. When the time comes to reveal the picture there are always loud complaints from the artist! 'Jesus on the Tube' fascinates pupils. He is there but no one notices. His neighbour looks away, rather as if scorning the strange figure next to him. Only Jesus has his eyes open and he seems to take up more room than anyone else. Another picture shows Jesus present at a table but only his hands are visible. People are similarly distracted, two can think only of each other, one is taken up with his drink. One picture appears to be of the crucifixion but Jesus is nailed to a tree. And the tree bears different fruits. Round the trunk winds the body of a snake. Underneath is a dark picture of war where a figure of Christ appears to be being trampled upon. This marvellous picture has many stories to tell.

Specific teaching on the concept of 'God'
What has already been said in discussing metaphors for 'God' indicates the need for some specific teaching on the kind of understanding of the word current within world religions.

The concept of God is as salient for any understanding of religion as is the concept of number for mathematics. It requires therefore time and some kind of structured development. The occasional discussion period, in which pupils express their current level of thinking about God, is no substitute for study in depth of how religious people understand 'God', why they do, and whether they are justified in so doing.

A lack of ability to think clearly about 'God' will adversely affect all other aspects of attempted RE. In all probability pupils will miss the point of the otherwise excellent work they may be doing on the phenomena of religion, its rites, customs, beliefs and moral values and so forth. All these gain their significance as 'religious' phenomena because of their underlying relationship to an understanding of 'God'. The only possible exception within the major world religions is Theravada Buddhism, but even here the concept of Nirvana is all-pervasive and has more features in common with an understanding of 'God' than with a Western secular atheist view. (See p. 98 for further discussion of this.)

Effective RE will help pupils develop specific skills concerning the concept of 'God'. Extensive time-allowance should be given to this. The temptation for teachers to cut off at this point and move on to something easier and less controversial is great, but the real value of RE lies in following the development through. Otherwise it is rather like spending several days journeying to a famous tourist site, but when we get there only allowing ourselves 20 minutes to see it. A possible way in might be the following, given in more detail on the website, together with other suggestions.

If God were...[16]
One of us has developed the use of metaphor as a way of expressing ideas about God in the classroom. It was developed originally from an idea in *New Methods in RE Teaching* by John Hammond and others.[17] It has been used successfully at Key Stages 3 and 4. The example given in Hammond's book was of work with 7- and 8-year-olds and we have no doubt that, given Petrovich's work with young children, it could be used successfully at Key Stage 2 and perhaps Key Stage 1.

First, tell the children that you are going to get them to get their imaginations working. Ask them to write down their answers to the following questions: If you were a colour, which colour would you be? Why? If you were a piece of furniture, which piece of furniture would you be? Why? Go on like this using whatever examples come to mind: animal, bird, flower, country, sound, car, television programme etc. You will find that children will suggest their own examples. So far as is practicable let the children talk to each other about their answers. Perhaps pair up those who have chosen the same colour, animal etc. and see if their reasons are the same or different. Did they find the exercise revealing in any way? Did it help them to understand themselves better? Could they devise a composite picture that would express their personality?

Now ask them to write down their answers to the following questions: If God were a colour which colour would God be? Why? If God were a piece of furniture, which piece of furniture would God be? Why? And so on. Pupils can choose one answer they are particularly pleased with, write it out and draw a picture to illustrate the aspect of God it expressed. So, for example, one Year 7 pupil with a reading age of 8 wrote out 'If God were a piece of furniture, God would be a wardrobe because He is open to everyone'. His picture showed a wardrobe with an open door. Inside the wardrobe was a picture of his family enjoying a day out at the beach. Another Year 7 pupil wrote 'God would be a rose because a rose is beautiful but you have to be very careful with them.' Her picture was a carefully drawn red rose with a thorn visible on the stem. In all the occasions that I did this lesson, no pupil ever attempted to draw God as a human being!

One Year 9 pupil was a very unhappy young lady and very resistant to RE. She had no time for God but she enjoyed this activity. Every answer revealed her view that God was unworthy of her attention. God, she said, would be a strong form of bleach since bleach destroyed living things and smelt horrible. I told her she was right not to believe in such a God.

Some quite profound insights about God can come to light this way which pupils then are willing to explore and take further. See the website for an example of particular insights that a Year 10 group came up with.

Imagination not only educates the emotions but extends the frontiers of knowledge and activates motivation. A prime purpose of RE should be to encourage it.

TO THINK ABOUT

A chance hearing of the Lord's Prayer produced the following conversation:

Child: What's heaven?
Adult: Don't know – I suppose it's where you go when you die.
The child asks again: But where is it?
Reply: Up there, in space somewhere.
The child, better acquainted with science than with religion, then asks: In space?
Reply: Well these ideas got around before people knew about space.
Child then asks: Why do they believe in it?
The adult replies: Oh, come on. Stop day-dreaming. Tidy your things up.

1 What will be the likely effect on the child's view of heaven if there is no further discussion at all in that child's life of 'heaven'?
2 What could, or should, the adult have said to make this an educationally helpful conversation?

NOTES

1 Stannard, R. (1989), p. 120.
2 Gunton, C. (1992), p. 10.
3 Hodges, W. (1977), p. 15.
4 Xenophanes, from his didactic poem on 'Nature'.
5 Voltaire, *Le sottisier* (xxxii).
6 Petrovich, O. (1989).
7 Phillips, J.B. (1932).
8 See e.g. Petrovich, O. (1999).
9 Petrovich, O. (2001).
10 Lucien Jenkins, *Music Teacher*, November 2005, p. 5.
11 This poem was written by Julie Gage and given by her teacher Elizabeth Ashton to Brenda Watson.
12 Richards, I.A. (1936), p. 180. On its application to religion see e.g. Soskice, J.M. (1985).
13 Black, M. (1971), p. 186f.
14 Burke, C. (1967), p. 34.
15 See Louth, A. (2002) for an excellent account of John's work on the role of the image.
16 See an article in *RE Today* (1995), vol. 12, no. 2, by Penny Thompson.
17 Hammond, J. et al. (1990), pp. 134–7.

CHAPTER 8

TRUTH-CLAIMS AND
THINKING SKILLS

'I'm quite good at thinking. I just need someone to start me up.' (8-year-old pupil).
How far does RE start them up?

We argue here that RE must enable pupils to learn how to think in order to evaluate for themselves the truth of religious belief. Without the development of such reflective, critical thinking skills, pupils have no means of resisting cultural pressures such as relativism or fully developing their religious understanding. We pay attention to the role of assumptions and how beliefs are formed. We suggest ways of handling truth-claims in the classroom, emphasizing the need to understand what is being claimed and setting out a cluster of criteria which can raise the possibility of evaluation.

A major task for RE is to help pupils forward in their thinking. It is not for teachers to tell them what to believe or value, but it is for them to try to equip pupils in such a way that they can enter into the debate and develop a sound and perceptive worldview for themselves. This involves – whether we like it or not – teaching them how to think; the capacity for being scholars in the true sense of the word has to be shared with everyone instead of being for an elite of specially gifted, specially privileged pupils.

The time-honoured expectation that pupils have to be told what to believe by authority in the form of parents, teachers or the state, can no longer operate today. In the modern world the reasons for accepting any particular authority can be and are challenged. It is as impossible as it is undesirable to try to put the clock back and treat the majority of pupils as being necessarily philosophical and theological infants incapable of any more. Their level of sophistication in other areas of life has become much more marked. This must happen with regard to RE too.

This is not incompatible with the teacher taking a line and defending it. Pupils expect 'Miss' or 'Sir' to have a view and to have some wisdom to impart as to what is and what is not a sound point of view on matters under discussion. It is good for pupils to have something to 'kick against' and, as Edward Hulmes argued a long time ago, a teacher's faith is a primary resource.[1] A major argument of this book is that teachers must not abandon their charges to their own devices when it comes to thinking and choosing in the matter of religion. Hulmes put it:

If children are not helped to understand the problem of conflicting commitments they may come to a point of indifference about them all, or uncritically assume that their variety signifies a defect in all institutional religion, and thus decide to have none of them.[2]

It is here that the teacher's commitment (which includes understanding) is so important. Here is a person who has come to faith and, it may be, struggles with doubts and perplexities. The young, if invited in to the thinking of such a teacher, can experience at first hand someone for whom faith is real and important. All of a sudden religion is real and vital. They can see that religion is taken seriously yet is not without its complexities.

THE IMPORTANCE OF DEVELOPING REFLECTIVE THINKING

There are many other reasons for giving careful thought to developing children's capacity for reflective thinking:

1 Such an emphasis in RE relates to the questions pupils actually ask. Even young children are interested in metaphysical questions.[3] The interest continues, even intensifies, during adolescence. The Head of Humanities in a large comprehensive school commented in the hearing of one of us, in a staff meeting about Year 9 general discussion groups on controversial issues, that 'in about half of such groups the question of God is brought in by some kid or other' and that he felt 'put on the spot'. RE is one of the few opportunities in the school timetable where such questions can be pursued in some depth.

2 Truth *per se* matters; beliefs and values based on a falsehood or mere prejudice are not only unstable but likely to cause much damage and hurt to the people holding them as well as to others who may become their victims. The twentieth century has seen many horrific examples of the power of wrong thinking, and this has often turned on matters of religion. Such an emphasis in RE can therefore help to guard against delusion and prejudice.

3 Such work would help to protect pupils from indoctrination from whatever source, religious or secular. Only thus, in fact, can over-pressurizing of the young be avoided – by developing their capacity to be able to think effectively for themselves.

4 Such work will also help pupils approach the diversity of religious beliefs in an open and non-dogmatic way without succumbing to the relativism which tends to regard different beliefs as just a matter of opinion. This will enable creative exploration of the well-worn comment 'but they can't all be right!' rather than saying there's no point in the question behind the statement.

Implications for RE

It is easy to understand, however, why teachers tend to run away from helping children to evaluate truth-claims. A minefield seems to open up: complexity, controversy, doubt, anxiety, anger, bitterness, bigotry, intolerance . . . all these are possible.

Yet by embarking on these difficult waters we are confronting what religion really is, not a safe cardboard version of it neatly packaged up for general retail. This is therefore preparing pupils for the real world.

Also this is the point at which RE really comes radically alive, where it shows the excitement and challenge of which it is capable. By comparison the seemingly safe approach is anaemic and superficial – it does not really engage pupils. This does. Everyone has deeply held opinions about the way things actually are, about reality, about truth. If teachers tap into this they plug into a powerhouse of emotional – and potentially intellectual – energy.

But we ought to make the perilous journey towards truth as safe as possible – can we ensure that at least beneficial results are *more likely* to ensue than unfortunate results? By 'beneficial' we mean those which accord with the six-fold valuing outlined in Chapter 1 as basic to education as to civilized living. We think certain guiding principles can help and offer starting-points for reflective thinking.

Before turning to these there are a number of misunderstandings which we hope to pre-empt.

Pre-empting misunderstandings

1   *Thinking involves more than problem-solving.* The Teaching Thinking movement and the drive towards teaching Philosophy in schools[4] has been an impressive development of recent years. The problem is that it tends to focus on problem-solving. Even where extended into thinking about values and beliefs, it tends to see this as largely problem-solving too – in this case 'How do I make up my mind what to do, what to value, how to live?' From one point of view this is right and necessary, but because of the context of our society generally – as discussed in Chapters 2 and 3 especially – the impression is very easily conveyed of relativism, that it is for pupils to conjure up their own values. The notion of the existence of a moral and spiritual order to which we need to relate rather than negotiating values for ourselves is normally quite weakly presented, if at all.

There is a need for a much more genuinely open approach to thinking, one which really does take all the options seriously, including the possibility that some values really are true and are reflected in the nature of reality.

2   *'We can't know anything for certain – all criteria are subjective.'* This is a very common attitude rendered more attractive by post-modernism. We agree that all thinking takes place in the context of uncertainty which cannot be neatly overcome by cast-iron reasoning. The provisional and on-going nature of all thinking, remaining open to the possibility of fresh evidence, is an important insight to which post-modernism has

rightly drawn attention. Every claim to knowledge bears unavoidably a subjective stamp unless all one is doing is playing a game where the rules are decided upon beforehand and then simply applied. So we are not arguing for some mythical dogmatic position. But it is important not to go to the opposite extreme and deny the possibility of meaningful talk about truth, and of what we say being nearer or further from the truth (see pp. 42–4 for discussion of this).

We talk of considerations, questions, reasons or criteria. But these must not be understood as knock-down rules to be applied in a purely objective fashion beyond challengeability. They remain considerations, and moreover considerations which gain their full effect in relationship with others. For all of us, as we puzzle over the immense problem of knowledge, it is cumulative evidence which counts as we gradually accumulate the insights by which we live and make sense of the world and our own and other people's experience of it.

It often happens that people dismiss so-called 'purely anecdotal evidence' in favour of something more objective. But this indicates the presence of positivism as discussed in Chapter 3 (pp. 34–9) – a highly challengeable position to hold. In fact anecdotal evidence is both unavoidable and necessary. All of us rely on our experience, and what we can learn of other people's experience through direct conversation with them, through studying them, through tradition, through accepting authority etc., and this understanding of our experience is always interpreted by us through our thinking about it, and emotionally trying to understand it (i.e. the feeling side of our natures) and through experimenting and testing and reflecting etc. This argues the need for, not the abandonment of, reflective thinking.

3   *Thinking is . . . ?* Certain stereotypes tend to come into people's minds when 'thinking' is mentioned. We list some of these in Figure 8.1. We think the term *reflective thinking* is useful to describe what we have in mind because:
(a) it has a quality of first-handedness and authenticity about it – a person's own thinking not somebody else's. In an unusual analogy Coleridge described people as 'tanks' or 'springs'[5] according to the way they borrow ideas from others: 'tanks' just take over ideas and store them like water; 'springs' adopt them, producing a stream of water and so making them their own. The one can easily become stagnant, the other has on-going vitality of its own.
(b) it is mindfully directed thinking, displaying a quality of attentiveness. Without this quality, nothing can be learned or understood. Yet it is important not to confuse attentiveness with the kind of frowning application traditional academic work has often encouraged. We have probably all experienced failing to see something and then later, as we do the washing-up or walk the dog, suddenly 'the penny drops', and we exclaim 'But of course . . . .'. Insight is like that: the quality of attentiveness must not be spoilt by our getting in the way of it – by the wrong kind of effort or by anxiety and feelings of self-doubt.

Figure 8.1 *What kind of thinker do you want to be?*

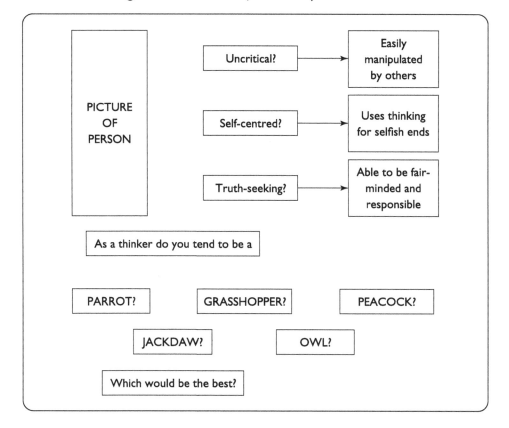

(c) thinking which is reflective is intimately linked with feelings, imagination and involvement in life, and is concerned about truth. Pure logic is only a small part of the thinking we habitually do, and can only be so because it is only appropriate for certain limited activities. In fact what we feel relates to what we think – the concepts we have, how we interpret situations, what we think ought to happen, and so on. And what we think relates to what we feel. Subjective reactions colour all we hear and see, and the words we use. Also there is a close connection between reason and emotion in other ways. The rational person *cares* about truth and is *disposed* to seek it.

Reflective thinking can perhaps be summarized by a quotation from the philosopher Basil Mitchell. He sees it as:

a matter of individuals attempting, incompletely, to make sense of the total environment in which they find themselves and to respond rightly to it. It is an activity which involves the whole person and calls for sympathetic imagination, sensitivity and constant self-criticism.[6]

Any view of RE that sees a split between a feelings/affective approach and a thinking /cerebral one is seriously mistaken, for both are involved all the time and cannot be separated (cf the fact/belief divide discussed in Chapter 3).

4 *'But isn't it much too difficult for most children?'* This is so common a reaction that it warrants a section on its own, even though reference to this was made in Chapter 7 (pp. 117–19). The short answer to this question is 'No'. Such thinking is for everyone, not just for the intellectually-minded. To do it one must be human, with feelings, experience, and some basic capability for getting on the wavelength of other people, as well as having a certain innate logical ability – the kind which enables a baby to learn unaided the mysteries of language. The capacity to make sophisticated discernment in thought-processes is within the grasp of almost everyone and constantly demonstrated in everyday life. It is this capacity to which RE must seek to relate, enabling transference of skills from the general to the religious sphere of enquiry.

If we want children to become philosophers in RE it is because they are already incipient philosophers, as for example Gareth Matthews has persuasively argued.[7] Reflective thinking is not beyond the capacity of any but the most severely mentally retarded. How far children take it, and especially the language they use and the sophistication with which they employ concepts, will obviously vary enormously, but none should be excluded because of a teacher's prior decision that they are not capable. How far they progress depends on many factors, but they will not progress unless given a chance.

An exaggerated and misplaced reliance on the research of Piaget and Goldman has encouraged teachers to have low expectations concerning children's abilities. Criticisms of that research have already been discussed in Chapter 7 (pp. 117–18). Young children do think – as Petrovich has shown (pp. 116–17). Limitations of expression and vocabulary can give the impression of naïvety, just as sophistication in language can hide naïvety in thought. A lively and optimistic search to find hidden depths and insights and questioning within pupils must replace negative attitudes towards children's capacity for thinking. In an illuminating interview on management, John Harvey-Jones made many comments as relevant to teaching as to management:

> One of the roles of management is to grow people's belief in themselves and raise their aspirations . . . They can do what they believe they can do but they sure as hell cannot do what their manager believes they cannot do. If you are told enough times that you

are incapable, you begin to believe it and lose the self-confidence you need to do your job. . . . Most people are switched on by recognition.[8]

This applies profoundly to pupils' capacity for reflective thinking.

In fact thinking cannot be avoided and it is crucial that people think as wisely as possible.

So how do we proceed? A useful way in is
1 to discuss with pupils different possible ways of knowing;
2 to discuss how beliefs are related to assumptions.

Grounds for beliefs and assumptions

Figure 8.2 suggests a number of reasons why we might believe something. These can evoke quite a lot of discussion at any age or ability level. Can you add more? Are all these reasons equally satisfactory? Discussion around these questions spawns many others such as:
1 Are there snags with any of them? – with all of them perhaps?
2 If so, on what basis can anyone *choose* a value or belief? or are we all just hemmed in tightly to whatever our parents or teachers or peer groups or the media or the government or a religious authority might say?
3 What in any case does this variety of possible authorities mean for people's freedom to begin to choose for themselves?
4 Are there dangers in 'going it alone' with regard to what we believe and value?

Figure 8.2 *Grounds for holding a belief*

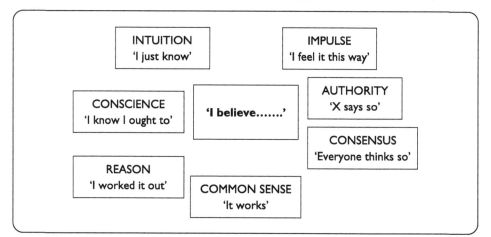

135

5 Arrange these grounds for believing something in an order of merit or of importance? How would you argue for the order you have chosen?

On taking things for granted

Assumptions It is important to appreciate that what we consciously say we believe
rests on all manner of things which we take for granted – assumptions. It is good
sometimes to try to clarify what these are.

We might start by some direct questioning or discussion, because what we take for
granted is on the whole what we never think about – of what we are almost certainly
mostly unaware. Class discussion or in groups, or individual written work, might include
some of the following, according to age, ability and interest:
(a) list some things you feel absolutely certain about;
(b) list some things you feel very uncertain about;
(c) why do you feel uncertain about them? – Is it because of your lack of experience
    or skill, or is it because no one can be certain of them?
(d) if no one can be certain of them, why?
(e) how do you rate the relative importance of the kind of things you have put down
    under (a) with what you have put down under (b)?
(f) on what grounds did you rate their importance?
(g) do you feel sure you're right in considering some things more important than
    others? How do you know you cannot be mistaken? And if you do not feel sure,
    does this matter?
(h) is it possible to doubt everything all the time?
(i) a great scientist and thinker of the seventeenth century, Pascal, once remarked:
    'Few speak of doubt doubtingly'. Think of an example of the point he was trying to
    make. (Here's one to get you started: 'Your view is just opinion', announced Mary
    with great conviction and emotion.)
(j) when we express strong doubts with such certainty we are taking certain things
    for granted – we are assuming something in the background which is beyond
    doubt. List some things you take for granted;
(k) list some things which someone you know or whom you have seen on television
    might take for granted;
(l) list some things which a Muslim, or Humanist, or Hindu might take for
    granted? In each case say why or why not;
(m) does it matter what people take for granted? Why? Why not?
(n) if you answered 'No' to question (m), what would you say to someone who does
    not take human rights for granted but regards it as perfectly in order to torture
    and kill people? If you answered 'Yes' to question (m), try to express the
    dilemma to which this gives rise.

Beliefs If an *assumption* is something we take for granted which we may not even
know we do, a *belief* is usually a collection of assumptions which are brought

together under an umbrella which is clearly articulated in words. Thus an environ-mentalist may say she believes in responsible care for the planet. But this rests on a number of assumptions such as:

Human beings have a moral responsibility not to be just selfish.
It matters what we leave our descendants.
The earth is something wonderful and life-giving.
It is also fragile and vulnerable.
Science and technology must not be destructive but used for good.
Sustainability matters.

Try making a mind-map of some of the assumptions behind these beliefs, some of them highly controversial:

Racism is wrong.
Women should not become priests or bishops.
Everyone has a right to euthanasia.
Schools can be objectively put into league-tables.
Classical music is elitist.
The past is dead; it's the present and the future we must bother about.

A STRATEGY FOR REFLECTIVE THINKING

The question now is to consider whether such fully-fledged beliefs and their largely unspoken feeder-assumptions are valid and true. To go about this we suggest a two-stage strategy.

The reason why we envisage two stages is neatly summarized in this quotation from C.S. Lewis:

> The first qualification for judging any piece of workmanship from a corkscrew to a cathedral is to know what it is – what it was intended to do and how it is meant to be used. After that has been discovered the temperance reformer may decide that the corkscrew was made for a bad purpose, and the communist may think the same about the cathedral. But such questions come later. The first thing is to understand the object before you: as long as you think that the corkscrew was meant for opening tins or the cathedral for entertaining tourists you can say nothing to the purpose about them.[9]

Stage 1: Being sure we understand what the belief under discussion really is
This is often much more complicated, especially with regard to religion, than many people think. Discernment is called for at at least six levels before seriously trying to evaluate whether a belief is true or not. They can be thought of as seven tests to be applied. Trying these out helps to ensure that we actually understand what we

are talking about and what the beliefs actually are. Figure 8.3 lists Levels of discernment necessary for understanding religion, with examples.

1 Communication test. This concerns the importance of understanding the words used and making sure that in an argument both sides mean the same by them. The problem of thinking we are attaching the same meaning to a word or action when we may not be can be appreciated humorously. Pupils can enjoy making up nonsense sentences like 'For goodness sake, put the table into the teapot!' or 'The house looked up and ran away.'

Conversations such as this can help even young children see the point:

> *Penny*: 'I love giraffes – I love stroking them on my lap – I'd love to have one for a pet.'
> *Daphne*: 'I would be scared out of my wits to have a giraffe – it's a wild animal and far too big for our garden!'

The same kind of mistake – usually entirely hidden from the people with the opposing views – can easily creep in to discussion about more serious matters, as shown in Figure 8.3.

2 Accuracy test. This concerns being fair with regard to what a belief actually claims. Accuracy matters in everyday life as it does in research. A famous example of the importance of checking whether the so-called facts are right occurred on the occasion of Charles II founding the Royal Society in 1660. At the inaugural meeting he posed this question: 'Why does water not spill over a bowl filled to the brim when goldfish are added?' Several months later, after much mental sweating, someone thought to ask, was the King right? They did the simple experiment and of course found that he was not!

Many wrong turnings in discussion and communication in general can be avoided, as unnecessary difficulties are pre-empted. A religious example is given in Figure 8.3. Another example might be attitudes towards Hinduism. The question is often asked whether Hindus believe in many gods and goddesses. Most Hindus would say that they do not, for they believe that at the heart of life is Oneness – Brahman – which manifests itself in an infinite number of forms. Veneration of the images is therefore for the devout Hindu worship of Brahman.

3 Integrity test. It is important when evaluating the truth of a belief to weed out of consideration any form of pretence or hypocrisy associated with the people claiming to hold the belief. This is an example of mismatch between statement and behaviour.

Figure 8.3 Six types of discernment necessary for understanding religion

1 COMMUNICATION
meaning of words

Applied to religion

These two people are not using the word democracy in the same way
A 'Democracy is the finest form of government.'
B 'It certainly is not.'
(A thinks of equality and liberty when the word 'democracy' is mentioned; B of football hooliganism and anarchic free-for-all.)

Fiona: 'I don't believe in God – science has disproved all that stuff.'
Mark: 'I do believe in God it makes sense to me as nothing else does.'
The disagreement here is at least partially one over the use of words. Fiona and Mark mean something quite different by the word 'God' such that they come to diametrically opposite conclusions.

2 ACCURACY
facts and honesty and avoiding making mistakes

In a doctor's surgery:
Patient: '4 tablespoons, did you say?'
Doctor: 'Good God no, 4 teaspoons.'

Many Protestants used to criticize Roman Catholics on the grounds that they worship the Virgin Mary. Yet this was in fact a pseudo-problem because Catholics do not worship Mary, but honour her as mother of the Christ whom they do worship.

3 INTEGRITY
no mis-match between belief and behaviour

A car driver indicates that he is turning right but goes straight on with disastrous consequences. Advice to drivers is to act according to the direction in which the wheels of the car are pointing, not trusting the signal given.

'I'll have nothing to do with religion – that vicar down the road couldn't care a damn for anyone.'
But the real question is, is he living his faith or is he a poor advocate of it?

4 SIGNIFICANCE
inner meaning of external words and actions

'They shook hands.' What did they mean by this? Did they agree? Were they just being polite? Were they deceiving each other?

'I can't stand all the incense, candles and ceremony, and above all the sermons, so I'm having nothing to do with religion'. This is a failure to appreciate what the outward forms are pointing towards.

Figure 8.3 (cont'd)

5 DISTINCTIVENESS WITHOUT SEPARATION both/and not either/or	'Are you a Darwinian or a creationist?' is a classic mistake (cf. Ch.10, pp. 170–72)
Holding together distinct parts within a greater whole Things can be inseparable even as they are distinguishable, as water = H_2O.	
6 CONTEXT historical sensitivity	The statement 'Jesus was the son of God' requires knowledge of its background (see discussion in Ch. 5 p. 85). It is interesting to compare the reactions of people from different religions to this statement. Most Hindus will be happy to say, 'Yes everyone is'. Muslims, however, are likely to say, 'No this is blasphemous. God is not a person who can have a son.' The Christian within the context of worship might say, 'Yes, his life revealed God in a special way'.
Understanding the background to a remark. The same remark can cause very different reactions in different settings. 'Stop talking' can be seen as plain common sense if everyone is talking at once, but if it comes from an over-talkative mother with a shy child it can have serious consequences on the child's character.	

Y talking to Z:
Y: 'Listening is so important.'
Half an hour later:
Z: 'I couldn't get a word in edgeways', muttered as he managed finally to get away.

What Y said may be right, even though Y fails to act by it.

The application of this distinction to religion is exceedingly important. Comments such as these are quite common: the newspaper headline: 'Religious mania behind terrorism?' It is easy to lump together under the heading of religion the political powermonger and the self-effacing saint, the ignorant victim of conditioning and super-stition with the thoughtful and intelligent worshipper, the sensationalist religious leader with the painstaking scholar. Unless we sort this out there is no hope of reaching any intelligent or sensible evaluation of religion.

These phenomena are as different as chalk from cheese. To eat chalk is as foolish as to try to write on a blackboard with cheese! Yet thousands of people do in effect do this when they reject religion because of the hypocrisy, superstition and dogmatism of some of its advocates, and when they accept religion because of their own taste for status, a safe life, or being hypnotized by the magnetism of some charismatic figure.

4   *Significance test.* Equally important for understanding of religion is the ability to distinguish between what is peripheral and what is central. The relative ease with which external forms and behaviour can be observed, and the degree of sensitivity required for penetrating their inner significance make this a special 'trap for the unwary'.

Regarding the significance of school uniform, for example, a Head might say to a visitor: 'The purpose of school uniform is so that pupils have a pride in belonging to the school.'

Later the visitor gets in conversation with a pupil.

Visitor: Why do you wear school uniform?
Pupil: Because I'd get into trouble if I didn't.
Visitor: So it doesn't make you feel as though you belong.
Pupil: Bloody hell no – I hate wearing it.

Scores of examples can be given from all the great religions, for this touches on the relationship of external words and actions to religious belief. This quotation from the *Muslim News* shows how important the distinction is, and what misinterpretation is possible if pupils are not helped sufficiently to see it:

In Islam, only the Qur'an is considered 'holy'. A teacher for example may hold up a prayer mat to signify a 'holy' object. The distinction between the mat being just an object upon which prayer is performed on and not the object of worship may cause problems.

(See Chapter 6, pp. 98–101 for further discussion on this as applied to religion.)

5   *Distinctiveness test.* It may seem an arid and dull activity to analyse and make distinctions. Wordsworth can be quoted:

Our meddling intellect
Mis-shapes the beauteous form of things.
We murder to dissect[10]

Yet his friend Coleridge could see a middle path – distinguishing, not in order to divide or separate, but in order to discern or understand. An obvious example is the relationship of a part to a whole. The hand can be distinguished from the body, yet it belongs to it in such a way that it cannot operate as a hand unless attached to the body – except in fantasy as in Ted Hughes' story of The Iron Man.

The difficulty which many people have in seeing this where religion is concerned is because of an either/or mentality. There are of course many cases where there is a necessary either/or in that if something is inherently contradictory, then choice has to be made. If I am writing on this side of the paper I cannot at the same moment be writing on the other side. Either the car engine is on or it is not. Either there is some cake left or there is not. Either there is money in the purse or there is not, etc. Similarly, as Andreas Whittam Smith pointed out in an article recently in the *Independent* 'There can be no tempering with torture. Either you oppose it or you go along with it.'[11]

But there is often a strong temptation to see things as either/or when they are in fact both/and. A graphic example was given me when on my first day of lecturing in a college of education a student came up and earnestly asked me: 'Do you believe the Bible – yes or no?' I was presented with a choice between just two positions when in fact there are many more possible ones.

6   *Context test*. This test highlights the necessity to understand the original context of a belief and make sure that something is not being wrenched out of that to a setting where it does not apply.

The question of context is extremely important. Take, for example the injunction 'Stop talking'. This makes sense in a theatre or doing some activity like bird-watching, but in a law-court where a witness is being browbeaten under cross-examination, or in a meeting where no one takes seriously an important point which is being made, it may be important that the injunction is resisted.

These are terribly obvious points, but we tend to forget them when dealing with complex and highly controversial matters which matter emotionally to us. Applied to religion the same statement can be received in totally different ways according to the context, for example, the phrase, 'Let us pray'. For an ordinary church service this can be regarded as absolutely matter of fact. If, however, this comes in a school assembly where there are many agnostics or atheists possibly present it can provoke the reaction, 'How dare they try to make us Christian'. If it occurs at the beginning of a committee meeting where something is going to be pushed through and the agenda manipulated it can provoke the reaction, '. . . hypocrites'. If it is said in the context of a vicar with a bereaved family who are deeply religious it can mean, 'Yes indeed, this will really help us'.

Before leaving Stage 1, readers may like to try the exercise in Figure 8.4 using the example of cheese to illustrate each level.

Stage 2: Evaluating the truth of a belief
This kind of thinking is leading on from the question of analysis to that of evaluation. The issue here is not only 'Where *do* I locate my response?' but 'Where *ought*

Figure 8.4 *Exercise on discernment levels using* cheese

Match the sentences with the six levels of discernment in Figure 8.2:
(a) 'Cheese and biscuits after the meal is a middle-class eating habit.'
(b) 'The *cheese* made an enormous noise and then flew off.'
(c) 'The wedge-shaped chalk may look like *cheese* but it doesn't taste like it.'
(d) 'Cheese is different from eggs and flour but in a soufflé is not separate from them.'
(e) 'I hate *cheese*' (because the Gorgonzola that mum eats smells horrible); 'I love *cheese*' (especially with toast for Saturday supper).
(f) 'Cheese is curdled butter.'

I to locate it in order not to be misguided, or plain wrong, or reveal my ignorance or blindness?' There is a need for criteria which relate to the basis upon which we evaluate anything. And these we need to share with pupils. Thus, about beliefs and values in science education, Michael Poole writes:

> In science education and in other areas of the curriculum more help needs to be given to students to enable them to discern where beliefs and values are located, how to spot where they follow from the subject matter or were imported at the beginning, what are the available options among them and what are appropriate criteria for testing their truth-claims and adjudicating between the ones on offer.[12]

A range of questions

Evaluating truth-claims: do the beliefs correspond to reality – are they right rather than wrong?

In order to decide whether something is sound or not, we can ask a number of questions. For example, with regard to the belief in the existence of God we can ask:

1 *Strict logic.* Is it logically satisfying or is there anything contradictory or inconsistent in believing in the existence of God?
2 *Explainability.* Can it offer an adequate, and perhaps more than adequate, explanation of the phenomenon of existence than a denial of the existence of God can?
3 *Comprehensiveness.* Is it inclusive of as many aspects of experience as possible, or is it exclusive, ignoring or dismissing many other aspects? – Is it welcoming potentially to all insights?
4 *Relevant authority.* Does it have the support of major well-tried traditions, or does it stand out on a limb as possibly idiosyncratic?
5 *Sustainability.* Can it be seen as sustainable in people's lives and through the centuries. Can it pass the test of time?
6 *Beneficial consequences.* Is the outcome likely to be beneficial – producing creative consequences?

7 *Openness*. Does it allow for the possibility of greater understanding or fresh insight? Does it lead to – even require – greater openness, or does it close the mind up?
8 *Positivity*. Is its thrust positive and not negative, referring to what is and not to what is not?

This is quite a battery of questions. The criteria they imply are summarized in Figure 8.5. Some of them have already been used in this book. In Chapter 3, for example, the first and the third, strict logic and comprehensiveness, were applied four times (pp. 37, 40, 44, 47f.) and the second, explainability, once (p. 35) and the sixth, beneficial consequences, three times (pp. 37, 41f., 48).

It is in weighing these up one against another – in balancing them and seeing them altogether cumulatively – that these criteria may become effective.

The use of the criteria
It is important to guard against certain misunderstandings, however. First, by themselves none of these criteria is foolproof. For example reliance on authority can be abused – called in when not necessary or appropriate. An example has already been given in the anecdote of Charles II on page 138. Authority can be mistaken and it can cover up ignorance with prestige and prevent people from thinking for themselves. This criterion can also be misunderstood as 'whatever is old is good'. Mistakes and ignorance can be handed on from one generation to another, habit can blind, and tradition can bind.

Second, the criteria become stronger as they interact with each other like interlocking links. See the quotation from Basil Mitchell in the 'To think about' box at the end of the chapter for an example.

Third, it is often helpful to consider the opposite – as Mitchell does here. The difficulty of expressing what we think adequately in matters concerned with assumptions and beliefs means that it is often easier to say what we do not agree with than what we do. For example, in applying the first criterion – logicality – belief in God is held by religious people to be more than a matter of logic. So to ask whether it is logical can be misunderstood because the request is inappropriate and inadequate. Yet most would want to agree that such belief ought not to be contradictory in any way, whilst bearing in mind the distinction between paradox and contradiction referred to at the end of Chapter 12 (pp. 209–10).

The value of the criteria
We do not claim any more for these criteria than that they raise at least the possibility of a belief being affirmable. The artistic eye, for example, will see what the pedestrian eye does not. Van Gogh could not possibly demonstrate the validity

Figure 8.5 *Eight possible criteria for evaluating beliefs*

EXAMPLE
The philosopher Kant spoke of being sure of 'the starry heavens above and the moral law within'. Is there a 'moral law within'?

CRITERIA	concerned with	
STRICT LOGIC	non-contradiction	The existence of much in the world that is evil doesn't contradict it because the moral law remains the ideal and judge of behaviour.
EXPLAINABILITY	order	It offers an explanation for the sense of right and wrong (as distinct from obeying or disobeying rules) which almost everyone has.
COMPREHENSIVENESS	wholeness	It includes all aspects of experience.
RELEVANT AUTHORITY	rootedness in tradition	Every major tradition ever known has believed in it.
SUSTAINABILITY	continuity	It makes for sustainability; without it life can easily become, as Hobbes put it, 'nasty, brutish and short'.
BENEFICIAL CONSEQUENCES	results	It is wholly beneficial unless understanding of it is corrupted ignoring 1 and 3.
OPENNESS	on-goingness of exploration	It is open because unselfishness creates space for others and frees the self from self-absorption.
POSITIVITY	harmony	It is positive creating an ideal of peace and harmony.

of his vision to someone who lacks that inner visual sense by which his greatness as an artist is perceived. Instead that sense has to be nurtured by more direct experience over a long period of time. This is why a child who grows up in an atmosphere where artistic beauty is in evidence and talked about and striven after has an enormous advantage over the child from a background of visual ugliness in which people are innocent of any artistic discernment.

For art, substitute science, languages, history and all the other curriculum areas including religion. Inner awareness is essential. What schoolwork can do, however, is help to arouse the desire for understanding. It can establish certain foundations, give pupils some strategy by means of which to proceed. It can especially help to remove unnecessary stumbling-blocks to the way forward for any given person. For example, no amount of arguing by itself will convince anyone of the truth of Genesis, 2–3, but knowledge of the possibility of interpreting it in different ways – which include the symbolic – can help people to think again about an easy dismissal of it. This can help to prevent simplistic denunciation of it.

If we do not ask these questions, can we be sure we have not abandoned the search at too early a point, so that we are like the police officer who judges too soon that the death in a detective story was a suicide and not a murder? Talk of on-goingness, openness to evidence, exploration, needs to be taken seriously. The problem is that many people tend to decide far too soon concerning religion that there is nothing there to search for – nothing important to be bothered about. Or they may decide that they have found the one true interpretation of religion.

This is very far from the attitude which almost all religions agree is essential for understanding and which is encapsulated in the parable of the pearl of great price. Maybe only to those of such a mind will religion or its truth be perceivable. As the advertising blurb puts it: 'Are you tuned in to the Win a Fortune Show?' Maybe that is the point: without being tuned in how can we know whether there is anything there or not? It is important to wrestle with questions of how far a belief corresponds to reality or is illusory. This is part of making sense of the world and of our experience in it.

Applying the criteria encourages such wrestling. These are all challengeable but nevertheless not negligible. Their cumulative force can serve to point out weaknesses, both in the content of a belief and in its expression in words, in a way which we can helpfully discuss with other people. Our awareness of the area under discussion, and our capacity for exercising choice, will increase through the effort of applying them, and balancing them against each other.

TO THINK ABOUT

The following quotation from Basil Mitchell illustrates the application of three criteria: (a) explainability, (b) comprehensiveness and (c) positivity

> The problem for the atheist is to provide a convincing account (*a) of religious experience, and with it of the entire (*b) religious history of mankind, which will do justice (*c) to its character and effects. Such an account has to be a purely naturalistic one (*a); it has to deny (*c) that these experiences are what they purport to be, namely, instances of human awareness (*b) of the supernatural. And it is important to notice that the onus is upon the atheist to show the reason why (*a) the experience is not (*c) to be trusted. Of course *no* experience is self-authenticating, but it is reasonable to accept claims made on the basis of experience (*b and *c) unless sufficient reason is produced (*a) for not doing so.[13]

1 Using three colours show how the 3 criteria (a)–(c) are intertwined in this argument.
2 How far do you agree with Mitchell?

NOTES

1 Hulmes, E. (1979), see especially ch. 2.
2 Ibid., p. 32.
3 Fisher, R. (1990), p. 245.
4 e.g. Lipman (1980), Fisher (1990) and many books by Edward de Bono and Tony Buzan.
5 Coleridge in a letter of 1811 referred to in Barfield, O. (1971), p. 6.
6 Mitchell, B. (1990), p. 210f.
7 Matthews, G. (1980).
8 Harvey-Jones in *Management Week*, May 1991, p. 80.
9 Lewis, C.S. (1941), p. 1.
10 Wordsworth: 'Intimations of Immortality'. See *The Penguin Book of English Verse* ed. John Hayward (1956), p. 264.
11 Smith, A.W., 27 February 2006.
12 Poole, M. (1990), p. 72.
13 Mitchell, B. (1990), p. 208.

CHAPTER 9

INTERPRETING SCRIPTURE

'Agreeing on some ground rules for how we read and interpret our sacred scriptures is probably the most crucial task facing Judaism, Christianity and Islam today.' (Rabbi David Goldberg)[1]

What is the place of the Bible in RE? The Bible must be properly taught as it is essential to an understanding of Christianity and, as the major Western religious text, has influenced Western civilization over a long period. As such it is inevitably a controversial and much debated text. We question reductionist approaches to the Bible and opt for an approach which looks for truth and opens up critical reflection. Pupils need to be taught to approach the Biblical material intelligently and we offer two examples of how a teacher might handle events of an historical nature in the classroom.

The last two chapters have examined the need for both emotional and cognitive engagement in order to understand religion. In this chapter we apply this to scripture which powerfully impacts on how people interpret their religion.

This chapter focuses on the Bible which includes Judaism as well as Christianity. It is the major scripture with which people in the West have wrestled and accepted or rejected. Much of what we say can be also be applied to the understanding of scripture in other religions: Hinduism, Buddhism, and Sikhism, and it is particularly pertinent regarding Islam (see below). The Bible in any case includes material relating to some of the prophets of Islam.

WHY TEACHING ABOUT SCRIPTURE IS IMPORTANT

The Bible used to be the staple diet of RE. Today it seems that any work on the Bible may have to be justified. A certain reluctance to grasp what is a difficult nettle is understandable. The Bible is not easy material: it can easily appear alien to people today. It is controversial and easy to offend somebody in the process of doing any work on it.

Yet all pupils need to be introduced to the skills of biblical interpretation. Judaism and Christianity cannot be understood without that. Whilst it is true that liberal and orthodox camps in both religions view the Bible differently in terms of authority and inspiration both nevertheless accord it reverence by giving it a unique and important place in worship. It may be reassuring that research done by the Biblos Project suggests that, despite secularization, pupils are 'not overwhelmingly negative towards the Bible. *Ambivalence* rather than overt *animosity* seems to characterise most pupils' attitudes.'[2]

The importance of teaching about scripture has been highlighted in recent years. One of the effects of the extremist Muslim terrorist attacks has been to direct the attention of moderate Muslims, as of non-Muslims, to the question of how the Qur'ān should be interpreted. It is indisputable that the suicide-bombers derive inspiration and comfort from their reading of the Qur'ān. It is therefore peculiarly important that a true and fair reading is taught. For the problem in a nutshell is this: that there are verses in the Qur'ān – as there are in the Bible – which, taken out of context and without regard for the import of the Qur'ān as a whole, do justify hatred and violence.

As Karen Armstrong[3] has pointed out, the damage is caused by 'concentrating obsessively on the more aggressive verses of the Qur'ān without fully appreciating how these are qualified by the text as a whole.' The overwhelming import of both Bible and Qur'ān is pro-love and anti-violence, so that the fragmented 'the-oracle-speaks' veneration of a particular text in the *Holy Book* is not being true to the spirit of any of the religions based on that Holy Book.

The crucial question is how can narrow, fragmented and insensitive views be overcome? RE certainly has a crucial role to play here. It should provide a safe haven in which highly controversial issues can be intelligently and empathetically explored. As the Biblos project concluded as a result of their quite wide-ranging research: 'While many factors affect pupils' attitudes towards the Bible, RE remains the most significant source of biblical literacy.'[4]

THE STATUS OF THE BIBLE AS SCRIPTURE

Emphasizing that the Bible should be studied 'like any other book' became almost a catch-phrase among scholars in the twentieth century. They were reacting against what was felt to be an over-pious approach to the Bible: in its extreme form the latter has been likened to 'bibliolatry', a term coined from the word idolatry to describe what can happen when the Bible is put at the centre of religion instead of the worship of God.

The non-pious approach may appear to be ideally suited to the study of religion in schools. But there are drawbacks. If it is the case that the world's scriptures are not just 'like any other book' – and who has decided and on what grounds that they are or are not? – then the methodology is flawed from the start. Furthermore, even *if* this is not the case, *if* the purpose of study is to understand religion, then we are not helped to do that by approaching scriptures in a way very different from how religious believers themselves do. A Muslim, for example, regards the Qur'ān as a Sikh regards the Adi Granth, namely, as a book that is unique.

Brenda Watson remembers being impressed by a conversation in India with Dr Sara Grant[5] who was involved in teaching the Upanishads to Indian students, both Hindu and Christian. The students were tending to find the work heavy-going, but she found that their degree of understanding was transformed when she adopted a quite different approach, one more in line with that of a Hindu guru. This involved a moment of silence at the beginning of a lesson, and then the recitation of a mantra, followed by the passage for study being intoned. She said that the atmosphere thus established, instead of being one of arrogant interrogation, became one of expectant enquiry. To Watson's comment that this did not meet Western ideas of openness and opportunity for criticism of the text, she replied that, so far from preventing criticism, it actually enabled it to be far more to the point. She said that they had far more searching discussion than would have been the case had an interrogative style been followed. And she countered Watson's comment further by asking whether an interrogative style was as open as it gave the appearance of being: does it not preclude from the start the possibility of any real understanding and openness to spiritual insight?

Many religious people indeed claim that the only way that scripture can reveal its secrets is to those who approach it with humility. Among Christians a style of participatory Bible study is much in evidence today. One recent book outlining such an approach begins with this story from East Africa.

A simple woman always walked around with a bulky Bible. Never would she part from it. Soon the villagers began to tease her: 'Why always the Bible? There are so many books you could read!' Yet the woman kept on living with her Bible, neither disturbed nor angered by all the teasing. Finally, one day she knelt down in the midst of those who laughed at her. Holding the Bible high above her head, she said with a big smile: 'Yes of course there are many books which I could read. But there is only one book which reads me!'

Interpretation of scripture

Reverence for the Bible, even if extreme as in this anecdote, does not equate with not thinking about it. RE needs to challenge the view, quite common both within and outside religion, which assumes that either the Bible has to be all of it and in every part literally true or it's a highly unreliable purely human document that Jews and Christians need take no more notice of than of a newspaper! This polarization of attitudes to the Bible is extremely unhelpful, for even the most out-and-out fundamentalist reader still interprets passages according to what is believed to be their intention – they do not believe that the sun literally 'stood still' for Joshua to win his victory, but that this is powerful poetic language.

It is not only those inclined to literalism who run the risk of polarizing attitudes to the Bible. The Loman Accelerated Symbolic Thinking programme (LAST)[6] strongly favours a symbolic interpretation. It implies that there are just three options: literal acceptance, rejection, symbolic interpretation, yet such polarization is seriously uncharacteristic of the Biblical material itself.

To appreciate the symbolic nature of much of the Bible should not lead to downgrading the importance of the historical question, 'what actually happened?' The key question is one of truth whether of historical truth or the truth of that to which the symbolism points.

Moreover, the Bible can be accorded real respect whilst acknowledging that fallible human beings were involved in its production and contents. There is real disagreement among religious people themselves on how the Bible should be interpreted, and in particular over the extent to which human error has been over-ruled by the Spirit of God in the writing, compiling and translation of scripture. This does however need to be discussed.

RE should introduce pupils to the range of possible approaches to the Bible from extreme conservatism to extreme radicalism.

Within Judaism there are three main groups usually known as Orthodox, Conservative and Reform. They have different attitudes to worship and to customs and these are related to a different approach to scripture. The Orthodox believe in a strict and traditional kind of approach, while both Conservative and Reform Jews consider that the tradition needs to develop and change to bring it into line with the modern world; they believe that in this way the timeless truth of the tradition can be appreciated today. Reform Jews tend to be more radical in the level of modern interpretation they advocate. There is a continuum between these three positions just as in views among Christians on their Bible. Figure 9.1 summarizes these positions.

How these different approaches work out in actual interpretation of a passage of scripture could be shared with pupils in a worksheet such as that on the website.

We need also to note that the fact of disagreement does not negate the value of a religious attitude to the Bible, any more than arguments among philosophers

Figure 9.1 *Spectrum of Jewish opinion with regard to the Bible*

Possible questions concerning the Bible

Authorship: Did *God* give the Bible?
'*God* spoke' [Orthodox]
'*God* spoke *and man* interpreted what he said' [Liberal Conservative]
'*Man* believed that God spoke' [Liberal Reform]

Authority: Must the Bible be accepted *literally*?
'You must accept what God has said, not pick and choose as though you know more than God' [Orthodox]
'You must be open to God's truth and ready to see it, and then work out what it means and how it should be understood' [Liberal Conservative]
You must read carefully what people have believed to be God's truth and accept what reason and common sense tell you' [Liberal Reform]

Reliability: Is the Bible true?
'It is true' [Orthodox]
'It is true but the way it is understood may vary according to the different perspectives of people' [Liberal Conservative]
'What is called true is relative; it may have been true for them but is not necessarily so for people today' [Liberal Reform]

Note:
If used in teaching all this could be within a big circle with the words: All Jews believe the Bible has a great deal of metaphor and symbolic language in it. The idea of a spectrum of opinion could be conveyed through colour coding.

rubbishes philosophy. Wherever people think strongly about something, there will be disagreements, and education is about coming to as close an understanding of the different views as possible before deciding for oneself what is most likely.

The Bible as historical source material

Scripture does not fulfil the same function in all religions. The status of scripture in Indian-derived religions is variable, normally important, and sometimes fundamental, but usually wearing the character of inspirational material associated with the handing-down of a great tradition – its uniqueness concerns its ability to infuse worshippers today with the same quality of spiritual seeking for enlightenment as that which motivated the great seers and gurus. In the Western religions, Judaism, Christianity and Islam, however, scripture fulfils that function but also another. For scripture there is regarded as embodying special revelation by God. The belief is that God has in a special and unique way influenced the course of human history. Revelation in these religions is linked to history. Their scriptures, therefore, for Judaism and Christianity are historical source material concerning that revelation, and for Islam, the Qur'ān itself is the revelation.

But this fact generates more controversy as to how much reliance can in fact be placed on the historical reliability of the Bible. The historical side of this is usually acknowledged by both Jews and Christians, but it is often spoken of as 'story'. Overuse of the word story in connection with biblical material can convey the impression that the gospels for example are not history. But an immediate retort from some people would be, 'But the gospels *are* story – they are certainly not history.' Yet this comment raises all the questions. Who says they are not history, and why? The gospels were certainly written in the form of history – purporting to be history.

As noted in Chapter 7, it is important that we take care over using the word *story* too readily to describe an episode. The word can easily give the impression that the content is just made-up like the story of Cinderella or other fairy-tales. We do not usually talk about the *story* of the French Revolution or the *story* of Hitler except if we mean we're going to try to present the information in an interesting way for people to hear.

The historical question in fact will not go away. Within Christian interpretation of Jesus there is in fact room for wide divergence, yet it always homes in on the Palestinian Jewish figure who taught and healed people in Galilee and was crucified in Jerusalem and who convinced his followers of his resurrection from the dead. To say it does not matter very much who he was, what he actually stood for, is to reinterpret Christianity in a way that loses touch with almost all Christians of all ages.

The fascination of the historical question about Jesus shows itself in unexpected ways in our society: the box-office success of films about Jesus and the phenomenal zillion-selling readership of Dan Brown's excitingly-written *Da Vinci Code*[7] making out that Jesus married Mary Magdalene and that they fled with their offspring to the South of France where they founded the Merovingian dynasty. The power of this fiction is that it purports to be founded on historical facts. RE should equip pupils to appreciate the highly-problematic nature of such claims.

The importance of work in the classroom on the Bible

Conveying skills of interpretation requires some ongoing work, for it is not possible or desirable to do this only very occasionally or in the odd lesson every now and then. It is particularly important that such work be done in primary as well as secondary schools because, if it is not, stereotypes develop in children's minds which it is very difficult later to replace. It is important to note that the objection raised by Goldman in the 1960s, that it is beyond children's capacity to understand, has been seriously challenged (see Chapter 5). Children will never develop the appropriate skills and concepts if they are never given the chance of so doing.

This is turning Goldman on his head as it were. His anxiety about Biblical work in the primary classroom was that children would learn things which later they had to unlearn. This is a serious consideration, but it applies all the more if Biblical work is *not* done.

The teaching of Easter may be taken as an example. The impression is easily conveyed to young children that this is about new life in spring, and Easter eggs, yet fundamentally it concerns Christian belief in the resurrection of Jesus. This appears to be very unpalatable content in today's world, and well nigh incomprehensible to the vast majority of pupils in schools. The educational requirement therefore is to help them to gain access to the idea, and to the evidence supporting it, so that they have some basis upon which to evaluate the Christianity which is based upon it.

In particular it is not enough to tell pupils what Christians believe, thus bypassing the question of historicity – for, as discussed above, Christians do not see it as just an imaginary story.

A POSSIBLE APPROACH TO SKILLS OF INTERPRETATION IN THE CLASSROOM

Pupils need introducing to three kinds of question. The first two questions correspond to the Stage 1 outlined in Chapter 8 (pp. 137–42), and the third to Stage 2 (pp. 142–4) which needs to be based on a sound understanding of Stage 1.

1   What kind of writings are in the Bible? Work could be done on the different kinds of material that are found in the Bible: myth, history, laws, material for ritual, prophecy, letters, teachings, fictional stories to make a point, parable, proverbs, expression of personal or political opinion, poetry. The point can be made that all these different kinds of writing require to be read and interpreted in quite different ways: to read a poem as though it were a law code is manifestly stupid. There is plenty of material published to help with this kind of introductory work.

2   What's it about? What did it mean to people in biblical times? Much sophistication is needed here to appreciate the complexity involved in attempting to answer such questions. We need to share with pupils problems of:
1 *Date*: that the Bible consists of writings produced over a long period – even 1500–2000 years – and that there are two significant contexts to note: that pertaining at the point of writing when writing was completed and that pertaining when the events occurred. Sometimes also a passage could be material of an even earlier period which was subsequently edited in later times and perhaps altered significantly.

2 *Language*: that the original language was Hebrew, Aramaic or Greek and therefore that we use a translation, and translation work is difficult. It comes as a surprise to many pupils to realize that the Bible was not written in English yesterday! Indeed a class of undergraduates one of us taught a couple of years ago thought this as well!

3 *Culture and customs*: that we have to discover as much as possible about very different ways of life from our own today, and enter imaginatively into them. It is important to note that we shall glimpse understanding much more easily if we avoid being immediately judgemental. For example, the sacrificial system of ancient Israel denotes an attitude to life so different from how most people today think, that a real effort of empathy and imagination is needed to understand it. And above all, they are needed to intuit what it is like for a society to believe in God, because this is so alien for many in our society today.

3   How true or meaningful are particular passages? These questions should be explored depending on the passage, and involve pupils' own thinking as well as what other people think.

(a) Did it happen? – if a passage claims to be history.

(b) Is it true? – if a passage claims to be teaching of some sort e.g. fictional story.

(c) Is it relevant and important for us? – if a passage claims to be of universal application.

Each question requires different criteria for approaching it. Thus for question (a) Did it happen? there is an important principle to appreciate: we need to give benefit of doubt to the text. This is how historians have to work in trying to understand what happened in the past. They have to presume that the evidence they have is trustworthy unless they have good reason to doubt it, for nothing can be proved conclusively anyway. Thus such questions as these need to be asked:

1 Is there any evidence against the passage being true?

2 If there is, how reliable is that evidence?

3 Is it greater than the evidence for the reliability of the text?

4 Why should we not trust the person/people who wrote it down and thought it happened?

5 What or whom are we trusting if we don't trust them?

For question (b) Is it true? we need basically to relate to two aspects of experience. Does it make sense of our experience of life as a whole? And how far does it square with our sense of right and wrong, with what is morally good/evil? This is a fundamental question to ask and whether we like it or not we have to rely on our total understanding to consider whether biblical injunctions advocating particular behaviour are morally justified for all time or are more reflecting their own time when perhaps certain knowledge was not available. This is what is at the heart of the dispute among Christians, for example over homosexuality.

For question (c) Is it relevant and important for us? we need to ask whether it is something universally important or only relevant for the time when it was written? To gauge whether it should or can transplant to a different age requires imagination and sensitivity to understand it in its own time, against its own context, and then to compare with the situation today. To over-stress the differences between the ancient world and our world today is just as bad a mistake as to underestimate the differences. Criteria to be used also include those in Chapter 8 on thinking skills.

An example: Luke 5:1–11; the call of the disciples and the
miraculous catch of fish
The first question to ask is:
1 What kind of writing is this, history? fictitious story? teaching? or what? Clearly this passage is written as history.
2 What is it about? Key-words needing to be understood are Capernaum, sea of Galilee, fishing in the time of Jesus, Peter, disciple.
3 Did it happen – how literally true is it?

Luke says it happened so we must give him benefit of doubt that it did unless we have strong grounds for not trusting him. Are there such grounds? Possibilities include:
1 It didn't happen at all because miracles don't and can't happen. Science has proved how the world works, and that's final. This isn't so watertight an argument as many of its advocates believe it is (see discussion below).
2 It happened as he said it did but it wasn't a miracle but just coincidence or clear vision by Jesus. Jesus just happened to have used his eyes more effectively to see movement under the water indicating the presence of a shoal of fish. The problem with this is that as a non-fisherman he didn't have the expertise and experience which the professional fishermen had, and they didn't spot the movement, so how likely is that?
3 Luke got a resurrection story mixed up with it like that in John 21:1–11 – a kind of visionary experience happened to the disciples convincing them that the spirit of Jesus survived death. Another miraculous catch of fish is made, again with Peter as the prime person to be impressed by it. The problem with this is that there is no evidence that Luke did this – it is only a conjecture, that Luke could perhaps have done so. But history is about what happened not about what might possibly have happened. Did William the Conqueror win the Battle of Hastings or not? We all know it's possible he could have lost it. The historical question is: did he? There is no evidence that Jesus did not in fact perform two miracles, the second after his crucifixion in order to convince Peter – by repeating the very same miracle which had so fired Peter's resolve to become a disciple back in the sunny days of Galilee – that he was forgiven for his ignominious betrayal of Jesus when he was arrested.

4 It happened just as Luke said it did. We can appreciate that there was good reason for Jesus to perform a miracle at the beginning of his ministry. It is no far-fetched consideration, for a lot was at stake. As an almost unknown teacher, Jesus needed disciples who would follow him, leaving their jobs and homes. This was asking a lot – for people just to down tools and follow a newcomer. An unusual event might trigger such a commitment.

What conclusion we reach regarding a passage such as this will be deepened by knowledge of certain skills and techniques for assessing the historical evidence. See the website for an example.

Such tests offer considerations – evidence to be taken into account. They do not give conclusive proof, and so the range of interpretations among Christians is as wide as that among Jews. Let us take, for example, the question of the Resurrection of Jesus which is of central importance for the understanding of Christianity. A consideration of the historical evidence concerning this unique event can illustrate some of the historical acumen which RE needs to share with pupils.

Views about the Resurrection of Jesus – background material for discussion

The likely impression that most pupils will have, owing to the general secularization of Western society (see Chapter 2) is that Christians who believe in the resurrection of Jesus are deluded on grounds already mentioned above regarding the so-called miraculous catch of fish. This way of thinking is so common that it is worth repeating what the problem is. Secularists tend to argue that:
1 The resurrection *could not* have happened because scientific laws forbid it, and
2 It *did not* happen because the historical evidence does not *prove* it did.

The important point regarding the first objection is that science purports to investigate the facts concerning the physical world. It ought not to decide *beforehand* what those facts are. If the resurrection did actually happen it was indeed unusual – a miracle – but this is exactly what it is claimed to be – unusual and a miracle. Therefore we cannot dismiss the resurrection on pseudo-scientific grounds but need to look at the historical evidence.

Norman Anderson in his book, *A Lawyer Among the Theologians*[8] argues that no one could question the actuality of this event unless indoctrinated with false suppositions. It is certainly true that much disagreement on how to interpret the Bible rests not on the material itself but on the assumptions which people bring to the material.[9] Thus a secularist assumption that such an event could not have happened is not itself historical evidence but a particular mind-set which people already have before they look at the gospels. Yet these are the primary source material which should only be set aside for sound *historical* reasons.

These points which relate to the nature of historical evidence in general are worth discussing in the classroom regarding the accounts of the resurrection of Jesus.

1 There are mistakes and inconsistencies in the accounts concerning the resurrection but this does not necessarily indicate unreliability except in small details. Indeed it may suggest authenticity in a way which carefully coordinated accounts would not. We give an example on the website of how to handle this question of the apparent discrepancies in the accounts of the resurrection with pupils.

2 The existence of Christianity owes its origin to this supposed event. All the evidence from the various parts of the New Testament including the earliest (the letters of Paul which happen to have survived) as well as the fact of Christianity and its beliefs and rituals, point to this conviction about the resurrection of Jesus as being central. The remarkable change in the disciples who had nothing to gain by being his followers – and much to lose, for it led to martyrdom for many – can be appreciated even by very young children.

3 If this event is doubted then stronger evidence for an alternative account should be given. Yet the variety of alternative explanations for the rise of Christianity, as well as for the existence of the resurrection narratives in the Gospels, argues for greater caution concerning scepticism about the accounts they give. As one scholar has put it recently, Jesus has been described as a political revolutionary, a magician, a Galilean charismatic, a Galilean rabbi, a Proto Pharisee, an Essene and an eschatological prophet. 'The plurality is enough to underline the problem. Even under the discipline of attempting to see Jesus against his own most proper Jewish background, it seems we can have as many pictures as there are scholars!'[10]

4 A particularly interesting point is the way in which alternative explanations for Jesus' resurrection tend to have even less evidence supporting them. They fall a long way short of any kind of proof. This does not seem to worry the scholars concerned, because they so often assume that if you can doubt something you should; it is enough for these alternative interpretations of Christianity to suggest another possibility. Paul *could* have invented the resurrection; Christianity *could* have originated in the cult of the sacred mushroom. Yet history is about what happened, not about the million possibilities which could have happened (see above).

5 The objection that the resurrection is unusual and unrepeatable and therefore did not happen cannot stand, for history is made up of unique occurrences. History seeks to unlock what happened in the past, and should not have a fixed idea of what that must have been like. The whole point of the great search for objectivity lies precisely here: that the historian may endeavour to let the evidence speak for itself.

6 It is often said that the Gospels were written by Christians with the purpose of putting Jesus in a good light. Yet such bias does not indicate the unreliability of everything a person says or writes, for it may be a justified bias – preference in the light of knowledge. A favourable reference given by a person who likes the can-

didate for a job is not automatically disqualified! Nor does the absence of bias necessarily, or even usually, indicate knowledge, for involvement with persons or events at some level is an essential means of acquiring knowledge.

The question of the historical evidence for the resurrection of Jesus is therefore something which should be looked at carefully in the classroom and not assumed to be non-existent.[11] The interpretation of Biblical material *is* controversial, and it is wrong to give the impression that it is not. The possibility of coming to different conclusions must be kept alive for pupils. Equally, however, to give the impression that religious faith does not relate to hard data carefully thought about is reinforcing a simplistic approach to the Bible which accords ill with the self-understanding of either Judaism or Christianity.

RE needs to open up the possibility for pupils of their own authentic exploration of Biblical material so that they can come to their own informed opinions on such matters. We want, as does the Biblos Project to *theologize*, i.e. to think theologically not passively – a phrase the Biblos Project adapted from Matthew Lipman's work on encouraging small children to *philosophize*. As they say in their conclusion:

> The theological search for truth in Biblical narrative is *not* an exclusive activity reserved for believers in God. All people, regardless of their beliefs and values, can engage with the text, whilst developing a greater awareness of its theological meaning and of their own theological assumptions, whether these be Christian, Jewish, Islamic, agnostic, atheist etc.[12]

TO THINK ABOUT

Williams backs science over Bible

The Archbishop of Canterbury does not believe that creationism – the Bible-based account of the origins of the world – should be taught in schools. 'I think creationism is . . . a kind of category mistake, as if the Bible were a theory like other theories.'

The debate over creationism or its slightly more sophisticated offshoot, so-called 'intelligent design' (ID) has provoked divisions. Most scientists believe that ID is little more than an attempt to smuggle fundamentalist Christianity into science teaching.[13]

1 What do you think the Archbishop meant by saying the Bible is not a theory like other theories?
2 What is unhelpful about this polarization of science and the Bible? (see Chapter 10, pp. 170–72)
3 What would be an educationally fair way of presenting serious differences of belief about the first chapter of Genesis?

NOTES

1 Rabbi David Goldberg (2006), letter to *The Times*, 17 January.
2 Copley, T. et al. (2004), p. 14.
3 Armstrong, K. (2005), 'Unholy strictures' in the *Guardian*, 11 August, p. 25.
4 Copley, T. et al. (2004), p. 17.
5 Conversation between Dr Sara Grant and Brenda Watson, 1973.
6 LAST associated with the Welsh National Centre for Religious Education.
7 Brown, D. (2003).
8 Anderson, N. (1973).
9 See e.g. Watson, B.G. (2004).
10 Crossan, J.D. (1991), p. xxviii.
11 For detailed discussion of these points, see Chapter 10 on 'The Resurrection of Jesus' in Watson, B.G. (2004).
12 Copley, T. et al. (2004).
13 Stephen Bates (2006), in the *Guardian*, 21 March, p. 1.

PART IV

EXTENDING THE CURRICULUM

RE AND THE REST OF THE CURRICULUM

> 'Overall learning is bound to be inefficient so long as it can't benefit from perception about the connections among subjects.' (James Moffat)[1]

Should the RE teacher be concerned about the interface between subjects? We argue that cross-curricular awareness is vital to good teaching in RE and discuss the contribution of RE in sample areas: citizenship, science, design and technology, and the teaching of modern languages. We offer two examples of RE-initiated cross-curricular units of work.

Much of this book has been taken up with helping RE teachers to think about their subject and how to teach it in exciting and challenging ways. We are used to thinking about 'the RE lesson', and agreed syllabuses specify what percentage of lesson-time should be given to the subject across the key stages. How far a school fulfils these requirements will be a matter for OFSTED to inspect. RE is judged at secondary level by its results as a GCSE subject and, to perform well, schools find that they have to spend every available minute on the examination syllabus. Often, at KS4, RE is struggling for a proper time allocation and it is nothing short of a miracle how RE teachers manage to get the good results that they do up and down the country.

WHAT IS THE POINT OF THE CROSS-CURRICULAR?

So is there any point thinking how RE relates to the rest of the curriculum and how the rest of the curriculum relates to RE? Is it not enough that we do a good job within our own parameters? The same question may be felt by teachers of other subjects. Increasingly at primary level attention is given to discrete subjects as targets have to be met in all subjects of the national curriculum. The 'integrated' day, where a theme was taken and addressed through all subject-areas is probably dead in all except the bravest and most confident schools. It is simpler and safer to tackle the targets systematically in subject-areas rather than create an integrated lesson or series of lessons and try to find spots where targets may be met. So, why think about and plan for cross-curricular work?

First, it happens all the time. All subjects inevitably speak volumes about other subjects, both positively and negatively. It is not unknown within a science faculty for patronizing attitudes towards biology to be expressed by the chemistry teacher! At a profound level shared beliefs, values and assumptions operate in every subject and activity in school. The marginalization of religion as a serious partner in the teaching of science, its possible contribution to modern foreign languages and so on reflects the difficulty our society and educational system has with religion. Society senses that religion has a place, even an important place, but does not know how to handle it and hopes that by giving it a slot in the curriculum it can get on with the rest of education untroubled by religious issues. Reductionism is a handy way of dealing with difficult matters but it is damaging and lacks all educational credibility. To turn a blind eye to what is going on in other subjects and activities of the school is to fail to notice some of the most important lessons that pupils are learning.

Second, all subjects in Britain are required to show how they are fulfilling the legal requirements to promote the spiritual, moral, social and cultural development of pupils and of society. Government initiatives in cross-curricular issues always seem to be in place.[2] This reflects the desire that education should have an element of the 'seamless whole' about it. All education is based on beliefs and values and it is really creative and constructive to reflect on what beliefs and values are being promoted through one's own subject area and that of others. A leading geographer, Patrick Bailey, has commented:

> I see geography as a very effective vehicle for raising issues and questions which go beyond purely materialistic considerations and far into the dimension which I would term spiritual . . . Love is a tremendously powerful principle of life and practising it will inevitably lead to actions which are of interest to geographers, concerned as they are to explain the observable effects of human behaviour.[3]

As an example he refers to urban studies and how

> The point is seldom made that all town development expresses the accepted values of societies . . . We do not have to invoke a spiritual dimension when we teach about the problems of cities; but to omit it is to leave out the most cogent reason why we should do something about the evils we describe.[4]

It is also entirely possible that we are promoting values and beliefs that are not true or good and therefore education should always preserve a place for debate and reflection. Education as we know it today is a powerful instrument and, in a culture which emphasizes standards and achievement, with a government which has made it a priority, it is all the more important that time be given to thinking about (and possibly) questioning what is going on across the curriculum.

Third, it must be a good thing for teachers to show interest in and concern for what is going on in other teachers' lessons. This promotes teamwork, compassion and sharing of good practice. It therefore helps relationships generally. It is good for pupils too to see that their teachers care about what others care about. Pupils need to understand that Miss is not just a science 'nut' and Sir is not just a theological 'boffin'. Penny Thompson remembers the sense of shock when her very clever and much-admired classics teacher expressed her interest in T.S. Eliot and her belief that prayer would preserve the life of Richard Dimbleby. Her pupil had assumed that she knew nothing about matters outside of Latin and Greek! Similarly today pupils used to look very worried when addressed in German in an RE lesson by Penny Thompson.

WHY SHOULD RE IN PARTICULAR BE INVOLVED IN THE CROSS-CURRICULAR?

There are several reasons why it is vital for the RE teacher to be interested and knowledgeable about what is going on in other areas of the curriculum and ready to make links in her own lessons.

The first reason is the rather obvious one that religion encompasses the whole of life. It is not just a whole-school issue but a whole-life issue. It is only our heavily secularized society that fails to see this. It is no coincidence that RE is probably the subject which already does more cross-curricular work than any other subject. RE is often linked with PSHE and Citizenship (hard to imagine Maths being so readily linked up) and for quite some time now has perfectly naturally adopted environmental themes. Creativity is innate to religious life. Links between music and art are very obvious and a visit to a Cathedral can provide an inexhaustible supply of references to other subjects. It is true that use of ICT may end up prioritizing information rather than wisdom[5] but it is also true that advances in technology can dramatically improve the quality of communication in RE lessons (see website). Religion uses diverse forms of language and can be a rich vehicle for language development without being untrue to its own forms of expression. Religion cannot help but be cross-curricular and fails to the extent that it is not.

Second, RE sits within the 'basic curriculum'. It is a further reflection of our uncertainty as to what to do with religion that RE has found itself rather grandly occupying a quaint area of the curriculum called 'basic'. The term was first coined by the 1988 Education Reform Act (ERA). It is unclear whether this was meant as a compliment to the subject or to exclude it from the ranks of the 'core' and what are now called the 'non-core foundation' subjects. Nearly twenty years on the term 'basic curriculum' appears to have fallen out of use. The phrase is still enshrined in law but the DfES and QCA websites today do not make use of the phrase. While RE is now acknowledged in all documentation and given parity of esteem in the sense that material for teachers and other interested parties can be accessed just like other subjects on its websites and in documentation, its role is nowhere acknowledged as 'basic', nor is attention given to what the word might mean. One site sponsored by the DfES lists RE after the 10 statutory subjects as 'an additional statutory area'.[6] It seems to be somewhat different in Wales where official documentation does make use of the term (though without discussing it).[7] It is possible that the term 'basic curriculum' was a creative (and politically motivated) response to concerns that RE was being sidelined in new proposals.[8] Nonetheless the fact that the term basic could be used of RE surely reflects a sense, however subliminal, of the important role of the subject. If a subject is basic then it relates to and supports all other subjects.

Third, RE is uniquely placed to question default secularism (where it exists) in the curriculum, a secularism which is damaging, not just to the chances of children taking religious life seriously, but also to proper debate about the future direction of society. Without proper attention being paid to religion in other areas of the curriculum it is likely that a secularist view of life will be indoctrinated by default. The teaching of a subject like History, for example, can so easily become one in which it is assumed that social, political and economic factors are all that matter in coming to understand the past. Even where religious issues force their attention on historians as in, say, the Reformation period, so often these religious topics are treated as a sub-set of the social, political and economic factors, not as valid aspects of history in themselves.

Moreover, the impression of religion given, where mentioned, may be quite belittling. For example, one of us recently in a Blackwell's bookshop chose four books almost at random from a selection of books for children on the Roman period. Each was extremely well-produced but could easily give readers the notion that religion is unimportant and irrelevant for today.[9] Religion formed a tiny part of the picture given and often the section on religion came after topics such as leisure. Roman gods and goddesses were generally described, but little attempt made at helping children to understand why people were religious apart from implying it was due to superstition and pre-scientific thinking. One book had a paragraph on 'Jews and Christians' under the general heading 'Beliefs and Superstitions'.[10] Christianity was usually mentioned only in the final section under 'Fall of the Roman Empire' thereby easily giving the impression that its decline was somehow caused by Christianity. This impression would be the more likely because Christianity was sometimes linked in the text with the repression of paganism. As one book put it 'Generally everyone tolerated the beliefs of others. The Christians were an important exception.'[11] The same book also spoke about 'the Christian god'[12] – a clear indication of a secularist perspective.

We stress that this indoctrination into secularism may well not be intentional but just happen as a by-product of never attending properly and fairly to religious perspectives. It is what pupils can take away with them from their schooling in a society where religion is on the whole not taken seriously, and often presented with distorted images of it. The null curriculum is powerful in its contribution to what pupils actually get from their time in school – the received curriculum (cf Chapter 2).

A further not unimportant reason is that an encounter between RE and other subjects is likely to spark off controversy and debate. Challenging stereotypes, encouraging real thinking through giving material with which pupils might not initially agree, and requiring close examination of the evidence is very invigorating and interesting and truly educative. Religion can be almost guaranteed to bring in controversy of this kind. Certainly the comments made by pupils who have experienced this type of RE indicate that this is the case. The Science and Religion Project gives examples of this.[13]

HOW TO DO IT?

We offer some examples here which should not be taken as comprehensive. The scope for cross-curricular work is very great and we can only offer a few suggestions. Elsewhere in the book we refer to other subject-areas such as English (Chapter 7, pp. 112–13), Art (Chapter 7, pp. 125–6, and Chapter 12, p. 206), and Philosophy (Chapter 8, passim).

Citizenship

It was once feared that citizenship would replace RE altogether. Impetus for this view was provided by David Hargreaves (former Chief Executive at QCA) who argued that non-denominational religious education had failed in its intention to provide moral foundations for pupils' lives and, outside of faith schools, should be replaced by citizenship: 'Attempts to bolster RE since 1988 have failed . . . moral education will in the future need to be more closely linked to civic education if it is to provide a common core of values shared across communities in a pluralistic society.'[14]

The idea of teaching citizenship (or civics as it used to be called) is not new and it would be good to introduce something of the ebb and flow of ideas that have led educationalists at one time to introduce discrete teaching and at another time to teach citizenship through immersion in ordinary subjects on the grounds that the standard curriculum is all about turning out good citizens. Where there is concern that schools are not turning out good citizens it is felt by some that the answer is not to introduce citizenship *per se* but to ask what is wrong with the teaching of ordinary subjects.

There is no doubt that citizenship has been brought in as a means of engaging pupils more actively in society and has an undeniable moral focus which, it may be felt, RE lacks. Hargreaves is right to point to a certain lack of rootedness about the way much RE is taught and it is true that relativism and subjectivism lurk in RE corners, often unobserved. In that sense the idea that citizenship, held to be a less controversial option, might be able to deliver the goods (in the form of a vision of the good and moral ideals) is understandable. But our concern in this book has been to argue that RE need not uproot pupils from traditional morality or leave them rudderless. It is also clear that citizenship is not without its own problems and can come across as value-free and ambiguous in its directives. For example, what exactly is meant by 'active citizenship'? It sounds very fine but one needs to ask 'active in what direction?' It may be better to have inactive citizens who observe the law and do not play loud music at night than citizens who actively flout the law and ignore conventions of politeness and consideration for others in their self-directed activities. The difficulty of 'taking a line' and providing uncontroversial moral direction is not solved by abandoning one subject and creating another. It could be argued that RE is better placed to teach a form of moral education that is undergirded by a plurality of interested parties than a merely 'secular' subject which sidelines religious insights and traditions. In the meantime citizenship is now a fully fledged contributor to the curriculum and offers natural links with RE.

Citizenship has, of course, a religious element in British society. Our very notion of what it is to be a good citizen is historically conditioned and religiously engaged. Pupils need to know this and reflect on the source of our ideas of good citizenship, whether that be in ancient Greek political theory or in the tradition of prophetic railings against injustice in society found in the Bible or elsewhere. Democratic dissent can be found in many books of the Bible and supremely in the figure of Jesus. Teachers could discuss what a good citizen is like in China, in Japan or in Iran. In what sense was the Buddha a good citizen? Pupils will be interested to know that for much of our history offences at law were tried in church courts and that King Alfred modelled his system of law on the Bible. This could lead to a discussion of the historic and existing relationship between Church and State. Why are there daily prayers in Parliament? Why is the monarch crowned in Westminster Abbey? What is the point of a national anthem? The ambiguity of the words of the national anthem which can be understood both politically and religiously could be explored. Some study of the arguments for going to war in Iraq will fit naturally into KS4 examination work. At the time when this was current in our newspapers the arguments for a 'just war', first put together by St Augustine in the fifth century AD, were continually referred to. The religious motivation of important icons such as Gandhi, Martin Luther King and William Wilberforce should be fully examined. Why can you drink alcohol in Europe but not in Saudi Arabia? Why are crime statistics in Saudi Arabia so very low? Pupils were extremely interested in a topic Penny Thompson did on this. The difference is stunning, and one of the reasons at least is that extended families are still common in Saudi Arabia and it is a serious disgrace to be found on the wrong side of the law. Families exert a greater authority than in the UK. Restrictions on alcohol may also have something to do with it! Pupils should be introduced to some Catholic social teaching which stresses the common good and (with older pupils) the principle of subsidiarity.

Social cohesion is something that citizenship is intended to address. At a recent gathering of Catholic secondary Heads the Archbishop of Birmingham had some profound things to say about society and what it means to be a person. Emphasis on autonomy and the importance of the individual, without any accompanying sense of what it means to be a member of a community with responsibilities and a formed moral conscience, has meant that society finds itself having to protect individuals from each other (since there are fewer and fewer morally binding patterns of behaviour that now restrain people). Laws and regulations multiply while restrained behaviour diminishes. Yet what motivates people is shared activity and goals, ordinary care and compassionate concern. The Archbishop said:

> What brings us together into social cohesion is that which is spiritual. What expresses the spiritual is our cultural heritage and creativity, which is most deeply rooted in religious endeavour. What sustains and completes our spiritual nature is the gift of religious belief. Social cohesion, then, is greatly served when the spiritual, the cultural and the religious are given their true and proper place.

> How ironic it is that in our public culture the opposite view has taken hold. Have we, quite simply, lost our nerve when it comes to the reality of religious belief? We have lost our nerve because, as a society, we have taken the road of relegating all these matters to the sphere of the private and seeking to build our society, our cohesiveness, on the material instead. There will never be a truly cohesive society that does not take seriously the spiritual quest of its people, in all the forms of that quest, and which does not give a space in its public culture for the religious beliefs of its people. The rigorously secular, liberal project of social cohesion is mistaken in its fundamental view of the human person and simply will not work.[15]

It is sometimes felt that Catholic schools (and other faith schools) perpetuate divisions and militate against cohesion. At the same time accepted wisdom celebrates difference and resists uniformity. Yet a religious identity enables human beings to 'develop sentiments of belonging and obligation' as Rabbi Jonathan Sacks puts it. Such sentiments are directly relevant to becoming a good citizen. A sense of belonging gives security. A sense of obligation leads to taking seriously injunctions such as 'love your neighbour', offering a welcome to the stranger and treating others with respect and consideration.

Further ideas may be found in a section of the non-statutory national framework for RE and in greater detail in the citizenship orders themselves where there are lots of useful suggestions for links between RE and citizenship.

Science

The interface between science and religion is, or ought to be, one of the most exciting areas to explore. It is certainly one of the most important, for confusion regarding the role of science and its success in offering a totally adequate explanation of the world is a major reason for the secularism of Western society. Unless science education provides room for education in beliefs and values, it easily conveys the impression that only science provides real knowledge, and religion in particular is a naïve, superstitious hangover from the past.

The challenge of post-modernism has impacted on science in that science has been called on to defend its pursuit of truth and seek to explain how it is not just one particular culturally-conditioned way of seeing the world. Dialogue with RE could be very helpful in encouraging pupils to think about the nature of science *per se*, as well as the beliefs and values upon which its practice is based, many of which have close affinity to religion.

It is important that this science–religion conversation is not left until Key Stage 4. Such issues and questions are talked about from Key Stage 1 upwards, because they are fundamentally of interest to everyone, including young children. As already discussed earlier – in Chapter 7 – even pre-school children think about questions of origin and meaning. Failure to allow children the opportunity to reflect with increasing knowledge on these questions means that they can fall prey to the false fact/belief divide in which science is on the fact side and religion on the belief side (see Chapter 3, pp. 35–6). This can remain a serious block in thinking throughout life. Recent discussion which Brenda Watson has had in the pages of the philosophy journal *Think*[16] shows how deep-seated are such misunderstandings. It is crucial to try to prevent them arising if possible – a stitch in time saves nine!

There is a great deal of published material to support work in this area.[17] It is also significant that there are science and religion components in the non-statutory national framework for RE. Ethical questions on the use of science and the implications of scientific enquiry are of obvious importance, but behind them lie notions of the nature of science and on what values and beliefs it is itself based. Fundamentally therefore the science–religion interface needs to focus on these philosophical questions. The following are just a few of the areas which can be pursued.

1 Teaching theories which purport to account for the existence of the world: evolution, creationism, intelligent design. This has become a highly political matter in the USA and sometimes in Britain and elsewhere. It is therefore particularly important that knowledge of these views is shared fairly and accurately, with emphasis on encouraging the search for evidence.

It is, in particular, wrong to give the impression that Darwinism can only be opposed by creationism. The argument for intelligent design is one taken very seriously by many scientists and philosophers. John Haldane, for example notes that the religious hypothesis on the existence of God

> ... explains both why science can work and why some of science's achievements are bad. The first because the world has an intelligible order to which science can conform itself; the second because there is also a moral order which the use of these scientific achievements may violate. Neither fact is something which science itself can explain. Yet both are explained on the assumption that the world is the product of intelligent design.[18]

2   Teaching the provisional nature of both science and religion. Here is how one scientist puts it: 'In science one makes progress on the basis of arguments concerning *levels of probability* rather than by chasing a fictitious boundary between the rainbow of "truth" and the base earth of "falsehood".'[19] In science as in religion it is necessary to make much use of models and metaphors which do not wear their meaning in a clear-cut straightforward way. As Ian Barbour puts it: 'All models are limited and partial, and none gives a complete or adequate picture of reality.'[20]

3   Challenging scientists who are strongly anti-religious. This is what, for example, Alister McGrath has done in his book *Dawkins' God: genes, memes, and the meaning of life.*[21] Francis Collins, Director of the Human Genome project, considers that in it 'Alister McGrath challenges Dawkins on the very ground he holds most sacred – rational argument – and disarms the master'.[22] Whether he does or not is an excellent question to put to pupils. In pursuing this question they can do valuable work on straight and crooked thinking. Michael Poole, brings out well the two-edged nature of arguments which can, like a boomerang, hit back at the sender: '*Dis*belief in God can equally well be compared to a computer virus.'[23] 'If young people are as easily taken in as Dawkins thinks, then the persistence of *atheism* could also owe much to the gullibility of young people.'[24] 'The charge of wishful thinking can equally well be laid against those who believe there is *no* God'.[25]

4   Teaching courteous debate. It is important that the search for truth does not get side-tracked into aggressive emotionalism. A reviewer of McGrath's book noted 'its relative lack of polemic' from someone capable of very forceful criticism.[26] This is how McGrath ends his book:

> I am sure we all have much to learn by debating with each other, graciously and accurately. The question of whether there is a God, and what that God might be like, has not – despite the predictions of over-confident Darwinians – gone away since Darwin, and remains of major intellectual and personal importance. Some minds on both sides

of the argument may be closed; the evidence and the debate however are not. Scientists and theologians have so much to learn from each other. Listening to each other we might hear the galaxies sing. Or even the heavens declaring the glory of the lord (Psalm 19:1).[27]

Design and technology

The National Curriculum Importance of Design and Technology Statement says that the subject:

- Prepares pupils to participate in tomorrow's rapidly changing technologies.
- Encourages pupils to think and intervene creatively to improve quality of life.
- Calls for pupils to become autonomous and creative problem-solvers as individuals and members of a team.
- Requires them to look for needs, wants and opportunities and respond to them by developing a range of ideas and making products and systems.
- Combines practical skills with an understanding of aesthetics, social and environmental issues, function and industrial practices.
- Encourages pupils to reflect on and evaluate present and past design and technology, its uses and effects.
- Helps pupils to become discriminating and informed users of products and become innovators.

An RE lesson might take this statement and ask pupils to discuss what values are being assumed in this statement. The teacher could suggest two values (from the list below) and see if pupils can come up with more. Prompt questions to help them would be to look at the statement and ask (a) 'What matters?' and (b) 'Why?' Get the pupils to go on asking the question 'Why?' until they feel they have come up with a satisfactory answer.

- that quality of life is important – it is more than a comfortable standard of living;
- that people's needs matter because people have unique significance;
- that aesthetic considerations matter – beauty is not an optional extra;
- that pupil's self-esteem and self-responsibility should be encouraged;
- that understanding of different cultures matters, as well as a sense of history;
- that the development of moral sensitivity is vital.

A unit of work for Year 7 pupils from the programmes of study found on the DfES website reads:

> With increasing concern for the environment, there is likely to be greater demand for carrying devices which can be used when travelling on foot or on public transport. Research carrying devices that already exist in different parts of the world, and use this information to design and make an environmentally friendly carrying device for someone in your local community.

What might an RE perspective offer if applied to the carrying-device task? Very little, some may consider, unless reference is made to the carrier-bag containing food for a Sikh gurdwara or a church social! Yet its major contribution would be in raising the meta-questions: Why should such tasks be thought important? Why develop such skills? Where pupils choose to design a bag for shopping or the conveyance of goods, it matters, in an acquisitive and consumerist society, that some interrogation of these values takes place. Pupils need to consider perhaps what difference it might make to how such tasks were performed if a person believed in the sacramental significance of everything that happens in this world.

In fact it would make a great deal of difference to both intention and practice. Such considerations affect not only assumptions but attitudes and outcomes also. Muhammad Akram Khan, for example, writes about the difference in both intention and practice which can or should exist regarding consumer behaviour in an Islamic economy which is shaped by Muslim beliefs and values. Of the seven points he cites, four are especially relevant:

1 Belief in the day of judgement extends the time horizon of one's decisions. Immediate utility of a product is replaced by considerations of reward in the *Akhira*;
2 The *Qur'ān* speaks of the material resources of the world as *hasanät, tayyibät, fadl Allah* and *ni'ma*, but they are basically a means to lead life in this world. They are not an end in themselves . . . The Prophet taught contentment (*qana'*) and thanksgiving (*shukr*), and subdued demand for material resources;
3 The *Qur'ān* has condemned both extravagance (*'israf*) and niggardliness (*bukh*) and has enjoined us to adopt an attitude of moderation in consumption;
4 The *Qur'ān* has condemned emulation in consumer behaviour . . . do not covet the bounties which God has bestowed more abundantly on some of you than others . . . Resources are a 'trial' for everyone, implying thereby that one who has fewer endowments faces a softer accountability.[28]

Using the above source material pupils could be asked to draw up a list of possible outcomes of different approaches to the task of designing a carrying device. Using the example of the device they have chosen to design, list what outcomes may result from:
(a) extravagant use of resources?
(b) niggardly use?
(c) trying to emulate those who have more money?

Go on to ask pupils to think about what difference it would make to the design of a product if one was motivated by considerations of (a) reward in the after-life and (b) the need to subdue demand for material resources? In what sense are resources a 'trial' for everyone?

Pupils could be given this list of possible outcomes and asked to think of examples of how the design of a product could lead to one or the other:

- responsible towards the environment *or* consumerist greed and increasing pollution;
- intelligent democratic citizenship *or* political repression;
- aesthetic awareness *or* creation of ugliness;
- enhanced status given to all people *or* devaluing of persons.

Modern foreign languages

The Foreword to the Modern Foreign Languages (MFL) Framework, intended to supplement the national curriculum programmes of study, says this:

> Learning foreign languages is increasingly important in a global economy and also has great value in terms of cultural and linguistic richness in our society, personal fulfilment and global citizenship and understanding. This *Framework for teaching modern foreign languages* underscores the vital importance of giving all pupils the tools to make direct and personal contact with other people and their cultures.

What view of the purpose of MFL is assumed by this statement? Clearly something is being said about the importance of languages for our economy but more is being said than this. Pupils are to learn a language in order to find personal fulfilment, become a citizen of the world and develop social awareness. A close relationship between culture and language is assumed, such that direct and personal contact is an important vehicle for understanding the culture of the other. We might agree with this sentiment but it is possible to understand the culture of France, for example, without a knowledge of the language and without direct, personal contact. Equally it is possible to have direct and personal contact without knowing the language of foreigners. This is particularly so for English people and, indeed, one writer has argued that it is pointless children learning a foreign language for more than a year if they have little aptitude for it.[29] Compulsory learning of foreign languages throughout secondary schooling was tried for a time but soon given up at Key Stage 4. Whatever the reason for the reluctance of pupils to learn a foreign language it certainly exists amongst less able pupils. A friend of one of us was asked to teach a class of Year 9 pupils at the lower end of the ability spectrum. She found it a great struggle. One pupil, sensing her difficulty, explained to her: 'We don't *do* French, Miss!'

While not departing from the statement of aims as officially promulgated is it possible to find a rather different motivation for MFL? One important expert in this area has argued that hospitality to the stranger, a biblical injunction of course, could give children the motivation that is badly needed.[30] When we travel to another country and seek to find out about and enjoy its richness we should say to children that not to seek to find out about and engage with language, something that is ever-present to both sight and ear, is a serious omission. Learning a foreign language can be pre-

sented as a way of extending a welcome and a deep appreciation of the other as a
fellow human being as opposed to seeing the foreigner as someone different whose
very strangeness means that they must conform to our ways before we can be
expected to show interest in theirs. This is a significant point when it is remembered
that many foreigners live and work in Britain. It can be particularly difficult for Germans
here and it is good that the MFL framework makes a point of commending the study
of post-Second World War history. It is unfortunately true that when pupils think
of Germany they immediately think of Hitler, and the concentration in history upon
twentieth century warfare does not help to counteract this.[31] RE needs to stress the
enormous contribution of Martin Luther, Music needs to dwell on that great
German, J.S. Bach (and one or two others!), History should review the remarkable story
of reunification and so on. In fact the framework for MFL offers considerable opportunity for this in its sections on cultural knowledge and contact. Mention is made of
links with media, art, music and history. It seems as though the framework has tried
hard to distance MFL from the tourist mentality which sees the point of learning a
foreign language as making it possible to find the toilets and find out where the bank is.

But here we hit upon a significant problem. If the point of learning a foreign language is to show hospitality and find out about the 'other' in a way that engages deeply
with who that person is and what she values then we have indeed entered upon a
rich vein of learning. It is of course why children (unlike religions in RE!) are not
expected to learn more than two languages. It is impossible to introduce children to
every aspect of culture and every aspect of language. The principles of selection become
extremely important. And here we need to point out a serious omission with the MFL
curriculum. Religion is not given a mention at all and the danger is that children
will presume that religion is not a part of modern cultures at all! Of course, one could
argue that MFL does not mention science, or maths or design and technology. And
this would be a fair point. But religion concerns that which affects people at a very
deep level, admittedly often a subconscious level. Most children learn European
languages, Spanish, French and German. The influence of Christianity upon these
countries has been profound and is on-going. Learning a foreign language in order
to welcome and understand the other must mean learning something about the way
religion has influenced culture and the people of these lands. One wonders if religion would be omitted in a similar curriculum dedicated to learning Arabic and the
countries where Arabic is spoken!

SUGGESTED CONTRIBUTIONS OF RE TOWARDS
CROSS-CURRICULAR EDUCATION[32]

Finally we offer two suggestions for some work in which pupils can be encouraged
to engage in-depth with what is fundamental in RE. The first uses a specifically

religious topic, the life of St Francis of Assisi;[33] the second is on the general theme of seeing, pointing towards the possibility of seeing things from a religious perspective.

The life and character of St Francis

There is a huge amount of material on St Francis which can be accessed easily by younger as well as older pupils to make interesting and challenging study. St Francis can be seen to be very relevant to life today, exemplifying many of its most worthwhile values such as freedom, independence, authenticity, integrity. He also clearly challenges at a deep level the consumerism and materialism which have become such marked features in the West. Yet his character lends itself to expression in paradoxes: unfettered by conventions, he was not a religious or political revolutionary; identified with the poor, he never campaigned against the rich but accepted with courtesy their hospitality; so deeply moved by meditation on the crucifixion of Jesus that he received the stigmata, yet he impressed all who knew him with his cheerfulness and joy.

Table 10.1 indicates how such study relates to key areas of cross-curricular interest today. We have not included ICT here as there is an important section on the website devoted to the role of ICT in RE.

Seeing – the view from Flatland

The purpose of this work would be to help develop awareness:

1 that we have each of us a particular perspective which makes it difficult for us to consider other ways of looking at things, especially if that would be uncomfortable to our set way;
2 that there may be such another way of looking which makes more sense of the whole of our own experience and that of everybody;
3 that if there is, we shall need to draw upon *all* the ways of knowing open to us to enable us to see this, otherwise our outlook may be just a flat two-dimensional one;
4 that we cannot in such matters *prove* we are right in such a way as to compel others to agree with us. Nor can they *prove* their way is right.

By opening up these questions the work should help encourage a fresh perspective on religion, as well as moral and social issues.

It is based on Edwyn Abbott's story of 'Flatland'.[34] The story focuses on a land that is entirely flat, and on what happened when one of its inhabitants, a Square, was visited by a Sphere from another world. The Square had enormous difficulty in trying to conceive of any other possible world, and after he did become convinced

Table 10.1 Key areas of cross-curricular interest and RE – Example: The life and character of St Francis

Financial capability	Citizenship	The world of work	ESD	PSHE	Inclusion	Creativity
Raises profound questions about the money-economy, the dangers of possessiveness and what to do about it.	Francis' relationship to the church of his day raises issues about how to question authority without stepping outside and giving up on it.	On what basis do we choose our work? How do we decide what job to take (or create)? Francis understood himself to be called by God to live and work in a particular way. What does this say to us?	St Francis could be the patron saint of the environment, with his love of animals and all created things.	The pursuit of health and the power of mind over body. Living simply without worry about possessions. Prayer and healing.	His respect for Clare and the impact of the Franciscan way of life on women today (e.g. an ashram in Pune, India). The profound effect of his teaching and example on spirituality.	Francis was a person of amazing creativity as shown in his prayers. The prayer beginning 'Lord, make me an instrument of thy peace' encourages creative action to bring joy, peace, love, faith, hope.[35]

he suffered persecution at the hands of those in authority in Flatland. It is a penetrating sociological as well as religious allegory.

The theme could be appropriate for younger children as well as upper primary and secondary. A helpful starting-point might be asking pupils to imagine a world in which there is no height, only breadth and length with such questions as:

1 What would Flatlanders themselves see? (What would a person coming towards them look like to them? What would a house which they were approaching look like to them?)
2 How might they know which was a house, and which a person, if they both were the same shape? (Touch or feel? Might they also *see* a difference?)
3 How would they recognize each other? (Might they talk to each other and touch each other and see who is who?)

The story could then be told. And discussion encouraged.

Possibilities for work in subject-areas include the following:
- *Mathematics*: the geometry of how a Flatlander could recognize the appearance and movement of shapes.
- *Science*: beginning to understand the theory of relativity – the story was reprinted in the Penguin Science Fiction Library (1987) precisely as an excellent introduction to this.
- *Art*: work on perspective: what Flatlanders can see; what we see is actually governed by what we already know and take for granted.
- *English*: problems in communication – the meanings given to words, literal and otherwise.
- *Social Studies*: expression and discussion of values which the Flatlanders had, for example sexism, elitism, and so on.
- *Philosophy*: *Flatland* focuses on how we can arrive at knowledge. The Flatlanders are like us who live in a world of time and space in which we find out about things through our five senses using our brains and how we feel about things. Is there a 'more-than-sphere' world? How can we find out? What might convince us?
- *RE*: connects the question of a 'more-than-sphere' world to the possibility of a spiritual/religious world which can be related to, but is radically different from, our world here, the existence of which we are unable to grasp just with our senses, brains and emotions. All the religions speak of such a reality which is more than this world of time and space and the denial of such a reality is what constitutes secularism. Consideration of this as a real possibility is what distinctively RE has to offer to the curriculum as a whole. We need to give pupils space to ask – if such reality exists how would we be able to become aware of it?

Ways of knowing tried out in the story parallel religious ways of knowing:

Flatland story	Religious revelation
1 Reasoning power using analogy	wisdom/teaching, especially through story and parable
2 Dreams and imagination	feelings and experiences which cause people to consider a different way of looking at things.
3 Presence of people who do see and understand	saints, sages, gurus . . .
4 Unusual happenings	miracles
5 Special experience	visions

The story could lead on to work on the science and religion debate. The story was written by a headteacher who was a theologian as well as a mathematician and scientist.

CONCLUDING COMMENT

Regarding the impact of the curriculum as a whole, the responsibility which teachers have is considerable, indeed awesome. Richard Pring, in his inaugural lecture as Professor of Educational Studies at Oxford (8 May 1991) argued the importance of the teacher's role. It is for them 'to uphold the standards which are at the centre of the best of liberal learning'. He summed this up by a letter from the head of a large high school in Boston, USA, which was sent to new teachers in her school.

Dear teacher,
I am a survivor of a concentration camp. My eyes saw
what no man should witness:
gas chambers built by learned engineers
children poisoned by educated physicians
infants killed by trained nurses
women and babies shot and burned by high school and
college graduates
so, I am suspicious of education.
My request is: help your students become human.
Your efforts must never produce learned monsters,

skilled psychopaths, educated Eichmanns.
Reading, writing, arithmetic are important only if
they serve to make our children more human.[36]

Pring comments: 'That ultimately is what we are preparing our students for'. All subjects have the responsibility to promote what is true and good. Are we to say that religion has nothing true and good to help us in this task?

TO THINK ABOUT

One of the most crucial areas for cross-curricular work is sex education. If RE does not contribute to what is offered to them here, in what respects are schools seriously short-changing pupils? (cf p. 28 in Chapter 2)

NOTES

1 Moffat, J. (1992), p. 79.
2 The 2000 review of the curriculum, for example, resulted in schools being asked to address the following topics across the curriculum: Education for Sustainable Development (ESD), Creativity, ICT, Literacy and Numeracy.
3 Bailey, P. (1986), 'The spiritual dimension', *TES*, p. 40.
4 Ibid.
5 See Broadbent, L. and Brown, A. (2002), p. 171.
6 www.teachernet.gov.uk; accessed on 17 February 2006.
7 See www.accac.org.uk; accessed on 17 February 2006.
8 See Thompson, P. (2004b), p. 112.
9 Usborne *Encyclopedia of the Roman World* (2001), DK Eyewitness *Ancient Rome* by Simon James (DK 1990/2002), Peter Ackroyd's *Ancient Rome: Voyages Through Time* and Pitkin Guides: *Roman Britain* (1996, 2002). It is fair to add that two other books were much fairer even though not much space was given to religion: *Find out about Ancient Rome* by Jane Bingham (Hodder Wayland, 2006) and Usborne *History of Roman Britain* by Ruth Brocklehurst (2006).
10 Usborne *Encyclopedia of the Roman World* (2001).
11 DK Eyewitness *Ancient Rome*, p. 62.
12 Ibid.
13 See www.srsp-net
14 Hargreaves, D. (1994), p. 34. He went on: 'The notion of a non-denominational core RE to be offered in all schools as a buttress to moral education is becoming less and less viable and should now be abandoned. The multi-faith pick 'n mix tour of religions easily trivialises each faith's claim to truth.' For a reply to Hargreaves see Jackson, R. (2004), pp. 126–42. See also Freathy, R.J.K. (2005).
15 See www.birminghamdiocese.org.uk
16 Watson, B.G. (2005), pp. 7–11.

17 e.g. Poole, M. (1995).
18 Haldane, J. (2005), p. 70.
19 Smith, D. (1993), p. 43.
20 Barbour, I. (2000), p. 180.
21 McGrath, A. (2005b).
22 Quoted on the front cover of McGrath's book.
23 Poole, M. (1996), p. 4.
24 Ibid., p. 5.
25 Ibid., p. 8.
26 Duncan Dormor in the *Church Times* (18.2.05).
27 McGrath, A. (2005b), p. 158f.
28 Khan, M.A. (1985), p. 243. See also two articles, Conway, R. (1990) and Riggs, A. (1990).
29 Williams, K. (2000).
30 David Smith. See Smith, D. and Carvill, B. (2000). The Charis materials from the Stapleford Centre give practical ideas. See www.stapleford-centre.org.uk
31 A friend of one of us is a German and does supply teaching. Pupils often ask her where she comes from. Having found out that she is German the next question is 'what do you think of Hitler, Miss?'
32 Reference may be made to the non-statutory national framework section called 'Learning across the curriculum: the contribution of religious education' pp. 14–18.
33 See e.g. Habig, M.A. (1972).
34 Abbott, E. (1987).
35 One famous prayer reads: Praised be my Lord God with all his creatures, and especially our brother the sun. Praised be my Lord for our sister the moon. Praised be my Lord for our sister water, who is very serviceable unto us and humble and precious and clean. Praised be my Lord for our mother the earth.
36 Quoted by Pring, R. (1992), p. 37f.

CHAPTER 11

WORSHIP AND EDUCATION

> The headteachers saw worship as the fulcrum by which the transformation of the school was levered. (Grubb Institute)[1]

We argue that worship and education are intrinsically linked. Furthermore pupils need to take part in worship in order to have a proper understanding of religion since worship is at the heart of religion. Increasing secularization makes it more important that schools offer pupils the experience of worship. Pupils need space in which to make their own personal response and we suggest ways of making this possible which respect the integrity of religious traditions while allowing commonality to be explored.

What sense can be made of the idea of a school worshipping and on a daily basis? Up until 1988 the law required the whole school to gather together for the daily act of worship.[2] This gives an important hint to the thinking behind it. The school gathers together each day to remember who it is and what it is for. The intrinsic value of gathering everyone together and focusing on what school is for is probably felt by most teachers and headteachers. A recent report into the turning around of three community schools which became church aided (Anglican) schools cited worship as a key factor in their success. The report states: 'Above all, the time for worship encouraged pupils to experience what it is to belong to something bigger than themselves and to look outwards to others.'[3]

Our discussion in this chapter on the role of worship needs to take account of what is really the purpose of education. Chapter 4 outlined three agendas common today which are not, in our view, educative (see pp. 60–63). So what is a school for? We would suggest that a school is a community dedicated to learning, a learning which seeks after (and therefore assumes the existence of) truth, goodness and beauty.

How can that be related to worship? For the religious believer, to worship is to focus on the goal of education and, as such, is never content with what is already 'possessed' or even experienced. Worship reaches out, rather than dictates or imposes. A religious understanding of education will mean that a school will try, and it is a tall order, to evoke a sense of wonder and thankfulness, to persuade those present of the meaningfulness of worship, such that pupils are encouraged to see something of the Mystery that is God and inspired to want to learn and apply themselves to their lessons, graciously given to them (!) in periods one, two and so on throughout the day.

Such an explicit religious view of education is properly at home in schools 'having a religious character'.[4] What however about community schools in which there may be large numbers of both staff and pupils who do not believe in God? The disquiet felt by so many schools at the legal requirement to incorporate worship for all relates to this fact of controversy. Many schools – perhaps most – can agree that it is important to come together as a school community and as a community dedicated to learning seen in terms of truth, goodness and beauty. But they may not agree on the Source of that learning being God.

There may be many things about school life that are not agreed upon of course and in some cases are bones of contention; uniform, policy on expulsions, length of school day, methods of assessment etc. A school has to take note of legal requirements and may take soundings within and without the school community before coming to a decision on these and other matters. It is the same with collective worship. The law allows considerable flexibility on the matter and it is up to a school to decide what is appropriate within the law. But a school cannot avoid taking a line on the matter of collective worship. One should not assume that a particular school community is averse to the worship of God. But, whatever line is taken, there will be a need to try to engage all those present, those who are unsure as well as those who are committed to a religious point of view.

So in this chapter we want to explore how opportunities for worship *can* be given to all without breaking that sense of community which is so prime a reason for assemblies.

THE CENTRALITY OF WORSHIP FOR UNDERSTANDING OF RELIGION

Opportunities in school for pupils to experience worship are a real asset for RE, for worship lies at the heart of religion. As H.D. Lewis used to say 'Religion begins in wonder'.[5] The saints and scholars of most of the world religions would agree. To ignore the dimension of worship is to miss out on something crucial for religious understanding.

It might seem possible to cover this aspect by units of work on worship and occasional visits to religious places of worship. These are important, but they do not fulfil the same function as enabling pupils actually to take part in worship. Externally observed rituals and symbols can be described but may actually serve only to obscure what is their real function – that of enabling the worshipper to focus on God.

For pupils to sense this they need to be able to experience it; there needs to be actual engagement.

Pupils should have such opportunities not just for the sake of learning about religion but so that, if they wish, they can perhaps find inspiration and help from such involvement. A newspaper article written just after the London bombings carried the heading 'Could prayer help youngsters cope with London bombings?'[6] Whilst religious schools should find such a thought unproblematic, the majority of community schools may feel decidedly uncomfortable at any suggestion that they should hold special worship for occasions like this. For they assume that a majority of people, staff and pupils, in their schools are not religious believers, and therefore that to take part in a religious service would be infringing people's integrity. Yet it does seem wrong to deny pupils in community schools the inspiration and prayer that is offered to pupils in other schools.

One factor that lies behind the nervousness felt about worship in community schools (and may equally be felt in schools having a religious character) is the sense that worship is incompatible with education. For education and worship have been widely assumed not to belong together. The idea dies hard that education is open while worship is closed, that education promotes a critical approach whilst worship encourages a passive receptive attitude, that education is exploratory and wide-ranging whilst worship is narrow-minded and dogmatic.[7]

Education and worship

How can we argue that education and worship can belong together, and moreover, that if pupils are to achieve in RE what they are capable of, exposure to the worship aspect of religion is in fact necessary? There are at least two main reasons.

First, such a presumed contradiction between education and worship is in fact based on serious misunderstanding. Chapter 3 outlined the fact/belief divide which attempts to separate reasoning from feelings. But this divide is deeply challenge-able (see pp. 34–8). What goes on in the classroom should and does involve the emotions as well as critical powers. And worship which is mindless and blind is not worship but superstition or obsession. Derek Webster, lecturer in the University of Hull, expresses the intellectual as well as affective aspect of worship like this

> School worship stretches pupils, asks them to look beyond themselves. If human society resembles a circle of people on a floating island, all looking inwards, then school worship is an opportunity to turn around and face an unknown, illimitable and mysterious ocean. Obviously worship is demanding of head and heart. It is like reading the *Phaedo*, for Plato asks his readers to ponder an argument and respond to the sweep of a vision which grants an eternal destiny. It is akin to heeding R.S. Thomas's words:

I had forgotten
   the old quest for truth
   I was here for. Other cares
held me.[8]

An understanding of worship along these lines is wholly in line with education.

Second, because pupils are growing up, in the West, in a highly secularized environment, opportunities for worship provide much-needed anti-indoctrination time. Paul Richardson sees the value of such opportunities for worship as 'an opportunity for children to express feelings and attitudes that are natural to them but which secular society encourages them to repress . . . Even children from families with no religious affiliation often have a sense of mystery and an awareness of values that can only be termed "religious".' He goes on:

> Unfortunately they are often embarrassed to talk about their spiritual experiences because they sense that secular society does not approve. They are afraid of being laughed at or thought stupid. Very often they lack the language in which to describe and discuss feelings and intuitions that are important to them.[9]

There is a powerful case for a willing suspension of disbelief in God as a counter-balance to the cultivation of doubt at other times. We too easily forget that questioning belief in God itself rests on certain convictions which are assumed. Why should they be assumed all the time, and never challenged?

THE CASE FOR WORSHIP-ENABLING ASSEMBLIES

This may be so, but why argue for what the law requires that 'All pupils in attendance at a maintained school shall on each school day take part in an act of collective worship' (subject to the parental right of withdrawal)?[10] The holding of voluntary assemblies is inadequate. This tends to leave pupils tied by their upbringing to particular forms or none at all, and even where choice is openly extended to pupils, a combination of secularism and peer-group pressure is likely to ensure that the choice is nominal only. Very few like to be associated with a God squad! That all pupils should attend such assemblies giving opportunity for worship is important because otherwise some will be educationally deprived.

Assemblies furthermore are major ways in which the school can be aware of itself as a community. This communal aspect is very important today because of the fragmentedness of so much of life, and because of the dangers of over-emphasis on individualism.

An additional and very valuable benefit of such assemblies is in providing time and quietness for pupils and staff to be able to reflect and not just react to what is presented to them. In a society full of bustle and change pupils badly need such times for quietness and reflectiveness, and opportunities to get on the wavelength of a different dimension to life.

COMBINING PERSONAL INTEGRITY WITH THE POSSIBILITY OF WORSHIP

The major educational argument against assemblies which are legally required and equate to an 'act of collective worship', has been, as Bernadette O'Keeffe's research revealed, that: 'In the majority of county schools collective worship is seen as an inappropriate activity because both pupils and staff encompass a wide range of religious beliefs and secular views.'[11] It has been pointed out many times that worship cannot be *required*, for it must be freely chosen. From a religious point of view whether what happens in school assemblies constitutes true worship is known to God alone. The same can in fact be said of services in church, synagogue, mosque, temple or gurdwara, also. Levels of participation in voluntarily-attended, as much as in compulsorily-attended, assemblies must be accepted.

What is crucial, however, is that in schools these different possible levels of participation are consciously spelt out. Pupils and staff need to know that they are not being presumed to offer worship by attending the assembly. It needs to be spelt out that there are two other ways of taking part open to everyone: that of educational enquiry, and that of finding something inspirational which is not worship (see Figure 11.1).

The level appropriate for all is that of an educational activity. Pupils should *take part* in such assemblies to help them find out about religion. Whether or not the content of the assembly proves to be inspirational or worship for any given pupil, such taking part develops educationally-desirable qualities of openness, empathy, imaginative thinking and the capacity for being still. Such qualities are required within every area of the curriculum so there should be no discontinuity between the assemblies and what forms the rest of the school experience. John Wilson pointed out that in such assemblies 'students are offered the act of worship to experience and criticize, not to swallow whole'.[12]

The 'worship' to be experienced and criticized in assembly – and Wilson was arguing for participation not just observation – can be in the content of the words and ritual, irrespective of whether they enable anyone in the room actually to worship. It is the giving the opportunity, or permission for, which counts. Whether, for anyone present, the impact is adoration rather than exploration does not concern us,

Figure 11.1 Three degrees of participation in assemblies giving opportunity for worship

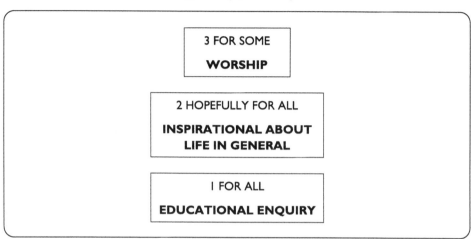

providing that the educational atmosphere in which the assembly takes place is appropriate. Obviously, if the worship content of words or actions were conveyed in an offhand trivializing way, the assembly could not be said to be offering more than a travesty of worship for consideration. But this is a question concerned with school management and practical arrangements.

Opportunity for quietness
Part of the great value of such assemblies is that pupils are *not* asked to reveal at what level they take part. This can remain known to each person in privacy. Such assemblies can therefore be times when staff and pupils can think things out for themselves without outside pressure. In this way such assemblies can perform a valuable anti-indoctrinatory function, helping all to achieve some real stillness and independence of thought.

Stillness is not the same as quietism. It is more like the natural rhythm of breathing in as well as breathing out. Attention only to the latter causes tension and breathlessness. The activist nature of our society makes it particularly important to help pupils experience some silence. The very difficulties involved in this indicate quite how necessary and important an educational task it is.

This underlines the value of frequency of assemblies because to learn stillness needs time, structure and regular opportunities for practising it. This is one of the most valuable skills that a school can encourage. We would express it as an entitlement on the part of pupils to be enabled to become familiar with well-established techniques of this kind. Time for quiet and reflection can be a most helpful start to the school day, sending pupils into the first lesson in a calm frame of mind.

There is also the matter of learning a discipline, just as in other areas of education. Worship is an activity which has to be learned and discovered over time. The Grubb report puts it like this:

> Do not pupils require to learn discipline in order to take authority for themselves? School worship is a form of discipline which provides a quality of life which is not available through other aspects of the normal curriculum. Whereas mathematics, science and the humanities provide growth especially in intellectual intelligence; and the arts, media and sporting activities contribute also to the development of emotional intelligence; is it possible that worship fosters moral, spiritual and social qualities which alongside the other subjects, lead to the development of the whole person in the context of society?'[13]

Of course, a wide variety of reactions can be expected from pupils. The Grubb report writes 'in times of reflection we all discover resistances in ourselves to change and some negativity is to be expected.' Individuals will only participate (to greater and lesser degrees) to the extent that they recognize its sense and to the extent that they love the goal of their education. The levels of consistency and reliability in the school generally will have a bearing on how pupils receive worship (and other aspects of their education too).

CONTENT OF ASSEMBLIES

The 1988 ERA inserted the words 'wholly or mainly of a broadly Christian character' into legislation concerning collective worship.[14] Schools may apply for a determination to be free of this requirement where their circumstances make alternative arrangements desirable. Some argue that this element of the legislation is damaging as it emphasizes difference and perpetuates division. The disadvantages of separate faith-groups, besides practical difficulties, include the possibility of their being divisive and reinforcing existing barriers of belief. It is this 'package' aspect of the worship dividing people into separate camps which is the real bone of contention. John Hull has argued that it stems from an unhelpful desire for purity which wants to exclude those who are 'outside the camp'.[15] On the other hand it is an undoubted fact that worship is not diffuse. It takes on the character of the tradition that perpetuates it. Traditions do change and interact but there must remain a core of belief and practice without which a tradition would lose its identity and worship would be colourless and lacking in conviction. Lord Jacobovitch argued that it was from going to a school which valued its Christian tradition of worship that he learned to cherish his own.[16] The law may be read as an attempt to balance these two concerns, something we try to do in what follows.

We want therefore to look again at the possibility of inter-faith assemblies which can effectively bypass the Christian versus multi-faith polarization.

Inter-faith assemblies

Developments in inter-faith dialogue in the past few decades have indicated that there is much that can be done in discovering a common core of belief, attitude and feeling within the major world religions. All the figures in Chapter 6 referred to common insight and/or a common task facing all religions.

Yet the whole area of inter-faith worship is fraught with difficulty and no one should approach it in a simplistic way. There is far more to it than simply choosing a reading from one religion, a prayer from another, and possibly a visual-aid from another. Ill-assorted assemblies can convey an impression of superficiality and be highly offensive to members of the faiths concerned. Of dubious educational value, they can become a subtle form of indoctrination – indoctrination into the beliefs and values associated with the particular type of pluralism which regards toleration as the highest virtue, on the grounds that all religions are basically saying the same thing. According to this view the fundamental one-ness of intention within all religions is taken as axiomatic, and diversity of forms of expression can become a source of celebration and not of either anxiety or controversy. Yet this is an inadequate view of religion as argued elsewhere in this book. The effect of mixing faiths together in this way will be to compromise and confuse pupils.

The protests of many members of different religions at different aspects of the facile medley approach calls for caution. A paragraph from a booklet by David Bookless, written for Christians, many of whom are worried by the idea of possibly compromising the integrity of their own faith by taking part in inter-faith worship, effectively summarizes as well as possible in a short space the kind of attitudes to be reckoned with from different religions.

> As well as different ideas of God and worship, the other faiths have very different attitudes to 'interfaith worship'. Most Orthodox Jews would reject it completely as *avodah zarah* (strange worship). Many Muslims would likewise reject it, although some would find serial acts (i.e. where worship of different faiths is presented in turn) and private prayer more acceptable. Sikhs generally have less problems, believing God to be at work in each faith, but some missionary Sikhs would reject pluralist approaches to the truth of all faiths. Undoubtedly the traditions within which 'interfaith worship' makes most sense are Hinduism and Buddhism, both of which tend to see different faiths as expressions of one reality. However, in all of these faiths there

are exceptions to the above, and the more mystical and liberal parts of each faith (Liberal Judaism, Sufi Islam) find it easier to worship together.[17]

He goes on to underline, however, that there is a range of approaches within each religion – none is monolithic, so that too much should not be made of rigid generalizations.

A way forward

Bookless draws up three principles which we would apply to the school situation in this way:

1 Inter-faith opportunities for worship should be *explicitly* discussed so that confusions and misunderstandings do not result.
2 There should be no attempt to gloss over the differences and difficulties – they should be acknowledged so that pupils realize they are entering an area of contemporary openness and discussion.
3 What is done in assemblies must be supported by and arise out of the kind of approach inherent in the RE they are receiving where opportunities for frank and honest discussion of religions is encouraged on the basis of critical affirmation.

This argues for a kind of assembly which focuses on general themes of deep religious significance, to which various religious traditions can contribute insights. The approach might be termed 'trans-religious' in that it does not evade the religions but allows them to point beyond themselves.

Such assemblies would be pioneering as discussed in Chapter 6. Suitable themes could include the following. A series of assemblies on each would be possible.

1 awareness of Mystery;
2 the use of symbolism in religion;
3 truth through metaphor;
4 problems of idolatry, superstition and hypocrisy;
5 the role of ritual in religion;
6 the inspiration of saints and holy people;
7 religious attitudes to the environment and to green issues;
8 religion and personal development;
9 religion and spirituality.

All these themes can help to illuminate all religious traditions. And yet they can do so in a way which is not in any sense imperialistic for any one religious tradition.

The pioneering role of such assemblies

'Open worship' is possible with its 'invitation to reflect on questions of meaning, purpose, values and commitments'. This *could* be a key-point at which schools could innovate and lead society instead of being led by society. It shows the way towards the possibility of worship-enabling assemblies which make sense religiously to people of different faiths without their having to resort to the cumbersome and possibly contentious procedures for opting out of the 'broadly Christian' requirement.

If schools can take up this challenge, and encourage in pupils an openness which nevertheless engages with religion at its central point, they will be performing a crucial task in preparing pupils for the real world. To be able to face controversy creatively, and learn how to be committed without being dogmatic, are invaluable skills which schools generally do too little about.

Every effort ought therefore to be made to see that worship-enabling assemblies do offer help in developing these skills. Especially important, as already discussed, is the capacity to be quiet, and engage in inner dialogue with oneself, so that perhaps a new perspective becomes possible. The ability to be still in this sense can help to release people from chains of conditioning of all kinds, as well as assisting the ability to think for oneself and make responsible decisions. In this way assemblies can help to promote creative dialogue between world religions.

QUESTIONS OF ORGANIZATION

There is plenty of latitude within the legislation for schools and RE teachers to fill it out in ways meaningful and interesting to themselves and their pupils. It is important to note that schools remain in control with regard to the how, when and what of the assemblies. How assemblies are run directly concerns RE teachers, for what goes on in assemblies can greatly help or hinder work in specific RE. RE teachers should be involved in encouraging and sometimes running assemblies which really do give space for all to reflect on religion.

Who is responsible?
While it is the responsibility of headteachers to see that such assemblies are held, they do not have to lead them themselves. Indeed, it is educationally desirable that many others are involved; other staff, pupils and perhaps parents or local churches and religious communities. A team approach to the task of preparing assemblies is likely to be more productive as well as realistic in terms of time and energy needed. In many schools classes in turn are responsible for special assemblies in which they share some of the work they have been doing. It is also feasible to set up an 'assemblies committee' jointly of staff and pupils to plan, monitor and revise assemblies. Part of the task of such a committee is to test the temperature in the school with regard to assemblies and suggest ways in which they can become more integrated into the life of the school.

There has been increased use since 1988 of visiting speakers and leaders or worship from different religious traditions. There is also more awareness from the religious side of the need for careful preparation of such involvement. The presence of outside visitors is valuable in making the assemblies more of an occasion, and giving variety and perhaps a religious visual aid, as it were, in the form of a person for whom religion is real.

Structure of assemblies

A great variety is possible. While some assemblies may be taken by particular classes and others led by visiting members of particular religious traditions, probably the 'bread and butter' assembly should require simpler planning and resources. It needs mostly to have at least four components:
1 some inspirational input: a reading, music, perhaps something visual;
2 space to reflect – a training in stillness and being able to be silent;
3 a specifically religious component in the form of an open invitation to take religion seriously;
4 short sentences explaining and reminding people of the educational purpose of the assembly, and that a consensus is neither assumed nor looked for.

Sharing the education focus

The latter point is crucial because it ensures that the assembly is impeccably educational and not perceived as indoctrinatory. Explicitly religious words and actions should be just as explicitly put into the context of a learning situation. Phrases such as 'let us pray' should be abandoned in favour of something more like the following:
1 'Let us listen to this prayer and, if we want to, silently say Amen.'
2 'Let us try to imagine what it is like to be a Christian/Muslim/Hindu as we sing/say these words.'
3 'Let us say this prayer/sing this hymn considering what we can, and what we cannot, personally agree with in it.'
4 'No assumption is made about your reaction to this hymn/prayer. Interpret it in whatever way is sincere for you.'

The three levels of participation open to people need to be articulated clearly to overcome the danger of wrong impressions. It is not enough for teachers to understand this. It must be communicated first and foremost to pupils, but also both via them and directly to parents and religious leaders of faiths to which pupils happen to belong. The theory must not be behind the scenes for them. It is what worship-enabling assemblies are about.

This may engender a fear that such hedging about instead of a simple 'Let us pray' may get in the way of the possibility of genuine worship. This need not happen, and should not happen, provided that the way in which the assembly is held is conducive to worship. The invitation silently to say, or not to say, Amen to a prayer should be said in a respectful, quiet and focused way. Because such an assembly really is inclusive in enabling all to participate without any feeling uncomfortable, this approach may well make more possible for more people some real experience of worship. In any case, the opportunity for reflection and meditation is invaluable in itself.

In all this it is the practice which counts and how it comes across to pupils. It may be that a school wants to offer prayers on behalf of the whole community and this may be combined with the sort of openness that we are recommending here. This respects the tradition of prayers offered in public life generally, such as prayers at State occasions, in Parliament and to mark Remembrance day and so on.

Stimulus material for assemblies
There is a great deal available in published sources, much of it very recent. Publishers appreciate the need for fresh material. Besides explicit assembly material, there is a lot concerned with religion which can easily be adapted for use in assemblies. A helpful article by Nicola Slee in reviewing some more unusual possibilities concluded with this paragraph:

> With such materials as these in the shops and on the shelves, there are no excuses for dull, introverted or narrowly monocultural acts of worship, and plenty of hints towards an interpretation of ERA's worship clauses which stays well within the letter of the law and, at the same time, fulfils all the criteria of good educational practice.[18]

Weblinks are given on the website. We close this chapter with one example of extracts which could be used in assemblies relating to the theme of *truth through metaphor* listed above (p. 190). The theme lends itself to a wide number of possibilities at every level from infant to sixth form.

The metaphor of the ocean
The inadequacy of human concepts in speaking of the Divine – or in trying to understand the Mystery at the heart of reality – leads religious people into exploring metaphor. The ocean is one example. The idea of ocean as symbolic could be introduced with a brief reference to the Greek word from which the name derives: Oceanus which in Homer refers to the great river encircling the whole earth – the great outer sea as opposed to the Mediterranean. By the seventeenth century it had come to be used metaphorically of an immense or boundless expanse of anything.

Ocean is often used as a metaphor for life, as, for example, in these lines from Longfellow:

Ships that pass in the night, and speak each other in passing.
Only a signal shown and a distant voice in the darkness;
So on the ocean of life we pass and speak one another,
Only a look and a voice, then darkness again and a silence.[19]

Ocean stands for voyages of exploration, for courage in leaving the safe and familiar and moving into the unknown, as in this poem by Gide:

We cannot discover
New oceans
Unless we have courage
To lose sight
Of the shore.[20]

Even more was this so in centuries before advanced nautical technology had made
travel as fast and common as today. To cross an ocean used really to be an advent-
ure when life was at risk. In the realm of beliefs and values and commitments, the
ambiguity and vulnerability of life preclude the possibility of 'terra firma' certainty.
As the Danish Christian thinker, Kierkegaard, used to say: 'we must learn to live over
70,000 fathoms of water'.

Ocean is a symbol for Reality within many religious traditions, especially in
Hinduism, Buddhism and Sikhism. One of the hymns in the Granth begins:

Thou art the ocean, all-knowing, all-seeing:
How may I a mere fish, know Thy extent?[21]

A prayer of the great Hindu scholar, Sankara, likens himself to a wave, rather than
a fish:

O Lord, even after realizing that there is no real difference between the individual and
Brahman, I beg to state that I am yours and not that you are mine. The wave belongs
to the ocean and not the ocean to the wave.

The imagery is also found in Christian hymns such as this by the seventeenth-
century writer John Mason. The third verse of his hymn 'How shall I sing that
majesty' runs as follows:

How great a being, Lord, is thine,
Which doth all beings keep!
Thy knowledge is the only line
To sound so vast a deep.

Thou art a sea without a shore,
A sun without a sphere;
Thy time is now and evermore,
Thy place is everywhere.

A single verse of a hymn like this can do much to wean people away from naïve concepts of 'God'.

TO THINK ABOUT

A tragic incident has occurred – perhaps the death of a pupil.

Choose some religious readings and prayers which, because of how they are introduced can be shared with all staff and pupils without any feeling uncomfortable.

NOTES

1 Grubb Institute (2002), p. 82.
2 The 1988 ERA made it possible for sections of the school to meet for worship and at different times of day. This was needed because secondary schools have large numbers of pupils and it is not possible to gather them together in one place, or it takes too long to do so.
3 The Grubb Institute (2002), p. 41.
4 This is the legal terminology for what are commonly called 'faith schools'. Community schools are schools 'not having a religious character'. This should not be taken to mean that community schools are secular. The law requires community schools to provide a daily act of worship which is 'wholly or mainly of a broadly Christian character'. Many church schools were handed over to state control in the years following the 1944 Education Act on the understanding that worship and religious education would continue to be provided.
5 e.g. Lewis, H.D. (1959), p. 104.
6 *Worcester News*, 12 July 2005.
7 The argument put forward in John Hull's *School Worship: An Obituary* (1975).
8 Webster, D. (1991), p. 251.
9 Paul Richardson (2006), *The Link – newspaper of the Diocese of Newcastle*, February, p. 2.
10 Education Act, 1996, Section 6.1.
11 O'Keeffe, B. (1986), p. 76.
12 John Wilson (1989), letter to *The Times*, 10 April.
13 Grubb Institute (2002), p. 41.
14 Amendments were introduced into the bill in the Lords which meant that the word Christian, qualified in certain ways, was inserted in clauses to do with both RE and collective worship. See Hansard, H.L. 3 May and 21 June 1988.

15 Hull, J. (1991b).
16 See Hansard, H.L. 3 May 1988, col. 419–21.
17 Bookless, D. (1991), p. 15.
18 Slee, N. (1991), p. 5.
19 Longfellow, *Tales of a Wayside Inn*.
20 Lines from Gide quoted in Hammond et al. (1990), p. 26.
21 Talib, G.S. (1975), p. 37.

CHAPTER 12

ENCOURAGING SPIRITUAL DEVELOPMENT

> 'An effective spiritual education will combine a hermeneutic of nurture with a hermeneutic of criticism. A good school will unashamedly induct children into the spiritual values and world-view which it considers to be of greatest worth, as well as insisting that children explore alternative possibilities.' (Andrew Wright)[1]

We discuss the problem of how the word spiritual is to be understood, and we give our own understanding of the term. The links between the spiritual and the religious are then explored, and in particular their relationship to experience. We suggest possible ways in the classroom of encouraging spiritual development through work in Art, and a focus on the religious/spiritual experience of St Francis and Sri Ramana.

By using the word spiritual in this final chapter, we are probably seen as implying that this is the ultimate goal of RE. It may be, but we first encounter the huge problem of how the word spiritual is to be understood. We begin therefore by discussing this in some detail, not just because of its importance in itself, but because the very controversy surrounding it is something to be shared with pupils, not dogmatically decided ahead of them. They need to appreciate and enter into the on-going debate about the spiritual and why it is important.

WHAT IS MEANT BY 'SPIRITUAL'?

It is notoriously difficult to define what one means by the word *spiritual*. At a conference on the future of classical music in our society held in London on 21 September 2005, the word *spiritual* was used a number of times. For example, listening to late Beethoven quartets was described as 'a spiritual experience'. What is meant by this? Why bother to use the word? At least three notions appear to be involved:

1 *Inspiration.* Musicians don't use the word spiritual of anything unless they mean to signify something of supreme importance – the mere use of the word indicates that this represents something incredibly precious and deeply meaningful to people, and authentic. The memory of something which they describe as *spiritual* will stay with people for years. It seems to have transforming power.

2 *Acceptance of Mystery*. It indicates something meaningful, but not in a way that can be described in clear-cut fashion. It is meaningful, but beyond what our conceptual equipment can cope with. It implies *transcendence* – a word also used many times at the conference. Because it is strictly ineffable, there are few attempts to define it. It is presumed that others either know what you mean or it will have to remain a mystery with a small m rather than experience of Mystery with a capital M. Most musicians who use the term will not want to use any kind of flowery language to describe it. They are content just to state it. And this supplies one reason for the power of music – that it does precisely transcend the need for words, which are inadequate.

3 *Assurance*. It relates to something beyond controversy for the person concerned – it's an aspect not of imagination or possible fantasy but of reality which they feel certain about. Other people may doubt its existence and may argue about its nature, but to the person concerned this shows they don't understand what is being spoken about.

The word 'spiritual' is thus often used in connection with aesthetic experience. Unfortunately, here too is uncertainty as to what the word means. This is not just an academic matter – it affects practice, for example in the arts. The art critic, Peter Fuller, considers: 'One worrying feature of recent years has been the fashionable appropriation of the language of the "spiritual" to defend work of a numbing vacuity.'[2] Part of the trouble is that the controversial element regarding how spiritual is understood has been submerged. Thus Lucien Jenkins[3] confidently asserts that the transcendent is only in the minds of those who use the word.

It is important therefore to try to achieve some clarity.

Definitions within education

The 1994 Education Act required schools to contribute to pupil's spiritual development. Parliamentary discussions showed an assumption that the teaching of Christianity in religious education would provide for pupils' spiritual development.

Three decades later, however, *The Supplement to Curriculum 11–16*[4] drew attention to the fact that the word 'spiritual' was no longer used solely in a Christian context. It gave two definitions. The first referred to 'inner feelings and beliefs' that are 'concerned with matters at the heart and root of existence'; the second confined the spiritual to the religious domain.

The latter is unacceptable because non-religious people talk about the 'spiritual'. Furthermore, we cannot equate the spiritual with the religious. True religion may be said to add to the spiritual a conscious relationship to the Source of the spiritual. Yet it is possible to have a real relationship without such consciousness, just as it is possible to talk about God without being spiritual.

The first definition is also unsatisfactory for, although it acknowledges that 'often these feelings and beliefs lead people to *claim* to know God', this emphasizes the uncertainty of what is claimed, and intentionally directs attention away from the content to the fact that some people are claiming it – in other words the human element is the focus of attention. Eight years later, *The Curriculum from 5–16*[5] disconnected spirituality from religion altogether.

In recent years government-sponsored documentation reflects both a secular and a religious understanding of spirituality (see Penny Jennings' article on the website). However, guidance for schools has focused on secular interpretations, on the grounds that this provides an inclusive approach. All pupils, regardless of their faith position, may be spiritually enriched, and by all curriculum subjects. Overall, the perception is that spiritual development, whether secular or religious, is understood to refer to the inner life and self-awareness, and is difficult to assess.

Andrew Wright

Andrew Wright has made a study of this question of definition in his book *Spirituality and Education*.[6] He gives this working definition: 'concern for the ultimate meaning and purpose of life'. Towards the end of the book he elaborates on the definition: 'Spirituality is the relationship of the individual, within community and tradition, to that which is – or is perceived to be – of ultimate concern, ultimate value and ultimate truth, as appropriated through an informed, sensitive and reflective striving for spiritual wisdom'.[7]

This brings in awareness of community and tradition and the word *truth*, but otherwise does not take us much further, for the qualifying phrase 'or is perceived to be' shows him trying to find a definition which is acceptable to all who want to use the word. And this has to focus on the human search for ultimacy, for only this can accommodate secularism. Nor does the phrase *the search for spiritual wisdom* define *spiritual* any further or guard against appearing to have reached agreement about something deeply controversial.

The problem is that Wright's definition of spiritual is already compromised in favour of a subjective approach which ignores the truth question because he speaks of 'four major modern philosophical traditions that have been instrumental in shaping contemporary spirituality'[8] instead of 'in shaping contemporary *attitudes to* spirituality'. For materialism denies anything beyond the empirically experienced value-free physical world, romanticism finds spiritual significance only in subjective, emotional intuition, and post-modernism simply rejects all truth-claims and calls on us to create our own personal spiritualities. Only one of these, critical realism, is capable of allowing spirituality to have any objective referent.[9]

So the question remains: why talk of the spiritual anyway? This is pertinent in the light of what he calls the 'do-it-yourself spirituality' advocated by Cupitt.[10] For is this not a contradiction in terms unless meaningless? Why bring spirituality in at all? Why not use terms such as 'management of your life' or 'what you choose to believe in and value' if it is assumed there is no spiritual *reality*?

The -isms of materialism, romanticism and post-modernism do indeed affect people's thinking about spirituality, but the effect is to secularize it, in which case using the word is like papering over the cracks to give a misleading impression that we are all talking about the same thing when we are not. This is not a good recipe for education.

Can we do any better?!
We see the spiritual as concerned with what transcends empirical existence – not to be thought of as primarily a quest so much as awareness of a reality to which we are able – indeed required – to relate. It is the element of facticity which needs to be stressed. Our preferred definition of the *spiritual* is that which is transcendent, which can be intimated in and through all aspects of life and which is grounded in the reality of God. Spirituality represents the level of a person's achievement in actually being on the wavelength of the transcendent which, in religions, is normally called God or Transcendent with a capital T.

That the existence of the spiritual may be contested we accept. It is true that some believe there is no such reality – that everything is in the end explainable in terms of molecules reacting on each other in the brain and nervous system. But that is a viewpoint like all others and should not masquerade as a required certainty. Our position is that the case for the controversial claim that there is such non-molecular reality must be put fairly to pupils and not be hidden or submerged by the constant bracketing of the phenomenological approach ('This is what X,Y,Z think') and the subjectivist agenda ('This is what I think'). Pupils must be given a proper chance to weigh the truth of what is believed.

Our definition separates what is meant by the word from whether people are right or not to believe in it. In principle, were the evidence to be available, the problem could be resolved. But we know it cannot be, because by transcending our modes of understanding and evaluation we cannot establish it as true or false beyond the possibility of challenging it. Therefore in education we must allow both possibilities to be presented. We should teach the spiritual realm (as defined) while also engaging with the opposite position held by the atheist/humanist. We should give the latter a fair hearing and be open to criticisms that are made of our own position, recognizing that such criticisms are an aid to further truth.

We suspect that is also what Wright wants. Nor does this have to be seen as 'a disembodied rational approach to analysis and critical assessment'.[11] All we have argued for earlier in the book regarding the importance of imagination and not assuming the fact/belief divide, points the way to a truly holistic approach.

It is crucial to appreciate that the spiritual is embedded within day-to-day living and experience. Figure 12.1 suggests a way of drawing attention to what the

Figure 12.1 *Distinguishing three planes of existence:*
the natural, the spiritual and the demonic

Ordinary plane:	**Spiritual plane:**	**Demonic plane:**
It is part of human nature	It is a qualitatively different attitude	The ordinary and spiritual capacities of people can become corrupt

EXAMPLE 1

To give in order to receive e.g. give a present so I get one back.	To give without thought of receiving anything in return, not even thanks, or to give when it costs far more than the person receiving suspects and therefore appreciates.	To give in order to manipulate, to make someone dependent, to show off, or to bribe.

EXAMPLE 2

To see things from one's own point of view, to measure the importance of things as they are important to *me*.	To see things really and seriously from someone else's point of view, to be really interested in what is of use or value or giving pleasure to *them*.	To be obsessively self-centred, or to use the knowledge which one has acquired to control others for one's own ends, or be willing to harm them if they stand in one's way.

EXAMPLE 3

To get pleasure from being successful, from being listened to with approval, from being acknowledged, from receiving applause.	To delight in other people's success and status, especially when lacking it oneself or even when the other's success is at the expense of one's own.	To delight in doing other people down, in working for their failure, in enjoying their misfortunes.

spiritual dimension is which makes it open to all, without prejudicing the real possibility of a religious dimension.

It refers to three radically different kinds of human behaviour and attitudes, one of which expresses ordinary human nature, one the 'spiritual' dimension, and one the reverse of both: what may be called the 'demonic', whether that word is understood symbolically or not.

Of course we are not here arguing for a return to a three-tier model of reality seen in literalistic terms. 'Supernatural' has had all kinds of misleading innuendoes associated with it – such as a separation between this world and another higher one. The spiritual plane is for all the great religions inseparable from the physical and psychological ways in which it manifests itself and becomes known by us, but yet it is truly distinguishable. Its relationship with the molecular 'vehicles' which express it is a non-reciprocal one: its presence can explain theirs, but they cannot explain it.

Spirituality is a genuinely different dimension to reality. To see it requires imagination, and yet it is not itself the product of imagination. Imagination is the faculty whereby we perceive it – or better, glimpse it – but imagination does not create it.

Relating 'spiritual' to 'religious'
The examples given in Figure 12.1 refer to the kind of experience well within the capacity potentially of everyone, and may be so much accepted as part of everyday life as to go unnoticed. For people to see these as consciously linked to 'spiritual' and religious experience, other qualities would normally be present. Three of these correspond to what was discussed above as being a likely meaning for musicians who use the term.
1 *Inspiration*. Used in its sense of 'being-breathed-in-to' and 'allowing' power to work within us. As a friend of one of us – who has only the most ephemeral links with any religious tradition – put it recently: 'We must learn to be *channels* not *engines!*'
2 *Acceptance of mystery*. Taking it for granted that the spirit is beyond our total comprehension, that this dimension cannot easily be put into words, or expressed adequately in any art form. It is to be pointed towards, implied, and therefore intuited. People see it or they do not. It is as primary as that. It cannot be proved or deduced. But people who glimpse it know its power and supreme attractiveness.
3 *Assurance*. Concerning the way things are, the great matters of life and death, the reason we are here – an inner certainty not imposed from without or dependent on other people's approval, nor reflecting chance moods.

There is perhaps a fourth which a religious view of life would add:
4 *Inclusiveness*. A sense of unity and seamlessness, awareness of the inter-relationship of everything. This is a very common feature of mystical experience – a transcend-

ing of language and categories of thought and distinctions of all kinds. The advaitic experience of Sri Ramana (see below) is a particularly striking example.

These four qualities or characteristics are only a beginning in attempting to say what spirituality is about. As such it is a dimension which meets us, not only in the arts or in religion but everywhere if we will let it, or which will elude us everywhere if we will not. Its natural language is one of symbol and paradox, and yet it is also utterly rational.

Signals of transcendence

The links between the spiritual dimension and religion are in fact close. Peter Berger spoke about 'signals of transcendence' which are given in and through our normal human experience.[12] People can immerse themselves in the spiritual dimension without being religious at all. Yet if these signals are really thought about, they can lead people to an awareness of religion.

Berger noted five:
1 the sense of order;
2 the phenomenon of play;
3 the experience of hope;
4 the concept of damnation – a sense of cosmic injustice to be put right;
5 the fact of humour.

Such aspects of life are normally just taken for granted yet, if thought about, they are at odds with a materialistic understanding of the world; they point to something other – something more.

We can add many other signals of transcendence present within ordinary and every-day experience. They can include:
1 a sense of wonder at beauty, especially the beauty of nature;
2 aesthetic experience;
3 the experience of personal rapport with other people;
4 altruism;
5 the fact of love.

Such signals of transcendence can often consciously give rise to an awareness of the need to use a different kind of vocabulary. A very striking example was told to Brenda Watson by someone who attended a dinner party in Moscow soon after Gagarin's space trip – the Gagarin who had reported that he did not see God in space (see p. 116). Apparently Gagarin said that when he looked out of the right window of his spacecraft and glimpsed the earth for the first time, he had an experience or sense of – and then he used a word which the interpreter did not know the meaning of, so he had to go to another table and ask another interpreter to help. After considerable discussion they came out with the word 'numinous'. Gagarin had had to search into the past for a word which perhaps he had heard from his granny!

Whether or not such factors develop religious awareness depends on the degree to which people can see a relationship between them and religion and can tease out the implications.

RELIGIOUS UNDERSTANDING OF SPIRITUAL

Moving now to a specific discussion of how uninhibitedly religious people use the word spiritual here is how Evelyn Underhill, speaking as a Christian, defines it. The spiritual life is one in which 'God and his eternal order have, more and more, their undivided sway'.[13] Different religions would express this in different ways. Buddhists for example would probably speak of it as progress towards a state of enlightenment in which persons are liberated from all false forms and images. In most religious traditions the concept of 'God' is invoked as the name for that Mystery which is at the heart of religion (see Chapter 6).

All major religions offer a deepening understanding of spirituality because of the way they enable people to be consciously in the presence of that Mystery. True religion makes spiritual progress easier because it provides a vocabulary, a structure and a community, all of which can help people to attend to this dimension. Religion also furnishes many inspiring examples as well as yardsticks to chart progress and guard against the hijacking of high intentions by evil forces, however these are understood. In a similar way, talk of the spiritual can help to revitalize religion. It is the goal of authentic religion and the judge of pseudo-religion.

RE should give access to the great spiritual traditions – the vocabulary used, and the kind of symbolism. In so doing, any hint of attempted indoctrination, conditioning, manipulation, even influencing and persuading, is misplaced because this dimension can only be grasped in freedom, or it is not grasped at all. It has to be experienced through people being able to be honest with themselves and reaching towards integrity. For each person is unique and it is useless as well as mistaken to try to be someone else. A recent anthology on spirituality has a quotation by Martin Buber from Rabbi Zusya when he said a short while before his death, 'In the world to come I shall not be asked why were you not Moses? I shall be asked why were you not Zusya?'[14]

'Be yourself' is, interestingly enough, a piece of advice at home in secularized Western societies as much as in traditional religion. But it is vital that this is seen not as legitimizing self-centredness, introspection or social irresponsibility, but as a means to ever deeper exploration of life in its totality. One of the best ways to do this is to study in depth particular people who have claimed to have religious experience.

WORK IN THE CLASSROOM GIVING OPPORTUNITIES FOR SPIRITUAL DEVELOPMENT

However the word *spiritual* is understood, an essential aspect is the development of personal awareness or attentiveness. For those who are happy with the distinction between *learning about* religion and *learning from*, this comes under the latter aspect.

Pupils need to relate whatever is happening or being studied to their own personal experience as a normal activity – an integrating process which should go on all the time. Because each person is unique, and has experiences which no other person has ever had quite in that way or in that combination of circumstances, this learning cannot be structured by teacher or syllabus or advisers from without, except possibly in certain exceptional situations where a sustained one-to-one relationship is possible or required. All the teacher can do – but it is a most important and fulfilling role – is to encourage self-reflection through appropriate teaching style. Reflectiveness should be seen as natural and part of the normal rhythm of daily life.

It is important for RE to engage explicitly with those aspects of experience which open up for many people a religious frame of reference. Pupils can be helped to appreciate the link between the spiritual dimension and religion, and to do this in such a way that the outcome is not assumed. Pupils may respond to seeing this possibility in different ways.

Elizabeth Ashton, as an experienced primary school teacher and then lecturer at Durham University, found that work on particular symbols could energize children into relating effectively to their own experience.[15] This helps them to produce work substantially more creative and thoughtful than what they have been able to do before. The poem, 'Lavender Lily', quoted in Chapter 7, is an example of this from one of her classes. It is an expression of the child's experience at several levels, especially an awareness of a love of nature. The poem reflects on themes such as poverty and death in a way seemingly detached, but yet at considerable depth indicating the writer has really been involved in what she was expressing.

The website carries a possible scheme of work on 'Seeing' as a way in.

EXPERIENCE EXPLORED THROUGH THE ARTS

A stepping-stone for many people is through the arts, seen not just as providing means of expression, but also as giving meaning and helping to structure experience. Here the central point is not to try to imitate arts education in RE, but to encourage links with what pupils do and experience in their arts education. In this way RE continues to do what it should without trespassing outside its domain unduly – it can focus on *religion*, while the arts retain their integrity and are not treated like 'visual aids' or 'follow-up work'. Also it promotes that holistic sense of the whole of life's experience being brought into harmony, including the discords.

The arts are especially important and effective in arousing spiritual awareness because they can speak directly at a feeling level, as well as being free from any slavish dependence on religious ideas which are often rejected out of hand by secularists. The arts therefore provide an invaluable way-in for many people. Veronica Williams, for example, has developed an interesting approach in connection with her work on art history. She has found that she can interest modern teenagers, and develop attitudes of stillness and attentiveness and reflectiveness, through detailed study of certain masterpieces. Involvement in the visual arts is one way in for many young people today.

With senior pupils a useful book is *Modern Art and the Death of a Culture* by Hans Rookmaaker, a Dutch art historian. This work of art history explores how culture affects art and vice versa. A study of the art and writings of Francis Bacon can open up debate about the loss of meaning and its relation to art. Bacon is quoted as saying: 'Man now realizes that he is an accident, that he is a completely futile being, that he has to play out the game [life] without reason . . . man can only attempt to make something positive by trying to beguile himself for a time . . . you see all art has become a game by which man distracts himself.'[16]

Like art, music provides an immensely satisfying spiritual experience for many people for whom religion is totally dead. Religious masterpieces such as the *Messiah* continue to exercise a fascination which is much more than enjoyment of good tunes.

STUDY IN DEPTH OF RELIGIOUS EXPERIENCE WHICH IS SPIRITUAL

It is important in coming to understand religion to appreciate the role of experience in the founding and development of it. Beliefs are not conjured up out of nothing but are rather a response to experience. There is always a certain mismatch between belief and experience, because the latter is untidy; it comes to us without our asking for it, while the expression in words of our interpretation of experience tends to have a more clear-cut, fixed character about it.

Sometimes discussions about religion seem to imply that, if it is not just something conditioned in people by their upbringing, it is the result of people trying to solve a problem – a kind of game of cognitive possibilities. Yet this is wide of the mark. Take for example Hugh Montefiore, the former outspoken Bishop of Birmingham who died recently. He claimed to have had a powerful and sudden conversion experience as a 16-year-old at Rugby School in the form of a vision of Jesus Christ such that, as he said, though he was a Jew in the morning, by evening he was a Christian.

The appeal to experience may be far from a conclusive argument for religion to the outsider. Hugh Montefiore *could* have been mistaken. The vision he had could have been some form of hallucination. But, unless there is good evidence to suggest it was a hoax or a mistake, is it for those who did not have the experience to dismiss out-of-hand the interpretation of the person who did have the experience? The fact that a member of a prominent Jewish family converted to Christianity in the course of one day, and who later in life admitted that he never really felt at home anywhere, is not good evidence that it was a hoax. Nor is the fact that he stood by that new commitment to the end of his long life an encouragement to interpreting his under-standing of it as will-o-the-wisp. It was for him an example of following where the evidence led him. Because he had had this experience which had convinced him of the reality of Jesus Christ, he must become a Christian even if that produces colos-sal misunderstanding by both family and friends and by his new co-religionists.

There are many examples of such determining experience which are emphatically not conditioned, because not comfortable for the situation or times in which the person lives. A study of, for example, St Francis of Assisi (cf Chapter 10) and the Hindu mys-tic Sri Ramana who founded a flourishing ashram in South India and died in 1950, could be illuminating. This could help to give substance to what is meant by the spir-itual dimension, for both of them lived out the kind of character expressed in the middle column of Figure 12.1. In addition, work on Sri Ramana can help to illumin-ate many of the 'inwardness'-exercises suggested by the experiential approach to RE, for he constantly advised devotees to meditate on the question 'Who am I?' The bonus with St Francis is in helping pupils to appreciate a depth in what it means to be a Christian which is so easily today seen at a superficial externalist level.

There are several striking similarities between the two, as Table 12.1 shows. Both had particular experience which was overwhelming in its impact upon them. Sri Ramana used to say that he had only one experience in his life; he spent the rest working it out. At the age of 16, alone in his uncle's house in Madurai, he describes how a sudden terror of death overtook him, and he found himself dramatizing the occurrence of death.

> I lay with my limbs stretched out as stiff as though rigor mortis had set in, and imitated a corpse so as to give greater reality to the enquiry. 'Well then,' I said to myself,

Table 12.1 *Similarities between Sri Ramana and St Francis*

Sri Ramana	St Francis	Similarity
Father a lawyer	Father a merchant	Middle-class background
Left home without saying where he was going	Feud with father led to court hearing before bishop	Unconventional attitude towards parents
Experience at Madurai when he was 16	Meeting with the leper; Praying before the crucifix in San Damiano; Hearing words from St Matthew's gospel	Overwhelming experience that changed the course of their lives
Life of a *sannyasin*	Life of poverty	Astonishing single-mindedness in pursuing the ideal
Ashram at Tiruvanamallai	Order of friars	Neither of them set out to found a community, but it happened spontaneously
'Birthday ode' etc. Composed *bhajans* – devotional song	'Perfect joy' etc. One of the first great poems in the Italian language: 'Canticle of Brother Sun'	Both excellent teachers using colourful, homely language; Both poets
Animals at ashram	Wolf of Gubbio etc.	Love of animals
Devotees included professors	Anecdote of his being able to resolve a difficult theological problem which defeated the scholars at Siena University	Not academic, but revered by academics as wise
Many came to him for advice	Anecdotes of his visit to Bologna, and to the Muslim Sultan	Peace-loving and active in trying to end feuds
Died of cancer without taking drugs of any kind	He became almost blind and died at the age of 44 from various diseases	Both endured great suffering with incredible stoicism

'this body is dead. It will be carried stiff to the burning ground and there burnt and reduced to ashes. But with the death of this body am I dead? Is the body I? It is silent and inert but I feel the full force of my personality and even the voice of the "I" within me, apart from it. So I am Spirit transcending the body.' All this was not dull thought; it flashed through me vividly as living truth which I perceived directly, almost without thought process. 'I' was something very real, the only real thing about my present state, and all the conscious activity connected with my body was centred on the 'I'. From that moment onwards the 'I' or Self focussed attention on itself by a powerful fascination. Fear of death had vanished once and for all.[17]

For St Francis there were a number of decisive moments, such as when he saw the leper. He dismounted from his horse and embraced the leper even though the thought of doing so was repulsive to him. He wrote in his Testament not long before he died: 'While I was living in sin, it seemed a very bitter thing to look at lepers; but the Lord Himself led me among them, and I had compassion on them. And when I left them, the thing that had seemed so horrible to me was transformed into happiness of body and soul for me.'[18] Another experience was when he was praying before the crucifix in San Damiano and it seemed to him that it gave him the message, 'Build my church', which he immediately interpreted quite literally as, 'Save this church from crumbling into ruins'. And the third occasion was in another church outside Assisi when he heard the reading from St Matthew's gospel about absolute poverty, and he became convinced that that was the path he had to follow.[19]

The self-authenticating nature of their experiences meant that neither of them was able to doubt them, yet the similarities must not blind us to certain differences. The experiences were interpreted quite differently, even though they produced remarkable resemblances in character. This raises the interesting question of whether by having different expectations the experiences were in fact different. Usually religious people tend to see these as different, Sri Ramana's being an experience of enlightenment and awareness of the Oneness of being, whilst St Francis's conveyed a sense of communion with God – a sense of a Presence revealing itself.

Such study can deepen RE as well as promote spiritual awareness across the whole curriculum. All religions furnish many examples.[20]

THE NEED FOR REFLECTION ON EXPERIENCE

As already discussed in Chapter 5, a doctrine such as the Christian belief in God as Trinity arose out of the way in which Christians experienced God as personal and in three quite distinct ways and yet as one. Logically this may not seem to make sense, yet for Christians it is like paradox pointing beyond a neat literalism to that reality which has impinged itself on them. Paradox defies logic, yet not by dismissing it but by teasing us to think wider and deeper and extend our horizons and challenge our starting-points.

Awareness of the possible truth of paradox is a most helpful way in to appreciating the nature of religious language as it wrestles to express experience. The theologian, Donald Baillie, used to give the example of two quite different kinds of maps – one showing hemispheres and the other straight. Both are needed to convey a spherical world in two dimensions, for although they contradict each other at every point to some degree, yet together they correct and balance each other in attempting the impossible, i.e. to convey an accurate impression in two-dimensional terms of the spherical world.

Such problems in expressing the insight arising out of experience cause some people to ask: Why bother? Why not just accept experience – why try to understand it and encapsulate it in words which will necessarily have an imprisoning effect upon the insight? T.S. Eliot spoke of 'the intolerable wrestle with words and meanings'.[21] Why take on such hard work?

Yet a person who has had this kind of experience cannot ignore it and is led on by the sheer facticity of it to seek understanding even though knowing that any knowledge gained will be partial and provisional. But then that, too, is a kind of knowing which perhaps deserves the rarely used word *wisdom*. Perhaps, in the end, that is what spiritual development is about: the gaining of that wisdom which enables a person to transcend both cognitive and emotional aspects of knowing and which enables the highest humanly possible quality of life, neither purely natural nor demonic.

TO THINK ABOUT

Spirituality concerns a quality of life which transcends the natural plane and resists what may be called the unnatural, evil or demonic.

1 By studying Figure 12.1 can you apply these distinctions specifically to religious practices?
   (a) reading the Qur'ān;
   (b) wearing a prayer shawl.

We give an example

going to church to enjoy belonging to a community	going to church to worship God	going to church to infiltrate political ideas

2 Explain why using the word plane can provide a link between secularist and religious understandings of spirituality such that the subjective connotations are overcome?

NOTES

1 Andrew Wright in Grimmitt, M. (2000), p. 176.
2 Fuller, P. (1990), p. 18.
3 Lucien Jenkins (2005), writing in *Music Teacher*, December.
4 DES (1977).
5 DES (1985).
6 Wright, A. (2000), p. 7.
7 Ibid., p. 104.
8 Ibid., ch. 2, p. 17.
9 e.g. Ibid., p. 29.
10 Ibid., p. 34.
11 Liam Gearon (2004), p. 22 critiques Wright.
12 Berger, P. (1969), pp. 70–96.
13 Underhill, E. in Garvey, J. (1986), p. 25.
14 Buber in Garvey, J. (1986), p. 5.
15 Ashton, E. (1989).
16 See also Northcote (1999). And a CD that has been produced '*Images of Salvation*', May 2004, available from www.york.ac.uk. Also Margaret Cooling, *Jesus through Art* and the *Bible through Art*, available from www.stapleford.ac.uk
17 Described in his own words, translated by Arthur Osborne (1970), p. 18f.
18 Described in his own words, translated by Leo Sherley-Price (1959), p. 200.
19 See e.g. J.R.H. Moorman (1963), pp. 11 and 19.
20 These books on Sri Ramana are in the Bibliography: Osborne (1970), Mahadevan (1976), Mahadevan (1977) and on St Francis: Moorman (1963), Sherley-Price (1959), Habig (ed.) (1973), Galli (2002). Wallet of materials on St Francis available from the Farmingtom Institute, Oxford.
21 Eliot, T.S., *Four Quartets*, East Coker II.

MEETING REQUIREMENTS

The bell rings and the teacher walks into the classroom. She closes the door, not being waited on hand and foot nowadays. A short walk to the table, likely to be the same size and shape as those provided for her pupils, and she is 'off'. In charge of all she surveys, she is the captain of the ship, eagerly anticipating steering her charges into interesting, exciting and productive waters. It all depends on her and, perhaps, the mood her pupils happen to be in that day.

The teacher is the one at the point of delivery. He or she is the one who counts and this book has been largely taken up with helping RE teachers to get a sense of their freedom and responsibility to make a difference. But, of course, it is not as simple as that. There are requirements which a teacher has to meet, authorities to satisfy and tests that pupils must take. Increasingly today accountability creeps in until the teacher may feel almost suffocated. What is crucial is that a teacher recognizes that requirements are servants to help in the task of teaching rather than masters intended to grind her down.

What then are the requirements? In England and Wales schools 'not having a religious character', often called 'community schools', must follow the Agreed Syllabus which is adopted by the LEA.[1] This is a syllabus drawn up by representatives of Christian denominations other than the Church of England and other religions, representatives of the Church of England (but not in Wales), teachers' associations and the local authority.[2] Agreed syllabuses first came into being in the 1920s as a response to problems encountered because of arguments over what could, and could not, be taught in the classroom. Groups of teachers and church representatives met with Board personnel to agree on what could be taught. This system, with certain modifications, is still enshrined in law today. The idea that a syllabus *permits* certain material to be taught is still quite strong. It is common, for example, for syllabuses to say that other material can supplement the syllabus.[3] The non-statutory national framework allows for the teaching of a wide variety of religions and secular philosophies in addition to Christianity and other principal religions. In voluntary schools which have a religious character it is possible for a more denominationally focused form of religious education to take place and there are many Diocesan syllabuses which are prescribed for study in such schools. Muslim, Jewish and Sikh schools may provide their own syllabuses in their voluntary-aided schools. Independent schools are entirely free of parliamentary legislation and may choose to provide RE or not.

It is important to remember that legal requirements, in many cases, give permission for things to happen rather than prescribe every detail. Lawyers often speak of 'provisions'. And legislation often gives wide discretion to those who have to make decisions.[4] The 1870 Forster Education Act, following heated debate, gave permission to the new school Boards to provide religious instruction in publicly funded schools. The London Board of Education ruled that 'the Bible shall be read . . .'[5] The permissive nature of RE is particularly clear because of the conscience clauses which allow parents to withdraw pupils, and teachers not to have to teach RE or participate in collective worship. The compulsory nature of RE in England and Wales lies in the fact that schools run by the local education authority must provide religious education but parents may decline the provision. There are diverse forms of provision for RE in these countries and across the world. Permissive legislation is likely to create diversity and, indeed, one of the main reasons for local determination of RE in England and Wales has been the need for RE to be responsive to local situations. Agreed syllabuses have in the past allowed a certain degree of latitude to take account of the interests of both teachers and pupils. This is generally still the case at the time of writing.[6]

But in an era of political pressure for ever higher standards, RE, like other subjects, is in danger of becoming increasingly tied down and prescribed. The push for ever higher standards in education has meant that teachers are coming under scrutiny as never before. One teacher of our acquaintance was inspected recently under the new 48 hour notice procedure. She was due to take a lesson for special needs' pupils and found herself writing seven individual lesson plans for one lesson in case the inspector arrived. Another teacher we know took up part-time teaching after the birth of her second child and was horrified to see how tied down teachers are to the syllabus – no freedom at all concerning what they teach. And she said the profession seemed to have become even more determined to assess and record every detail of children's work. Certainly the push is on for RE to take assessment more seriously with OFSTED reporting that, despite improvements in assessing RE, there is 'much more to be done'.[7] Syllabus providers in all types of school are being encouraged to use the eight-level scale found in the non-statutory national framework for RE.

We think it is important to retain a sense of balance in all this. Lack of proper syllabus construction and total lack of assessment can be just as unhelpful as too much prescription and an obsession with assessment. One of us in recent years has been asked to go in to 'help with RE' in the absence of a teacher in two schools. In one school the syllabus consisted of a long list of topics and in the other there appeared to be no resourced syllabus at all. School policy was to rely on the professional judgement of the teacher. Clearly such a system breaks down when the teacher is absent! A carefully planned syllabus which takes account of what children have already learned, reflects some awareness of what children are learning in other subjects, builds in progression and incorporates methods of assessment which enable children to see what they need to do to improve is of enormous help to the RE teacher. A good syllabus frees a teacher to develop really interesting schemes of work and lesson plans. It is usual for the RE department (or co-ordinator in primary schools) to develop schemes of work and a good department will encourage monitoring of the latter so that they are kept under review and modified where necessary. Lesson plans are usually the responsibility of the teacher and ingenuity is generally welcomed here and good ideas shared in regular departmental meetings which are the norm in secondary schools.

The important thing, as we said earlier, is that a teacher does not let the structures which are in place to support the teaching become a clamp tying them down at every turn. Such structures include 'non-statutory national framework', Diocesan policy, schemes of work, attainment targets, agreed syllabus, eight-level scale, behaviour policy, paired assessment, pupil self-assessment, reporting procedures, SOW, Key Stage (KS2) scores, CATS predictions, target grades, curriculum review etc.

Why assess in the first place? Several arguments suggest that assessment is counter-productive. Assessment may be felt to be inappropriate in some aspects of RE and indeed the framework states as much: 'not all aspects of religious education can be assessed. For example, pupils may express personal views and ideas, that, although integral to teaching and learning, would not be appropriate for formal assessment.'[8] It involves an element of subjectivity on the part of the teacher and the criteria selected. It is time-consuming and a burden for teachers who may have between 500 and 600 pupils at any one time. It can promote comparison between pupils (and between schools) which can result in a feeling of failure for many. It encourages the wrong kind of motivation and discourages learning for its own sake.

On the other hand it may be argued that if an aspect of RE cannot be assessed can we be sure that it can be taught? The non-statutory framework may be wrong in claiming that some things must not be assessed on the grounds that they are personal. This is not to say there are no difficulties or concerns to be acknowledged. The Birmingham agreed syllabus is under review at the time of writing. Its draft document on assessment states:

> The views and ideas people hold are constantly subject to such assessment. We may regard them as deep or shallow, ill thought out or well-ordered, badly supported or soundly argued. What may be wrong is to assume there are set answers to perennial questions, or to assume that many of the most important concerns in religious life are open to public scrutiny or that everything should be made public.

All assessment is open to the charge of subjectivity. However criteria need to be shared with pupils and, increasingly, this is becoming the norm. Certainly it can be time-consuming but there are strategies to help. One example of good assessment practice in the 2004/5 OFSTED subject report of RE cited the use of classroom assistants and the contribution of the RE co-ordinator. A report published by OFSTED in 2003 suggested that the best schools had introduced sampling or staggered marking for teachers. In the former case a teacher marks five or six books a week and in the latter a teacher marks a set of books every so often. Assessment nowadays increasingly does not give pupils grades which encourage comparison. Rather they are given individual targets within fairly broad levels and this has encouraged weaker pupils to (a) feel that they are really cared about and (b) see observable improvements in their work. Does assessment discourage learning for its own sake? It may do but good teaching should counteract this since the teacher himself will exhibit the joy of learning and discovery. Pupils should be encouraged to think that one day they may emulate their teacher. And this does involve passing examinations!

Perhaps the most important thing about assessment is that it should aid learning and motivate pupils. A teacher should not assume that whatever form of assessment they find themselves asked to operate is necessarily fulfilling either function. Critical affirmation is needed here too! When pupils have been given a substantial piece of work to complete it is always encouraging to them to have a personal comment made upon their work and insights. Reading out their work to the class is a wonderful affirmation and spur to do well next time. What a teacher has to be careful about is that it is not the same pupils' whose work is always read out. Group work can overcome this to an extent. Formative assessment, whereby a piece of work is set as part of the syllabus but also used for assessment purposes does not require extra planning or effort. Assessment can be through oral contribution, either in answer to a question or as part of a learning task, such as the learning of Psalm 23 or something similar. It can be a photograph of a pupil carrying out an investigation or the record of an interview on tape. The possibilities are endless and assessment can be undertaken by pupils themselves. Feedback to pupils should always be constructive: 'here is an example of how to construct an argument . . .'. Rather than 'you need to learn how to construct an argument'. Clearly, if marking reveals a common misconception, the teacher can take time to deal with it next lesson. The discovery of a common mistake can be used to develop next year's lesson plan.

What about levels? In assessing the level at which a pupil is working in RE at KS2 a teacher may make use of English KS2 scores, reading ages and predictions of CATS scores which are routinely carried out in Year 7. On the other hand these scores may not always be appropriate. One of us used to deliberately not read reports on Year 7 pupils at first so as not to prejudge them. After the first few weeks and having formed an opinion of those pupils who showed exceptional insight and promise, she would read the scores. Inevitably some of the weaker pupils had shone in her lessons. Spiritual insight may not be the same thing as a verbal reasoning test or reading age! The good teacher will build something into the levels of assessment to take account of such insight. Assessment must become part of the armoury of a good teacher. It is not of itself the solution to difficulties in learning in RE. Good teaching may be.

NOTES

1 Generally there is only one. However, there is provision in law for an authority to adopt more than one syllabus if the religious backgrounds of the children make it desirable.

2 For a good explanation of the SACRE see '*So you're joining your local SACRE . . .*'. It is available from the National Association of SACREs: www.nasacre.org.uk. For a guide to both bodies see *SACRE and ASC: a guide,* by Penny Thompson: www.angelfire. com/pe/pennyt/

3 An interesting example of this is the rider in the 1988 ERA to the effect that the prohibition against the use of denominational formularies is 'not to be taken as prohibiting provision in such syllabus for the study of such catechisms or formularies.' Education Act, 1996 s.376 (2).

4 See Harte, J.D.C. (1989), p. 36.

5 See Hilliard, F.H. (1963), ch. 1.

6 The 2006 Birmingham agreed syllabus, in draft form, makes specific statements about the role of the professional judgement of the teacher and, in particular, the need for the syllabus to avoid over-prescription.

7 OFSTED subject report (2004/5). See www.ofsted.gov.uk

8 Non-statutory framework for RE (2004), p. 35.

REFERENCES AND RECOMMENDED READING

Abba, R. 1992. *The Nature and Authority of the Bible*. Cambridge, James Clarke.

Abbott, E. 1987. *Story of Flatland*. Harmondsworth, Penguin Books.

Abdel-Malik, A. and Abdel-Malik, K. 1995. *Celebrating Muhammad: Images of the Prophet in Popular Muslim Poetry*. Columbia, SC, University of South Carolina Press.

Adams, K. 1990. Changing British attitudes. *Royal Society of Arts Journal*, CXXXVIII, 5412, pp. 826–34.

Ainsworth, D. 1968. *Aspects of the Growth of Religious Understanding in Children aged 5–11*. Unpublished thesis for Advanced Diploma in Education, Manchester University.

Anderson, N. 1973. *A Lawyer Among the Theologians*. London, Hodder & Stoughton.

Anthony of Sourozh. 1986. *The Essence of Prayer*. London, Darton, Longman & Todd.

Appleton, G. 1985. *The Oxford Book of Prayer*. Oxford, Oxford University Press.

Ashton, E. 1989. *Religious Education and the Unconscious*. University of Durham unpublished MA thesis.

Astley, J. 1992. Will the Real Christianity Please Stand Up? *British Journal of Religious Education*, 15, 1, pp. 4–12.

Astley, J. 1994. *The Philosophy of Christian Religious Education*. Birmingham, AL, Religious Education Press.

Astley, J. and Francis, L.J. (eds) 1996. *Christian Theology and Religious Education: Connections and Contradictions*. London, SPCK.

Bakhtiar, L. 1976. *Sufi: Expressions of the Mystic Quest*. London, Thames & Hudson.

Barbour, I. 2000. *When Science Meets Religion: Enemies, Strangers, or Partners*. San Francisco, Harper.

Barfield, O. 1971. *What Coleridge Thought*. Connecticut, Wesleyan University Press.

Barnes, L.P. 1997. Religion, Religionism and Religious Education: Fostering tolerance and truth in schools, *Journal of Education and Christian Belief*, 1, pp. 3–25.

Barnes, L.P. 2001. What is wrong with the phenomenological approach to Religious Education? *Religious Education*, 96, pp. 445–61.

Barnes, L.P. 2002. Working Paper 36, Religious Education in the secondary school: Thirty Years On. *Journal of Education and Christian Belief*, 6, 1, pp. 61–77.

Barnes, L.P. 2006. The Misrepresentation of religion in modern British (Religious) Education, unpublished paper presented to the Hope RE Colloquium.

Barnes, L.P. and Kay, W.K. 2002. *Religious Education in England and Wales: Innovations and Reflections*. Leicester, Religious and Theological Studies Fellowship.

Barnes, M. 1989. *Religions in Conversation*. London, SPCK.

Barnes, M. 1991. *God: East and West*. London, SPCK.

Barton, J. 1991. *What is the Bible?* London, SPCK.

Bausor, J. and Poole, M.W. 2003. Science Education and Religious Education: possible links? *School Science Review*, December, 85 (311), pp. 117–24.

Beck, C. 1990. *Better Schools: a Values Perspective*. Lewes, Falmer Press.

Begbie, J. 1992. The Gospel, the Arts and Our Culture. In H. Montefiore (ed.) *The Gospel and Contemporary Culture*. London, Mowbray.

Berger, P. 1969. *A Rumour of Angels: Modern Society and the Discovery of the Supernatural*. London, Penguin Books.

Bigger, S. 1991. Assessing Religious Education. *Journal of Beliefs and Values*, 12, 1, pp. 1–4.

Black, M. 1971. Models and Metaphors. In I.T. Ramsey (ed.) *Words about God – The Philosophy of Religion*. London, SCM.

Board of Education. 1931. *The Primary School* (The Hadow Report). London: HMSO.

Board of Education. 1938. *Secondary Education* (The Spens Report). London: HMSO.

Bobrinskoy, B. 1986. Revelation of the spirit; language beyond words. *Sobornost*, 8, 1, pp. 6–14.

Bookless, D. 1991. *Interfaith Worship and Christian Truth*, Cambridge, Grove Worship Series 117, Grove Books.

Borgmann, A. 1991. *Technology and the Character of Contemporary Life: A Philosophical Inquiry*. Chicago, University of Chicago Press.

Borowitz, E.B. 1979. *Understanding Judaism*. New York, Union of American Hebrew Congregations.

Broadbent, L. and Brown, A. (eds) 2002. *Issues in Religious Education*. London, Routledge Falmer.

Brown, D. 2003. *The Da Vinci Code*. London, Corgi Books.

Brown, J.M. 1980. *Men and Gods in a Changing World*. London, SCM.

Burke, C. 1967. *God is for Real*. London, Fontana Books.

Carr, D. 1995. Towards a Distinctive Conception of Spiritual Education. *Oxford Review of Education*, 21, pp. 83–98.

Carroll, J. 2001. *Constantine's Sword: The Church and the Jews*. Boston and New York, Houghton Mifflin Company.

Chappell, K.R. 1991. *Investigating Jesus*. London, Edward Arnold.

Chater, M. 2005. The personal and the political: notes on teachers' vocations and values. *Journal of Beliefs and Values*, 26, 3, pp. 249–59.

Chesterton, G.K. 1995 [1904]. (reprint) *Orthodoxy*. San Francisco, Ignatius Press.

Chesterton, G.K. 1912. *What's Wrong With the World?* London, Cassell.

Claxton, G. 1990. *Teaching to Learn*. London, Cassell Educational.

Clifford, R. 1991. *Leading Lawyers Look at the Resurrection*. Oxford, Lion.

Cobb, J. 1990. Beyond Pluralism. In G. D'Costa (ed.) *Christian Uniqueness Reconsidered: The Myth of Pluralistic Theology of Religions*. Maryknoll, NY, Orbis Books.

Cohn-Sherbok, D. 1991. *A Dictionary of Judaism and Christianity*. London, SPCK.

Cole, J. 1988. *God in his World Today*, Oxford, Amate Press.

Comenius, J.A. 1990. *Panegersia, or universal awakening* (A.M.O. Dobbie, Trans.). Sheffield, Sheffield Academic Press.

Conway, R. 1990. The influence of beliefs and values on technological activities – a challenge to religious education. *British Journal of Religious Education*, 13, 1, pp. 49–55.

Conway, R. 1999. *Choices at the Heart of Technology: A Christian Perspective*. Harrisburg USA, Trinity Press International.

Cooling, M. and Cooling, T. 1992. Christianity in the primary school, *Resource*, 14, 3.

Cooling, T. 1994. *Concept Cracking: Exploring Christian Beliefs in School*. Nottingham, Association of Christian Teachers.

Cooling, T. 2005. The search for truth: postmodernism and religious education. *Journal of Beliefs and Values*, 26, 1, pp. 87–93.

Copley, C., Copley, T., Freathy, R., Lane, S. and Walsh, K. 2004. *On the Side of the Angels: The Third Report of the Biblos Project*. Exeter, University of Exeter Press.

Copley, T. 1997. *Teaching Religion*. Exeter, University of Exeter Press.

Copley, T. 2005. *Indoctrination, Education and God: The Struggle for the Mind*. London, SPCK.

Copley, T. 2006. Review of the Non-statutory National Framework for Religious Education. *British Journal of Religious Education*, 28, 1, pp. 102–104.

Copley, T., Freathy, R. and Walshe, K. 2004. *A Summary of the Main Findings of the Biblos Project 1996–2004*. Exeter, University of Exeter School of Education and Lifelong Learning.

Corless, R. and Knitter, P.F. 1990. *Buddhist Emptiness and Christian Trinity*. New York, Paulist Press.

Cracknell, K. 1986. *Towards a New Relationship – Christians and People of other Faith*. London, Epworth Press.

Cragg, K. 2005. *A Certain Sympathy of Scriptures, Biblical and Quranic*. Brighton, Sussex Academic Press.

Crossan, J.D. 1991. *The Historical Jesus: the Life of a Mediterranean Jewish Peasant*. Edinburgh, T. & T. Clark.

D'Costa, G. 1988. *Faith meets Faith – Interfaith Views on Interfaith*. London, British and Foreign Schools Society RE Centre.

D'Costa, G. 1990. *Christian Uniqueness Reconsidered*. New York, Orbis Books, Maryknoll.

D'Costa, G. 1996. The Impossibility of a Pluralist View of Religions. *Religious Studies*, 32, pp. 223–32.

Doble, P. 2005. Whose confession? Which tradition? (A preliminary critique of Penny Thompson, 2004a). *British Journal of Religious Education*, 27, 2, pp. 143–57.

Douglas, M. and Tipton, S. (eds) 1983. *Religion in America*, Beacon Press.

Dunn, J.D.G. 2005. *A New Perspective on Jesus*. London, SPCK.

Dunne, J. 1991. *The Partings of the Ways: Between Christianity and Judaism and their Significance for the Character of Christianity*. London, SCM/TPI.

Durham Commission. 1970. *The Fourth R, The Durham Report on Religious Education*. London, National Society.

Egan, K. 1988. *Primary Understanding*. London, Routledge.

Ehrman, B.D. 2004. *Truth and Fiction in The Da Vinci Code*. Oxford, Oxford University Press.

Felderhof, M.C. 1995. Is There a Place for the Religious Voice in Public Education? *Journal of Beliefs and Values*, 16, 1, pp. 21–6.

Felderhof, M.C. 1999. On Understanding Worship in School (Part 1). *Journal of Beliefs and Values*, 20, 2, pp. 219–30.

Felderhof, M.C. 2000a. On Understanding Worship in School (Part 2). *Journal of Beliefs and Values*, 21, 1, pp. 17–26.

Felderhof, M.C. 2000b. Religious Education, Indoctrination and Freedom. In Nils, G. Holm (ed.) *Islam and Christianity in School Religious Education*, Religionsvetenskapliga Skrifter no. 52, Abo, 1–25.

Fisher, R. 1990. *Teaching Children to Think*. Oxford, Basil Blackwell.

Francis, L.J. and Thatcher, A. (eds) 1990. *Christian Perspectives for Education*. Leominster, Gracewing.

Freathy, R.J.K. 2005. *Religious Education and Education for Citizenship in English Schools, 1934–1944*. Unpublished Ph.D. Thesis. University of Exeter.

Fuller, P. 1990. *Images of God*. London, The Hogarth Press.

Furedi, F. 2004. *Where Have All the Intellectuals Gone?* London, Continuum.

Galli, M. 2002. *Francis of Assisi and His World*. Oxford, Lion.

Garvey, J. 1986. *Modern Spirituality: an Anthology*. London, Darton, Longman & Todd.

Gearon, L. 2004. *Citizenship Through Religious Education*. London, Routledge/Falmer.

Goldman, R. 1964. *Religious Thinking from Childhood to Adolescence*. London, Routledge & Kegan Paul.

Goldman, R. 1965. *Readiness for Religion*. London, Routledge & Kegan Paul.

Gollancz, V. and Greene, B. 1962. *God of a Hundred Names*. London, Victor Gollancz.

Grimmitt, M. (ed.) 2000. *Pedagogies of Religious Education*. Great Wakesing, Essex, McCrimmons.

Grubb Institute. 2002. *Becoming Fit for Purpose, Leading Transformation in Church Schools*. London, The Grubb Institute.

Gunton, C. 1992. Knowledge and Culture: Towards an Epistemology of the Concrete. In: H. Montefiore (ed.) *The Gospel and Contemporary Culture*. London: Mowbray.

Habig, M.A. 1973. *St Francis of Assisi – Omnibus of Sources*. London, SPCK.

Haldane, J. 2005. *An Intelligent Person's Guide to Religion*. London, Gerald Duckworth and Co.

Halstead, J.M. and Reiss, M.J. 2003. *Values in Sex Education: From Principles to Practice*. London, Routledge/Falmer.

Hammond, J., Hay, D., Moxon, J., Netto, B., Roban, K., Straugheir, G. and Williams, C. 1990. *New Methods in RE Teaching – an Experiential Approach*. Harlow, Essex, Oliver & Boyd.

Hanson, R.P.C. 1984. *The Making of the Doctrine of the Trinity*. London, Anglican and Eastern Churches Association.

Hargreaves, D. 1994. *The Mosaic of Learning*, London, Demos.

Harries, R. 1987. *Christ is Risen*. London, Mowbray.

Harris, M. 1988. *Women and Teaching*. New York, Paulist Press.

Harte, J.D.C. 1989. The Religious Dimension of the Education Reform Act, 1988. *Ecclesiastical Law Journal*, 5, p. 36.

Hay, D. 1990. *Religious Experience Today: Studying the Facts*. London, Mowbray.

Hilliard, F. 1963. *The Teacher and Religion*. London, James Clarke.

Hinnells, J.R. 1984. *A Handbook of Living Religions*. Harmondsworth, Penguin.

Hodges, W. 1977. *Logic*. Harmondsworth, Penguin Books.

Hooker, R. 1989. *Themes in Hinduism and Christianity*. Frankfurt, Verlag Peter Lang.

Hooker, R. and Sargant, J. (eds) 1991. *Belonging to Britain*. British Council of Churches/ Council of Churches of Britain and Ireland.

Hookway, S.R. 2004. *Questions of Truth – Developing Critical Thinking Skills in Religious Education*. Norwich, RMEP.

Houghton, J. 1988. *Does God Play Dice? A Look at the Story of the Universe*. London, Inter-Varsity Press.

Hull, J. 1975. School Worship: An Obituary. London, SCM.

Hull, J. 1989. *The Act Unpacked*. Birmingham, Christian Education Movement.

Hull, J.M. 1991a. *God-talk with Young Children*. Birmingham, Christian Education Movement.

Hull, J. 1991b. *Mishmash: Religious Education in Multi-cultural Britain: a Study in Metaphor*. Birmingham, Christian Education Movement.

Hull, J.M. 1996. A Critique of Christian Religionism in Recent British Education. In: J. Astley and L.J. Francis (eds) *Christian Theology and Religious Education: Connections and Contradictions*. London, SPCK.

Hull, J.M. 2000. Religionism and Religious Education. In: M. Leicester and S. Modgil (eds) *Spirit and Religious Education*. London, Falmer Press.

Hulmes, E. 1979. *Commitment and Neutrality in Religious Education*. London, Geoffrey Chapman.

Hulmes, E. 1989. *Educational and Cultural Diversity*. London, Longman Group.

Hyde, K.E. 1991. *Religion in Childhood and Adolescence*. Birmingham, AL, Religious Education Press.

International Religious Foundation. 1991. *World Scripture: a Comparative Anthology of Sacred Texts*. New York, Paragon House.

Ipgrave, J. 1999. Issues in the Delivery of Religious Education to Muslim Pupils: Perspectives from the Classroom. *British Journal of Religious Education*, 21, 3, pp. 146–57.

Ipgrave, M. (ed.) 2004. *Scriptures in Dialogue: Christians and Muslims studying the Bible and the Qur'an together*. London, Church House Publishing.

Islamic Academy. 1991. *Faith as the Basis of Education in a Multi-faith, Multi-Cultural Country; Discussion Document II*. Cambridge, Islamic Academy.

Jackson, R. 1997. *Religious Education – An Interpretive Approach*. London, Hodder & Stoughton.

Jackson, R. 2004. *Rethinking Religious Education and Plurality: Issues in Diversity and Pedagogy*. London, Routledge Falmer.

Jeffreys, M.V.C. 1955. *Beyond Neutrality*. London, Pitman.

Jeremias, J. 1971. *New Testament Theology: Volume One*. London, SCM.

Jones, G.L. 1999. Teaching Contempt: the Jew through Christian eyes. *Journal of Beliefs and Values*, 20, 1, pp. 5–20.

Kay, W.K. 1997. Phenomenology, Religious Education and Piaget. *Religion*, 27, pp. 275–83.

Kay, W.K. and Smith, D.L. 2000a. Religious Terms and Attitudes in the Classroom (Part 1). *British Journal of Religious Education*, 22, pp. 81–90.

Kay, W.K. and Smith, D.L. 2000b. Religious Terms and Attitudes in the Classroom (Part 2). *British Journal of Religious Education*, 22, pp. 181–91.

Keast, A. and Keast, J. 2005. *Framework RE I*. London, Hodder Murray.

Kettle, D. 2005. *Gospel and Our Culture Newsletter*. Cambridge, Gospel and Our Culture network.

Khan, M.A. 1985. Resource Allocation in an Islamic Economy. *The Islamic Quarterly*, XXIX, 4, pp. 241ff.

Kirkwood, R. 1990. *Looking for Proof of God*. London, Longman Group.

Knitter, P.F. and Corless, R. 1990. *Buddhist Emptiness and Christian Trinity*. New York, Paulist Press.

Lewis, C.S. 1941. *A Preface to Paradise Lost*. Oxford, Oxford University Press.

Lewis, C.S. 1945. *The Great Divorce: A Dream*. London, Geoffrey Bles.

Lewis, H.D. 1959. *Our Experience of God*. London, Allen & Unwin.

Lipman, M., Sharp, A.M. and Oscanyan, F.S. 1980. *Philosophy in the Classroom*. Philadelphia, Temple University Press.

Louth, A. 2002. *St. John Damascene*. Oxford, Oxford University Press.

Ludemann, G. 1997. *The Unholy in Holy Scripture: the Dark Side of the Bible*. London, SCM.

McGrath, A. 2005a. *The Twilight of Atheism*. London, Rider.

McGrath, A. 2005b. *Dawkins' God: Genes, Memes, and the Meaning of Life*. Oxford, Blackwell.

McGrath, A. (general ed.) 2006. *The New Lion Handbook: Christian Belief*. Oxford, Lion Hudson.

Macquarrie, J. 1968. *New Directions in Theology Today: Volume 3, God and Secularity*. Cambridge, Lutterworth Press.

Magee, J. 1958. *Reality and Prayer*. London, Hodder & Stoughton.

Mahadevan, T.M.P. 1976. *Ramana Maharshi and his Philosophy of Existence*, 3rd edn. Venkataraman, Tiruvannamalai, S. India.

Mahadevan, T.M.P. 1977. *Ramana Maharshi, the Sage of Arunacala*. London, Unwin Paperbacks.

Maple, G. 2005. Exploring Religion in School: an Anglican Response. *Journal of Christian Education*, 48, 2, pp. 43–57.

Marks, J. 2001. *Faith In Education*. London, Civitas.

Marsden, G. 1997. *The Outrageous Idea of Christian Scholarship*. New York, Oxford University Press.

Matthews, G.B. 1980. *Philosophy and the Young Child*. Cambridge, MA, Harvard University Press.

Maxwell, N. 2005. Science Under Attack. *The Philosophers' Magazine*, 31, pp. 37–41.

Milbank, J. 1997. *The Word Made Strange*. Oxford, Blackwell.

Mitchell, B. 1980. Religious Education. *Oxford Review of Education*, 6, 2, pp. 133–9.

Mitchell, B. 1990. *How to Play Theological Ping Pong*. London, Hodder & Stoughton.

Mitchell, B. 1994. *Faith and Criticism*. Oxford, Clarendon Press.

Moberly, W. 1992. 'Old Testament' and 'New Testament': The propriety of the terms for Christian theology. *Theology*, XCV, 763, pp. 26–32.

Moffat, J. 1992. *Harmonic Learning: Keynoting School Reform*. Portsmouth, NH, Heinemann.

Montefiore, H. (ed.) 1992. *The Gospel and Contemporary Culture*. London, Mowbray.

Montefiore, H. 2002. *Looking Afresh: Soundings in Creative Dissent*. London, SPCK.

Moorman, J.R.H. 1963. *Saint Francis of Assisi*. London, SPCK.

Morris, R.W. 1994. In *Values in Sexuality Education: A philosophical Study*. Maryland, University of America.

Mott-Thornton, K. 1998. *Common Faith, Education, Spirituality and the State*. Aldershot, Ashgate.

Newbigin, L. 1983. *The Other Side of 1984: Questions for the Church*. Geneva, World Council of Churches.

Newman, J.H. 1979 [1870]. (reprint) *A Grammar of Assent*. Indiana, University of Notre Dame Press.

Nichols, A. 1999. *Christendom Awake*. Edinburgh, T. & T. Clark.

Northcote, V. 1999. *Using Art in RE; Using RE in Art*. London, The National Society.

O'Hear, A. 2001. *Philosophy in the New Century*. London, Continuum.

O'Keeffe, B. 1986. *Faith, Culture and the Dual System*. Lewes, Falmer Press.

O'Keeffe, B. (ed.) 1988. *Schools for Tomorrow: Building Walls or Building Bridges*. London, Falmer Press.

Orwell, G. 1984. *Animal Farm*, London, Chancellor.

Osborne, A. 1970. *Ramana Maharshi and the Path of Self-knowledge*. London, Rider & Co.

Parrinder, G. 1990. *A Dictionary of Religious and Spiritual Quotations*. London, Routledge.

Petrovich, O. 1989. *An Examination of Piaget's Theory of Childhood Artificialism*. University of Oxford, unpublished PhD thesis.

Petrovich, O. 1999. Preschool Children's Understanding of the Dichotomy Between the Natural and the Artificial. *Psychological Reports*, 84, pp. 3–27.

Petrovich, O. 2001. Postmodernity: Science points to God. *UPI News*, 21, p. 41.

Phillips, J.B. 1932. *Your God is too Small*. London, Epworth Press.

Polanyi, M. 1964a. *Personal Knowledge: Towards a Post-critical Philosophy*. New York, Harper & Row.

Polanyi, M. 1964b. *Science, Faith and Society*. Chicago, University of Chicago Press.

Poole, M. 1990. Beliefs and Values in Science Education: a Christian Perspective (Part 2). *School Science Review*, June, 71 (256): 67–73.

Poole, M. 1992. *Miracles – Science, the Bible and Experience*. Milton Keynes, Scripture Union.

Poole, M. 1995. *Beliefs and Values in Science Education*. Maidenhead, Open University Press.

Poole, M. 1996. *Science and Christianity 10. A Reply to Richard Dawkins*. Oxford, Farmington Institute: Farmington Papers.

Poole, M. 2002. Explaining or explaining away? The concept of explanation in the Science–Theology debate. *Science and Christian Belief*, 14, 2, pp. 123–42.

Priestley, J. 1991. RE – the hub of the curriculum. *RE Today*, Summer, 8f.

Priestley, J. 1992. Whitehead Revisited: Religion and Education – an Organic Whole. In: B.G. Watson (ed.) *Priorities in Religious Education*. London, Falmer.

Pring, R. 1992. *Academic Respectability and Professional Relevance*. Oxford, Clarendon Press.

QCA. 2004. Religious Education – the non-statutory framework for religious education. London, QCA/DfES.

Quoist, M. 1966. *Prayers of Life*. Dublin, Logos Books, Gill and McMillan.

Race, A. 1983. *Christians and Religious Pluralism*. London, SCM and New York, Obis. (2nd edn 1993)

Raeper, W. and Smith, L. 1991. *A Beginners' Guide to Ideas*. London, Lion.

Ramsey, I.T. 1971. *Words about God – The Philosophy of Religion*. London, SCM.

Religious Education Council. 1990. *Handbook for Agreed Syllabus Conferences, SACREs and Schools*. London, REC.

Richards, I.A. 1936. *The Philosophy of Rhetoric*. London, Oxford University Press.

Riggs, A. 1990. Biotechnology and Religious Education. *British Journal of Religious Education*, 13, 1, pp. 56–64.

Rookmaaker, H.R. 1994 (reprint of 2nd edition). *Modern Art and the Death of a Culture*. Leicester, Apollos. First published by IVP in 1970.

Roques, M. 1989. *Curriculum Unmasked: Towards a Christian Understanding of Education*. London, Monarch Publications.

Rose, D. 1992. *Towards an Understanding of Religious Diversity in School*. Roehampton, Fulton.

Ross, C. 1991. *Leading Lawyers Look at the Resurrection*. London, Lion.

Ryeland, G. (ed.) 1991. *Beyond Reasonable Doubt*. Norwich, The Canterbury Press.

Sacks, J. 1991. *The Persistence of Faith*. London, Weidenfeld & Nicolson.

Sankey, D., Sullivan, D. and Watson, B. 1988. *At Home on Planet Earth*. Oxford, Basil Blackwell.

Sayers, D.L. 1949. *Creed or Chaos*. New York, Harcourt Brace.

Schools Council. 1971. *Religious Education in Secondary Schools*: Working Paper 36. London, Evans/Methuen.

Sherley-Price, L. 1959. *St Francis of Assisi*. London, Mowbray.

Slee, N. 1989. Conflict and Reconciliation Between Competing Models of Religious Education: Some Reflections on the British Scene. *British Journal of Religious Education*, 11, 3, pp. 6–35.

Slee, N. 1991. Windows on Worship: a Review of Some Recent Resources for Assembly. *Journal of Beliefs and Values*, 12, 2, p. 5f.

Smith, D. 1993. *Being an Effective Expert Witness: the technologist in the courtroom*. London, Thames Publishing.

Smith, D. 1999. *Making Sense of Spiritual Development*. Nottingham, Stapleford Education Centre.

Smith, D. and Carvill, B. 2000. *The Gift of the Stranger: Faith, Hospitality and Foreign Language Learning*. Cambridge, Eerdmans.

Smith, H. 1991. *The World's Religions*. San Francisco, Harper.

Smith, R. and Standish, P. (eds) 1997. *Teaching Right and Wrong*. Stoke-on-Trent, Trentham Books.

Soskice, J.M. 1985. *Metaphor and Religious Language*. London, SCM.

Stannard, R. 1985. *Science, Psychology, and the Existence of God*. Occasional Paper 19. Oxford, Farmington Institute for Christian Studies.

Stannard, R. 1989. *The Time and Space of Uncle Albert*. London, Faber & Faber.

Starkings, D. 1993. *Religion and the Arts in Education: Dimensions of Spirituality*. London, Hodder & Stoughton.

Steiner, G. 2003. *Lessons of the Masters*. Cambridge, MA and London, Harvard University Press.

Stewart, I. 1989. *Does God Play Dice – The New Mathematics of Chaos*. Harmondsworth, Penguin Books.

Stone, I. 1986. *The Origin – Biography of Darwin*. New York, Doubleday.

Swinburne, R. 1986. *Evidence for God*. London, Mowbray.

Talib, G.S. 1975. *Selections from the Holy Granth*. New Delhi, Bell Books Vikas.

Taylor, J.V. 1978. The theological basis of inter-faith dialogue. *Crucible*, pp. 4–16.

Teece, G. 2005. Traversing the Gap: Andrew Wright, John Hick and critical religious education. *British Journal of Religious Education*, 27, 1, pp. 29–40.

Thatcher, A. 1991. A critique of inwardness in religious education. *British Journal of Religious Education*, 14, 1, pp. 22–7.

Thatcher, A. 2004. The Curriculum of a Christian University. In: J. Astley, L. Francis, J. Sullivan, and A. Walker (eds) *The Idea of a Christian University*. Milton Keynes, Paternoster.

Thiede, C. 1991. *Jesus: Life or Legend*. London, Lion.

Thiessen, E. 1993. *Teaching for Commitment: Liberal Education, Indoctrination and Christian Nurture*. Leominster, Gracewing.

Thompson, P. 1995. If God were . . . *RE Today*, 12, 2, pp. 30–31.

Thompson, P. 2003. Critical Confessionalism for Teaching Religion in schools: A UK Case Study. *Journal of Christian Education*, 46, 2, pp. 5–16.

Thompson, P. 2004a. Whose Belief? Which Tradition? *British Journal of Religious Education*, 26, 1, pp. 61–72.

Thompson, P. 2004b. *Whatever Happened to Religious Education?* Cambridge, Lutterworth Press.

Thompson, P. 2004c. *Fitting out the Framework: How to Use the National Framework to Deliver Good Religious Education*. Occasional Paper no. 7, Liverpool.

Thouless, R.H. 1953. *Straight and Crooked Thinking*. London, Pan Books.

Tillich, P. 1957. *Systematic Theology*, Vol. 2. London, Nisbet.

Trigg, R. 1973. *Reason and Commitment*. Cambridge, Cambridge University Press.

Trigg, R. 1998. *Rationality and Religion*. Oxford, Blackwell.

Trigg, R. 2005. *Morality Matters*. Oxford, Blackwell.

Vardy, P. 1988. *And if it's True?* London, Marshall, Morgan and Scott.

Vardy, P. and Arliss, J. 2003. *The Thinker's Guide to God*. Hants, John Hunt Publishing.

Wansbrough, H. 2006. *The Story of the Bible: How it came to us*. London, Darton, Longman & Todd.

Ward, K. 1991. *A Vision to Pursue*. London, SCM.

Ward, K. 2004. *What the Bible Really Teaches: a Challenge for Fundamentalists*. London, SPCK.

Watson, B.G. 1987. *Education and Belief*. Oxford, Blackwell.

Watson, B.G. 1988. Children at School: a Worshipping Community. In B. O'Keeffe (ed.) *Schools for Tomorrow: Building Walls or Building Bridges*. London, Falmer Press.

Watson, B.G. (ed.) 1992. *Priorities in Religious Education: A Model for the 1990s and Beyond*. London, Falmer.

Watson, B.G. 2004. *Truth and Scripture*. Vale of Glamorgan, Aureus.

Watson, B.G. 2005. Should Philosophy Replace Religious Education? Reflections following Brendan Larvor's article 'Tu quoque, Archbishop'. *Think*, 9, pp. 7–11.

Watson, B.G. 2006. Is atheism a 'faith' position? *Think*, 12, pp. 43–8.

Watson, B.G. and Ashton, E. 1995. *Education, Assumptions and Values*. London, David Fulton.

Webster, D. 1991. School Worship. *Theology*, XCIV, 760, pp. 45–53.

Webster, J. 1998. *Theological Theology*. Oxford, Clarendon Press.

Wenham, J. 1992. *The Easter Enigma*, 2nd edn. Guernsey, Paternoster Press.

Wiles, M. 1992. *Christian Theology and Inter-religious Dialogue*. SCM.

Williams, K. 2000. Why Teach Foreign Languages in Schools? A philosophical response to Curriculum Policy. *Impact*, 5, ed. J. White. Philosophy of Education Society of Great Britain.

Williams, R. Archbishop of Canterbury. 2004. *Belief, Unbelief and Religious Education*, paper given at 10 Downing Street, www.archbishopofcanterbury.org

Wilson, A. (ed.) 1991. *World Scripture: a Comparative Anthology of Sacred Texts*. New York, Paragon House.

Wilson, A.N. 1991. *Against Religion: Why We Should Try to Live Without It*. London, Chatto & Windus.

Wingate, A. 1988. *Encounter in the Spirit*. Geneva, WCC Publications.

Wingate, A. 2005. *Celebrating Difference, Staying Faithful: How to Live in a Multi-Faith World*. London, Darton, Longman & Todd.

Wink, W. 1990. *Transforming Bible study – a Teacher's Guide*. London, Mowbray.

Wright, A. 1997a. Hermeneutics and religious understanding. Part one: the hermeneutics of modern religious education. *Journal of Beliefs and Values*, 18, 2, pp. 203–16.

Wright, A. 1997b. Hermeneutics and religious understanding. Part two: towards a critical theory for religious education. *Journal of Beliefs and Values*, 19, 1, pp. 59–70.

Wright, A. 1998. *Spiritual Pedagogy*. Abingdon, Culham College Institute.

Wright, A. 1999. *Discerning the Spirit: Teaching Spirituality in the Religious Education Classroom*. Abingdon, Culham College Institute.

Wright, A. 2000. *Spirituality and Education*. London, Routledge/Falmer.

Wright, A. 2003. *Religion, Education and Post-modernity*, London, Routledge/Falmer.

Wright, A. and Brandon, A.-M. (eds) 2000. *Learning to Teach Religious Education in the Secondary School*. London, Routledge/Falmer.

Wright, N.T. 2006a. *Evil and the Justice of God*. London, SPCK.

Wright, N.T. 2006b. *Simply Christian*. London, SPCK.

Yeaxley, B. 1925. *Spiritual Values in Adult Education*. Oxford, Oxford University Press.

Young, F.M. 1991. *The Making of the Creeds*. London, SCM.

NOTE ON RESOURCES

There is much material available to help with teaching RE. The following website has a very full and up-to-date list:

www.theredirectory.org.uk

INDEX